IN HER OWN NAME

In Her Own Name

The Politics of Women's Rights Before Suffrage

Sara Chatfield

Columbia University Press   New York

Columbia University Press
Publishers Since 1893
New York   Chichester, West Sussex
cup.columbia.edu
Copyright © 2023 Columbia University Press
All rights reserved

Library of Congress Cataloging-in-Publication Data
Names: Chatfield, Sara, author.
Title: In her own name : the politics of women's rights before suffrage / Sara Chatfield.
Description: New York : Columbia University Press, 2023. | Includes bibliographical references and index.
Identifiers: LCCN 2022050224 (print) | LCCN 2022050225 (ebook) | ISBN 9780231199667 (hardback) | ISBN 9780231199674 (trade paperback) | ISBN 9780231553230 (ebook)
Subjects: LCSH: Women's rights—United States—History. | Married women—Legal status, laws, etc.—United States—History. | Women—Suffrage—United States—History.
Classification: LCC KF390.W6 C43 2023 (print) | LCC KF390.W6 (ebook) | DDC 342.7308/78—dc23/eng/20230105
LC record available at https://lccn.loc.gov/2022050224
LC ebook record available at https://lccn.loc.gov/2022050225

Cover design: Milenda Nan Ok Lee
Cover image: Lenorko © Shutterstock

To Margaret Eleanor and June Elizabeth

Contents

Introduction   1

CHAPTER ONE
Life Under Coverture and How It Changed   10

CHAPTER TWO
Married Women's Rights Reforms in American
Political Development   33

CHAPTER THREE
Social Movements and State Power: Reform in State Legislatures   57

CHAPTER FOUR
Constitutional Conventions as Key Reform Moments   88

CHAPTER FIVE
Decentralized Reform and Policy Diffusion   130

CHAPTER SIX
Courts as Collaborators and Catalysts   149

Conclusion	169
Methods Appendix	177
Acknowledgments	191
Notes	193
Bibliography	221
Index	235

IN HER OWN NAME

Introduction

In 1839, Mississippi's legislature passed a law exempting a married woman's property—primarily enslaved human property—from debts incurred by her husband. Over the next several decades, Mississippi would pass laws expanding married women's economic rights further, culminating in a statute that one newspaper called "the most radical" in the United States.[1] How was Mississippi—not well known for being a vanguard of feminist policy making—a pioneer in married women's property rights? This question can be answered at least in part by considering the man who introduced Mississippi's first Married Women's Property Act in 1839: Senator Thomas Hadley. Hadley was in financial trouble and sought both debt relief through a personal bill that would forgive his debts to the state and financial benefit from a married women's property act.[2]

A decade later, in a vastly different political and economic context than antebellum Mississippi, delegates convened in Monterey to draft California's first constitution. They debated whether to include protections for married women's separate property and what those protections should look like. One delegate argued that without a provision guaranteeing married women's ownership of property they brought into a marriage, men would never convince wealthy women to move west and marry them.[3] The desire to induce wealthier women to move west had implications not just for the marriage prospects of single men but for the project of settlement.

Between 1835 and the ratification of the Nineteenth Amendment in 1920, married women's economic rights were expanded significantly around the nation. The puzzle for political scientists is how these statutes and constitutional provisions passed at all in a time when women's political power was severely constrained in multiple ways, including no right to vote in most states. Before such laws were enacted, the common-law doctrine of coverture dictated that women became civically "dead" upon their marriage vows—and in this era, almost all women married, given the limited opportunities for economic survival as a single woman. The law saw husband and wife as united in one legal identity, an identity that was of course defined and controlled by the husband. This meant that any property owned by a single woman before marriage—often inherited from a relative or received as a gift—now belonged to her husband, who could manage or dispose of it as he saw fit.

Over the course of the nineteenth century, all states passed at least limited (and often quite expansive) reforms granting married women a variety of new economic and legal rights. These laws varied but could include provisions protecting a wife's separate property from the debts of her husband, granting her management and control of that property, and expanding other related rights, such as the ability to sign a legal contract or appear in court under her own name. Though these reforms usually started in state legislatures, they were then interpreted by state courts and often enshrined in state constitutions. Even as these laws expanded (some) married women's economic citizenship dramatically, in both design and practice they contained elements of both inclusion and exclusion. Most, though not all, married women's property laws were race neutral in terms of their language. But in practice the intended beneficiaries were propertied white women, and this set of reforms had negative consequences for Native and Black women as a class, although individuals could sometimes take advantage of the new laws.[4] The reform of married women's economic rights in the states was a major period of both democratization and liberalization but—as with many democratizing policy changes—included meaningful exclusionary and illiberal elements as well.

Why and how were women's economic rights expanded before they had the right to vote and often in the absence of an organized women's movement? The story of women's rights in the United States often begins with the story of the suffrage movement, but economic rights reforms took place decades earlier. Why would men in power—legislators, convention delegates, and judges—expand women's economic rights, presumably at the men's own expense? The short answer is that it was not necessarily at their own expense, and it was often in fact in their economic and familial interests as well as in the interest of the states and territories they represented to do so. We can see the long answer through three interrelated stories.

The first is the story of male legislators and convention delegates who had compelling reasons to expand married women's rights in ways that benefited them. The precise reasons varied by time and place, but sometimes they were personal: relieving family debt, fathers protecting family assets that would eventually be inherited by their daughters (and potentially by their grandsons), and legislators in frontier states hoping to attract women to areas with substantial gender imbalances. Male political actors also sought to build state power through the protection of married women's property, passing reforms that protected the institution of slavery and aided settlement of the frontier alongside expanding women's rights. Married women's rights became a ready solution to all sorts of societal, political, and economic problems of the 1800s and early 1900s and were employed for reasons as varied as temperance to debt relief. Rights expansions were meaningful but also limited; women's groups sometimes demanded even more dramatic changes to property arrangements within marriage, but these demands were typically viewed as too radical or too disruptive to domestic harmony. Male political actors limited reforms to those with a clear benefit to themselves.

The second story is how these motivations were channeled into state political institutions. After state legislatures passed married women's economic rights reforms, specific cases arose that required interpretation by state courts. Unlike the conflictual and interest-group-driven battles in the courts that we might first think of when we hear about courts' role in the political process, there were few cases in the nineteenth and early twentieth centuries where state courts clearly acted in strong opposition to state legislatures in the issue area of married women's economic rights. Even while state courts were collaborating with legislative bodies, though, their rulings on limited reform legislation revealed the inconsistencies and complex real-world implications of these laws, prompting legislative and constitutional bodies to respond. This complexity created an iterative, incremental reform process, such that the typical state would pass multiple reforms over the course of decades. As new western states joined the Union and southern states redrafted their constitutions after Reconstruction, state constitutional conventions also became an important site for the guarantee of women's economic rights, even in contexts when those conventions were otherwise extremely rights restrictive. One institution alone was typically not enough to secure strong versions of economic rights reforms; it was through working their way through multiple state institutions that rights were gradually and incrementally expanded over time.

The third and final story is the spread of these laws across the Union. No state acted in isolation when it came to married women's economic rights. There was no national mandate from Congress or the Supreme Court, nor would there have been given the nineteenth-century view that property rights were the exclusive jurisdiction of state governments. Yet each of the states and territories passed some form of married women's economic rights reform between 1835 and 1920. States frequently borrowed ideas and even cribbed language wholesale from each other, often explicitly calling on another state's experiences, successes, and failures. This story shows how rights reforms can spread among the states when national coordination or control is absent.

MARRIED WOMEN'S ECONOMIC RIGHTS IN AMERICAN POLITICAL DEVELOPMENT

This research makes important interventions into our understanding of American political development (APD). The APD literature thus far has not extensively examined the development of married women's property rights in the states. Most commonly, these reforms are treated as minor examples or even simply mentioned in footnotes. Yet examining these reforms more robustly allows for new insights into our understanding of how gender, federalism, and liberalism interacted in the development of American state power.

First, this book contributes to our understanding of the role of federalism and state institutions in the development of both individual rights and state power in the nineteenth century. As part of marriage and family law, married women's property rights were nearly exclusively the responsibility of state governments. States and territories with dramatically different political cultures and histories with women's rights converged on the same policy solution of married women's economic rights, often using identical language in statutes and constitutions. Knowing the process by which a policy expanding rights came to fit multiple state-level goals helps us understand how nationwide policy development can take place despite the lack of top-down coercion or coordination. The book thus also adds to an existing literature on states' rights expansions and constitutional reform, outlining new mechanisms by which both statutory and constitutional diffusion have developed.[5]

Married women's property acts also provide an important example of the ways in which the state employs identity—in this case gender as well as race and marital status—to build state power. Gretchen Ritter writes that "gendered understandings have been available for use in advancing political agendas or in legitimating political change."[6] The granting of new property rights to married women allowed states to pursue enslavement and settlement agendas. By "protecting" enslaved human property, antebellum southern married women's property acts kept slave-owning families solvent during economic turmoil, increasing the economic stability of slaveholding women while casting enslaved women and men as property to be "protected" from the debts of their enslaver's husband. Meanwhile, male politicians on the frontier saw white women as crucial to the project of settlement, a civilizing force that would boost territories' population numbers high enough for them to apply for statehood and to be central players in permanently seizing land from Native people. Here, too, it is clear from the design of the laws and the context in which they were embedded that only a certain group of women were meant to benefit from married women's property acts and that other groups would have their rights stripped from them.

Relatedly, the development of women's economic citizenship through married women's property acts shaped and constrained the boundaries of these developments. As can be seen through the operation of identity in these reforms, these laws helped define the ideal or desired citizen. They expanded married women's economic citizenship but also delineated in important ways which women got to enjoy that fuller citizenship. By their very nature, they had the most impact on women with property to protect, and many had bureaucratic requirements such as registration or the use of separate bank accounts that further limited how many women could realistically benefit from them. Around the country, male political actors liberalized married women's economic rights with respect to the market to the extent that they thought it was necessary to allow for the development of efficient and workable property rights in a commercial economy. But they took care not to interfere with the husband–wife relationship as it was defined at the time more than was needed to accomplish this goal and left women's place in the economy partially but not fully liberalized because of an enduring commitment to gender hierarchy. That being said, despite these limits, this series of reforms represents a major instance of democratization in American political development, and, thus, understanding both the extent of and the constraints on that democratization is crucial for understanding women's place in U.S. democracy.

Finally, scholars of APD have written extensively about the role of liberalism in American political culture.[7] As Duncan Bell notes, the term *liberalism* is "employed in a dizzying variety of ways in political thought and social science."[8] In this book, I use the definition of liberalism that is most prominent within the APD literature, which emphasizes individualism, economic opportunity, liberal democracy, as well as the absence of feudalism and rigid class divisions.[9] A major theme in this literature is the idea that Americans were not, after all, "born liberal"; the process of liberalization and the limits of liberalism are crucial for understanding political development in the United States.[10] The liberalization of married women's economic rights in the mid-1800s and early 1900s has received less attention in these studies than reforms around labor law, citizenship, and civil rights.[11] This early period of development is particularly important for understanding the processes of liberalization and rights expansions in the United States because these reforms took a different trajectory than those in many other issue areas. Although married women's property acts did liberalize many of the feudal elements of coverture, they left in place core features of the gender hierarchy and strengthened racial hierarchies; after the acts' passage, these liberal and illiberal elements of marriage continued to coexist, often uneasily, for decades. As discussed already, reforms happened almost entirely at the state level, with state institutions playing distinctive roles. In particular, courts played a less conflictual and more collaborative role in the development of married women's rights than in the development of many other rights expansions.

PLAN FOR THE BOOK

I take a multimethod approach to exploring the development of married women's economic rights reform. The study ranges from 1835, when Arkansas Territory enacted the nation's first married women's property law that dealt specifically with protecting a married women's separate property, through 1920 with the ratification of the Nineteenth Amendment of the U.S. Constitution. I examine case study data from a subset of states and territories around the nation to allow for close analysis of materials such as constitutional convention minutes, newspapers, and state court cases. I also analyze the passage of multiple reforms and the text of both statutory and constitutional provisions using quantitative methods to examine broader patterns and connections between states.

Chapter 1 provides key background information, describing the conditions of married women under coverture and the basic outlines of the reform period that followed. I describe the major contours of married women's economic rights across time and space, identifying five key categories of reforms in the states and mapping their passage. This chapter also summarizes what we know about married women's property reforms from previous literature across multiple academic disciplines. In chapter 2, I outline my theory and major arguments, highlighting how interstate and intrastate reform processes across multiple institutions combined to bring about reforms to married women's economic rights.

Chapters 3 and 4 analyze the reform of married women's economic rights in state legislatures and state constitutional conventions. Largely using case study evidence, both chapters explore the ways that the enactment of new rights for women could be leveraged by both parties and political actors across the political spectrum to achieve a variety of political goals. In particular, actors in the two venues were able to use these new rights as vehicles for both inclusion and exclusion, simultaneously granting some women fuller economic citizenship while reinforcing the exclusion of others. I emphasize that male political actors' often conflicting motivations led to an ambivalence around married women's property legislation that ultimately limited its potential.

Chapters 4 and 5 also explore the spread of reform language and concepts throughout the states. In constitutional conventions and state legislatures, political actors borrowed readily from other states, attempting to learn from both successes and failures in other places. In chapter 5, I use event history analysis to estimate the likelihood of specific reforms being enacted over time. Importantly, I find that although there are connections among the different types of economic rights granted to married women during this reform period, in most places they were passed at different times and for varying reasons. No one factor predicts early or late passage of all five reform types, but rather distinctive patterns are exhibited for the different types of reforms. I also study the spread of reforms by examining the transmission of text between states with an analysis of statutory and constitutional text based on plagiarism software.

Finally, chapter 6 concludes the tour of state-level institutions with state courts. Courts played a catalytic role in the development of married women's economic reforms, most often interpreting married women's property laws narrowly. These narrow interpretations were not necessarily out of line with the intentions of state lawmakers, whose attempts to balance economic rights for women with state protection of women could lead to complex, conflicting statutes. As courts interpreted these statutes in ways that increased confusion and decreased predictability in credit markets, popular pressure grew for simplifying the law and granting more expansive rights to married women.

In some ways, this account of rights reform is depressing. It underscores just how little agency women of the nineteenth century enjoyed and the ways in which more powerful elite male actors held sway over the form, extent, and impact of rights expansions. But the account is also hopeful. The expansion of rights doesn't necessarily require that a group already hold political power or have the capacity to actively organize and campaign in every state. Law can take on a life of its own and flow outward through states, which learn from and compete with one another.

Reform ideas can spread even without highly organized activism in each statehouse. Policy can change, and rights can expand even when group members cannot take their demands to the ballot box. And the reforms that took place through the passage of married women's property acts paved the way for further democratization of women's role in both the political sphere and the economy.

CHAPTER ONE

Life Under Coverture and How It Changed

To understand the developments in married women's economic rights that took place at the state level from 1835 to 1920, it is crucial to understand what came before these reforms. What was life for women like before the passage of married women's property acts? The first section of this chapter explores women's lives under coverture as well as ways that married women could carve out exceptions for themselves and gain more independence during this early period.

Next, I examine the actual reforms, providing an overview of the data at the center of this book. To understand what happened and when, I sort reforms into five categories that I see as being most important to the married women's economic rights reform project: a married woman's ability (1) to hold separate property free from her husband's debts, (2) to control and manage that property, (3) to hold her wages or earnings as separate property, (4) to write a will, and (5) to engage in business.[1] I provide sample language that demonstrates the different ways states framed these rights and map the passage of these rights over time and space.

Finally, I review what we know about married women's property rights reforms from a variety of academic disciplines, including history, law, sociology, and economics. Scholars from numerous fields have analyzed these reforms using their own disciplinary perspectives. I synthesize the major contributions from this previous work and highlight how a perspective grounded in American political development can expand our understanding of the dynamics of reform.

WOMEN'S LIVES UNDER COVERTURE

Prior to the 1840s, married women's property rights and their legal and economic identities more broadly were governed largely by a legal doctrine known as coverture. Coverture was based on the British common-law system, which was adopted by all of the colonies and eventually by most states.[2] Linda Kerber describes coverture as being "based on the assumption that married women had neither independent minds nor independent power."[3] Single women certainly faced legal barriers to full political and economic citizenship—suffrage being one major barrier and another being state-level prohibitions on women engaging in certain professions, such as law and medicine. Yet when it came to many economic and legal rights—including owning and managing property, signing legal contracts, and appearing in court—single women were formally treated like men under the law.[4] This was not the case for married women.

From the moment a woman said her marriage vows, her legal identity was completely subsumed into her husband's; she ceased to have an independent identity under the common law. Coverture entailed a host of legal disabilities, many of which related to married women's economic rights.[5] Married women could not own property, had no right to their wages, and could not write wills, sign legal contracts, take out mortgages or other loans, or file for bankruptcy.[6] As Marylynn Salmon discusses in her excellent account of the law concerning married women's property before reforms were passed, husbands even had the power to limit their wives' ability to shop at specific local shops and to prevent them from purchasing particular items.[7] If a woman inherited property from a relative or received it as gift, it belonged to her husband and could be seized by his creditors.[8]

The lack of a separate legal identity went beyond property rights. A wife could not appear in court under her own name, sue for personal injury, or testify against her husband.[9] As head of household, the husband had custody of a couple's children, with limited exceptions, and even had the power to designate in his will someone other than their mother as their guardian.[10] Even a wife's body was not considered her own. Marital rape was not considered a crime; women could seek legal redress for domestic violence only in the most extreme of circumstances; and men determined the family's place of residence and had the right to physically restrain their wives from leaving that place.[11]

In sum, women's lives under coverture were severely constrained. Women didn't just lack voting rights—they had little to no sources of independent power at all.[12] Not all these legal disabilities were reformed during the period under study in this book; for example, reforms to marital-rape laws did not begin to be made until the 1970s, and married women did not have legally protected independent access to credit until the passage of the federal Equal Credit Opportunity Act in 1974.[13] Yet the reforms that were enacted were surprisingly sweeping given the dearth not only of married women's political power but also of their economic, legal, and social power.

Although the common law and married women's legal status under it was strict in theory, exceptions abounded. For instance, in some states married women could run businesses (and engage in activities such as contract writing and making loans as part of those businesses), at least under certain limited circumstances. Called a *feme sole trader*, a woman might be permitted to engage in market activity if, for example, her husband provided written permission, if her husband abandoned her, if he were insane or imprisoned, or if the woman sought a special exemption through the state legislature or a local court.[14] Feme-sole-trader policies were considered necessary for married women whose husbands could not provide them with basic living expenses and provided a way for some of these women to avoid falling back on public support, thus solving the problem of dependency on the state. But these exceptions to the common law varied dramatically among states and, of course, did not apply more generally to all married women, only to those who fit specific qualifications and had the resources to avail themselves of these laws. Further, although women who qualified under these statutes had some measure of independence in running their businesses and making independent legal decisions, their profits ultimately still belonged to their husbands.[15] A woman who was abandoned by her husband might be able to run a business in his absence in order to support herself and her children, but she faced the potential of losing any economic gains from this business if he chose to return.

Another major exception to the common-law status of coverture was the use of equity (in some states called "chancery") courts to make special arrangements outside of common-law rules. Originally based in appeals to the king's chancellor, these courts developed in Britain as a way to "offer[] special remedies when none were available at [common] law"; they were based "in the concept of fairness as opposed to legal strictness."[16] The idea was that these special petitions could be brought before judges in situations when the common law was considered too harsh.[17] Not every state adopted equity courts, but those that did allowed married women to make use of legal instruments not available to them in common-law courts, where they had no independent legal identity. In addition, before marriage, women (or their families) could negotiate marriage settlements that altered the common law of coverture in a variety of ways. For example, the wife's separate property might be set aside so that it was not accessible to the husband but instead was managed by a third-party trustee, often a male family member, such as a father or brother. Before marriage, some women negotiated for more autonomy, such as the ability to make independent decisions about their separate property, as if they were single.[18]

Like feme-sole-trader policies, equity courts had their limitations. Many states either never established equity courts or eliminated them at some point. Particularly in northeastern colonies, equity courts were often seen as costly and slow as well as having an unsavory "association with the prerogative powers of king or governor."[19] Even where equity courts existed, they were expensive and required legal expertise (or access to legal representation) to take advantage of, and so only wealthier women could utilize them in practice.[20] To a large extent, the purpose of these policies was to keep control of property within a woman's family of origin rather than to empower her specifically.[21] Sandra F. VanBurkleo estimates that, at most, 8 percent of married women were able to take advantage of antenuptial agreements and similar equitable mechanisms to protect property they brought into their marriage.[22] Further, because the type of property rights granted by equity courts was by special petition, each situation was treated in an ad hoc manner and not linked to broader economic or legal rights for women as a group.[23]

Finally, some U.S. territories and states did not base their marital-property rights system on the British common law but were instead heavily influenced by the Spanish or French civil-law systems. This influence took a variety of forms. For example, Louisiana adopted a civil-law system wholesale, whereas California operated almost entirely under the common law with a special carve-out for marital-property rights that borrowed heavily from civil-law understandings of marriage. In contrast to the common law, which was based on judicial precedent unless state legislatures chose to make explicit exceptions, all of civil law was based on written legal codes.

Under civil law, a married woman did not lose her legal identity and had more access to the court system. After marriage, property owned by either spouse before the marriage or acquired by them afterward was generally considered community property, jointly owned by both the husband and wife. However, although married women technically held (joint) ownership of this property, this condition served primarily as a way to keep that property within her family of birth, not to empower her economically. While the couple was married, and both spouses were alive, community property would typically be placed completely under the husband's control and management.

Scholars have differed on the extent to which community-property regimes had a meaningful impact either on the lived experiences of married women or on the pace of reforms.[24] Because traditional community-property rules, like the common law, lodged management rights solely with husbands, they did limit married women's ability to engage with the broader economy in meaningful ways. As a result, the states with community-property regimes passed married women's economic rights reforms that looked very similar to those of the rest of the United States, often using very similar language. Even in Louisiana—which diverged most extremely from common-law traditions—married women's legal and economic rights were reformed during this same period in ways similar to other states'.[25]

As a more general point, despite the existence of various exceptions, limitations, and variations to coverture, women fundamentally lost a major part of their civic and economic identity after marrying. Married women living before economic rights reforms were severely constrained across multiple dimensions of their lives. And most women did marry:

90 percent or more of women older than thirty-five were married during this period,[26] meaning that almost all women of this era could expect to fall under the rules for married women at some point during their lives.

MARRIED WOMEN'S ECONOMIC RIGHTS REFORM IN TIME AND SPACE

Thus, the typical married woman living in the United States in 1820 would have had extremely limited legal and economic rights. Regardless of whether a woman lived in a common-law or civil-law state or whether equity courts provided limited relief for wealthy women, she lost most of her economic rights upon marriage. A century later, she would have substantially expanded powers and protections around a host of economic and legal matters. Starting in the 1830s, states and territories began to chip away more systematically at the doctrine of coverture in ways that—often slowly, gradually—began to open up economic and legal rights for married women. In some ways, these reforms were not radical, and certainly there were real limits to what they would accomplish. But by 1920 and the ratification of the Nineteenth Amendment, the various married women's property acts and related reforms enacted throughout the country did represent a fundamental shift in the way married women were treated under the law and in their relationship to the state. Although some illiberal restrictions remained, in most states the law acknowledged a separate legal identity for married women and allowed them to hold property and make contracts as if they were single.

These reforms occurred despite the facts that women had the right to vote in only a few states and the political system as a whole was relatively hostile to women's economic and political equality. In any given state, reforms tended to become more expansive and rights granting over time, although there are some exceptions.[27] What exactly did these reforms look like? Table 1.1 provides a working definition for each category of reform, sample statutory language, and descriptive statistics. I describe here in more detail how each reform worked in practice.

The most basic and often the earliest of these reforms allowed married women to hold certain types of property separately from their husbands, referred to here as "debt-free separate estates." This sort of law

TABLE 1.1
Definitions, Sample Language, and Descriptive Statistics for Reform Categories

Reform	Working Definition	Sample Language	Descriptive Statistics
Debt-free separate estates	Explicit definition of married women's ability to own a separate estate and explicit exemption of that estate from her husband's debts	"That the property owned by any married woman, before her marriage, and that which she may acquire after marriage, by descent, gift, grant, devise, or otherwise, and the increase, use, and profits thereof, shall be exempt from all debts and liabilities of the husband, unless for necessary articles for the use and benefit of the family. Provided, however, That the provisions of this act shall extend only to such property as shall be mentioned in a list of the property of such married woman as is on record in the office of the register of deeds of the county in which such married woman resides" (Dakota Territory, 1862).	*Number of states with passage by 1920*: 47. *Date range*: 1835–1890. *Median year of first passage*: 1855.
Control and management	Married women granted general powers of control and management over their separate property, including sales and mortgages. These powers were more sweeping in some states than in others and sometimes included limitations on sales of real estate.	*Strong version*: "That the real and personal estate of every female acquired before marriage, and all property, real and personal, to which she may afterwards become entitled, by gift, grant, inheritance, devise, or in any other manner, shall be and remain the estate and property of such female, and shall not be liable for the debts, obligations and engagements of her husband, and may be contracted, sold, transferred, mortgaged, conveyed, devised or bequeathed by her, in the same manner and with the like effect as if she were unmarried" (Michigan, 1855).	*Number of states with passage by 1920*: 45. *Date range*: 1848–1919. *Median year of first passage*: 1873.

		Weak version: "Any woman, hereafter married, may, while married, bargain, sell and convey her real and personal property, and enter into any contract in reference to the same, in the same manner as if she were sole; but no conveyance of any real property, (except a lease for a term not exceeding one year,) and no conveyance of any shares in any corporation, shall be valid, without the assent, in writing, of her husband, except with the consent of one of the judges of the supreme judicial court, or of the court of common pleas, or the judge of probate, to be granted, on her petition, in any county, on account of the sickness, insanity or absence from the Commonwealth, of her husband, or other good cause; and her husband, if within the Commonwealth, shall have such notice of the petition as the judge or court may order. This petition may be presented to, and granted by, any such judge in vacation, as well as in term time" (Massachusetts, 1855).	
Earnings	Earnings and wages granted status as separate property with control-and-management rights like those granted for other separate property (i.e., inheritances, gifts, property owned before marriage, etc.).	"That a married woman shall be entitled to receive, use and possess her own earnings, and sue for the same in her own name, free from the interference of her husband or his creditors: Provided, this act shall not be construed to give to the wife any right to compensation for any labor performed for her minor children or husband" (Illinois, 1869).	*Number of states with passage by 1920*: 40. *Date range*: 1843–1919. *Median year of first passage*: 1873.

(continued)

TABLE 1.1
Definitions, Sample Language, and Descriptive Statistics for Reform Categories (*continued*)

Reform	Working Definition	Sample Language	Descriptive Statistics
Sole trader	All married women have the right to operate a business and sign contracts, not subject to limitations such as a husband's abandonment or permission or a court's finding of competence. In some states, "sole-trader" status is explicitly mentioned; in others, statutes refer to a broad right to contract for married women.	*Sole-trader language*: "Any married woman may carry on trade or business and perform any labor or services on her sole and separate account, and the earnings of any married woman from her trade, business, labor, or services shall be her sole and separate property, and may be used and invested in her own name" (Nebraska, 1871). *Contract language*: "The contracts of any married woman, made for any lawful purpose, shall be valid and binding, and may be enforced in the same manner as if she were sole; and her separate property shall be holden by attachment, or levy on execution, in any suit brought to enforce such contract, but she shall not be liable to arrest, on any writ in such suit, or on any execution issued on a judgement recovered in the same; *provided* that nothing in this act shall be so construed so as to affect any suit now pending" (Maine, 1866).	*Number of states with passage by 1920*: 39. *Date range*: 1807–1919. *Median year of first passage*: 1874.
Wills	Married women have the right to bequeath their separate property in a will, without a husband's permission.	"A married woman may dispose of all her separate estate by will, without the consent of her husband, and may alter or revoke the will in like manner as if she were single. Her will must be executed and proved in like manner as other wills" (California, 1874).	*Number of states with passage by 1920*: 48. *Date range*: 1808–1901. *Median year of first passage*: 1868.

codified the sort of rights that had been available to wealthy women through equity courts by granting *all* married women separate estates for certain types of property. The property covered by separate-estates laws varied but often included property the woman had owned before marriage, property that she inherited, and gifts to her from anyone other than her husband. It might include real estate, personal property such as clothing and household goods, and in some states enslaved humans. This separate property would typically be required to be registered in the area where the woman lived and would then no longer be liable for her husband's debts. Although some debt-free separate-estate laws were more expansive, many provided only for the ownership of separate property and the protection of that property from creditors. These laws functioned primarily as a form of family-level debt relief, and all control and management of a wife's separate property—and sometimes any profits gained from use of that property—remained firmly with the husband. In some antebellum southern states, these debt-relief acts were limited to or specifically named enslaved human property, making it clear that white women were the primary intended beneficiaries of the reform.

In some states, debt-free separate-estate laws were combined with reforms that allowed married women control and management over that separate property, but in other states these more expansive laws, which I call "control-and-management" statutes, came later. Laws allowing for control and management of separate property sometimes allowed married women to act as a feme sole (a single woman) with regard to their separate property—that is, with broad powers to buy, sell, lease, and mortgage that property. Other states and territories passed in-between measures that allowed a married woman to control her property in some ways but not in others; for example, she might use her separate property as collateral for a loan to educate her children but not to engage in land speculation. When I refer to control-and-management statutes, I am generally referring to the more expansive versions of these acts, which allowed women full control over their separate property. That said, some states passed only weaker versions of these laws that still placed some limits on married women's control of their property, especially the sale of real estate, and these weaker versions are still included in the data. These more limited control-and-management laws would typically require a husband's consent for real estate sales or long-term leases and sometimes provided for judicial override.

A third type of reform, typically referred to as "earnings acts," gave married women ownership over their wages. Wages had historically been seen as a different type of property than real estate, personal property, and enslaved human property and thus were often covered by different legislation.[28] The key defining feature of earnings acts was that they classified earnings or wages as separate property to be treated like other types of separate property. Thus, they varied in the amount of power they granted to women. Earlier earnings acts passed before control-and-management statutes might grant only limited control over wages but exempt them from a husband's debts, or they might even limit the dollar value of earnings that a married women could control. Later earnings acts passed alongside or after control-and-management statutes were more expansive in the economic rights they granted to married women. Accordingly, as with other types of married women's economic rights reform, states sometimes passed multiple versions of earnings acts over the years.

Fourth, "sole-trader" provisions allowed married women to conduct business under their own name and on their own account as well as to sign contracts as if they were single. As discussed earlier, even before the wave of married women's economic rights reform that began in the 1830s, some states had long granted sole-trader rights for a small subset of married women, but there were significant limits to these policies. Here, I focus on laws that granted sole-trader rights to *all* married women regardless of a husband's status or permission, though some states did require a married woman to publicly register her intent to operate as a sole trader in some way. In some states, statutes explicitly referenced rights to carry on trade or business, whereas in others the language focused on a broad right to contract as if one was single. Sole-trader laws were often combined with earnings provisions, allowing married women both to conduct business and to retain ownership of their earnings from that business.

Finally, married women in many states also gained the right to write their own wills, without their husband's permission, regarding their separate property: I refer to these policies simply as "wills" laws. The reform of the right to bequeath property to others spans the largest period in this study, beginning in the early 1800s and continuing after

1920. Nonetheless, I include testamentary power in my discussion and analysis because this right is so closely tied to other property rights and because some states passed laws relating to wills alongside and packaged with other married women's property rights.

In addition to defining categories of reform, we also want to know where and when these policies were enacted. For each state, I have identified the earliest reform passed that meets the definitions listed in table 1.1, although later reforms might further clarify or expand women's economic rights. More details on the process of identifying the dates of these reforms as well as a full table of dates of reform for all states and territories can be found in the "Methods Appendix." Note that, as discussed earlier, each of these reform categories could be broader than these working definitions, and details could vary from state to state.

Figure 1.1 gives a sense of the pace of each reform over time. This type of graph is called a "violin plot": it gets wider in periods when many states were passing a particular reform and narrower during periods when no or few states were passing that reform. The U.S. maps in figures 1.2–1.6 provide a different way of visualizing reforms by providing information on particular types of reforms in both time and space. For each map, lighter shades indicate passage of a given reform before and around 1835, and progressively darker shades indicate passage over the decades up to 1920. States that passed a particular reform after 1920 are indicated with a crosshatched pattern.[29]

Even these figures do not fully capture the story of married women's economic rights reform because states often refined and expanded rights in various ways after the passage of initial statutes. The figures also do not represent the extensive legal activity that was taking place in state courts around married women's property rights. I address both of these topics elsewhere in this book through the use of case study evidence throughout the narrative as well as through a focus on the importance of state courts in chapter 6.

STUDIES OF MARRIED WOMEN'S PROPERTY RIGHTS ACROSS DISCIPLINES

Scholars from different disciplines have analyzed the passage of married women's property acts and related reforms. As a result, what we currently

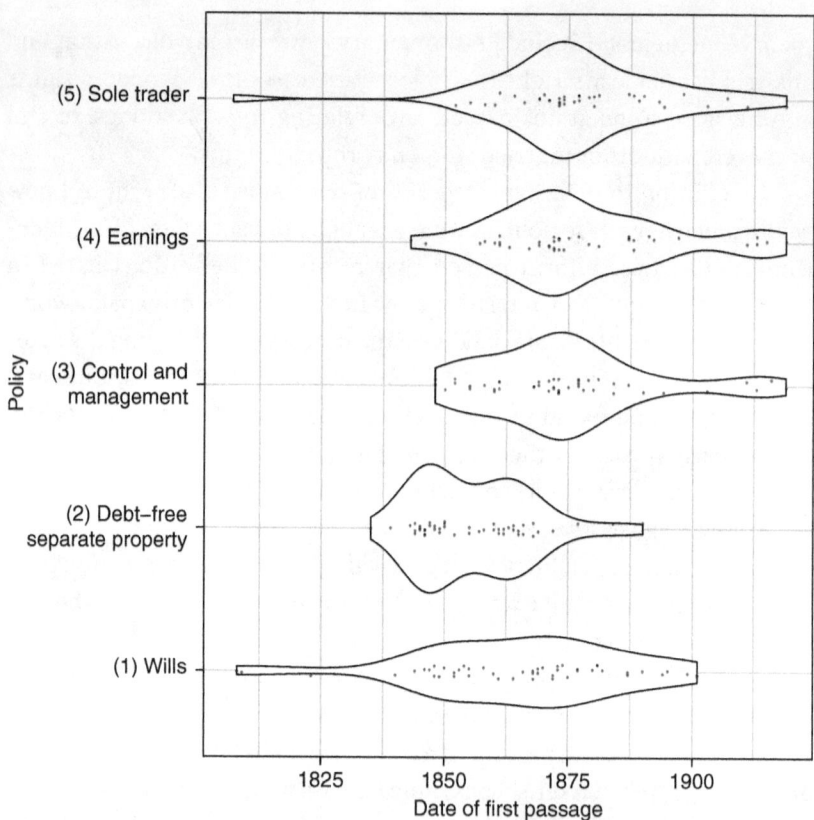

FIGURE 1.1. Dates of passage of married women's property rights reforms.

know about these reforms reflects different disciplinary perspectives, priorities, and methodologies. In this section, I outline findings from two major perspectives on the reform of married women's economic rights. The first perspective comes largely from historians and legal historians and is based primarily on case study methods. These studies typically focus on the historical context and processes of reform passage as well as on legal responses. The second perspective comes primarily from economics and is characterized by medium-N studies that look for nationwide patterns in both the predictors and the consequences of married women's property rights reforms. Both perspectives provide important but differently focused insights into the development of married women's economic rights.

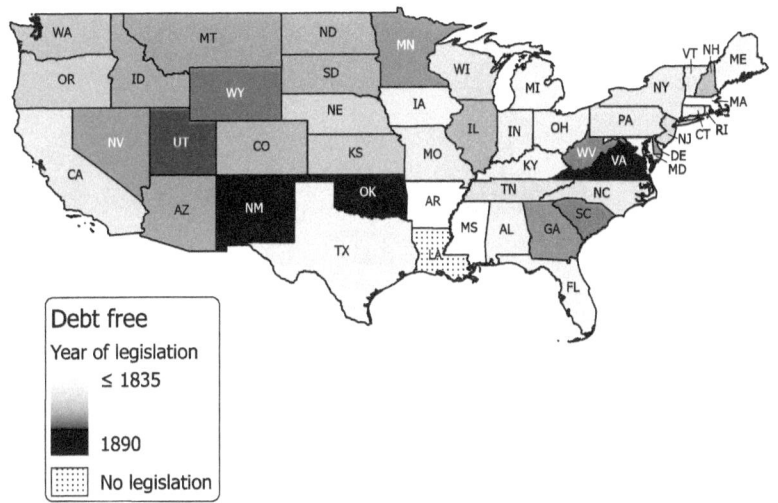

FIGURE 1.2. Passage of debt-free separate-estates reforms. Sources for all maps are listed in the "Methods Appendix" in the section outlining how statute dates were determined.

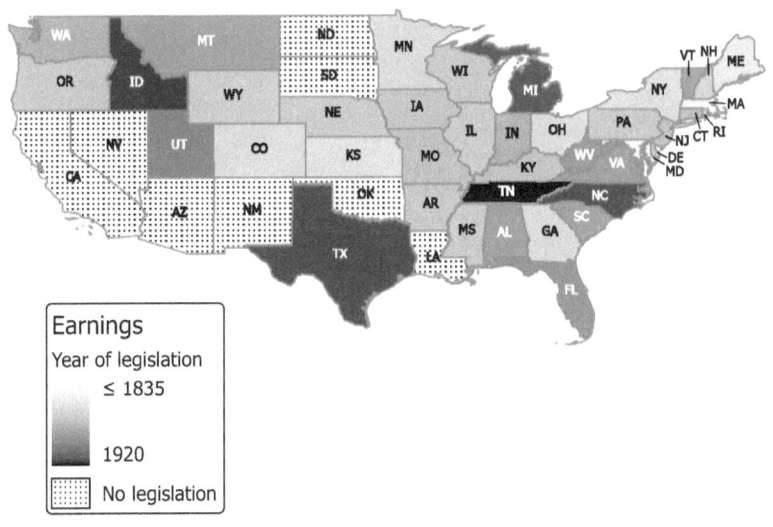

FIGURE 1.3. Passage of earnings acts.

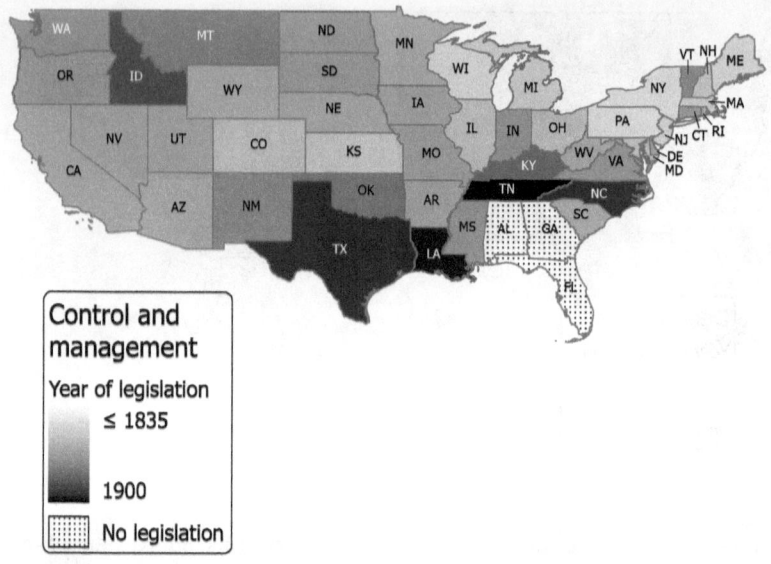

FIGURE 1.4. Passage of control-and-management rights reforms.

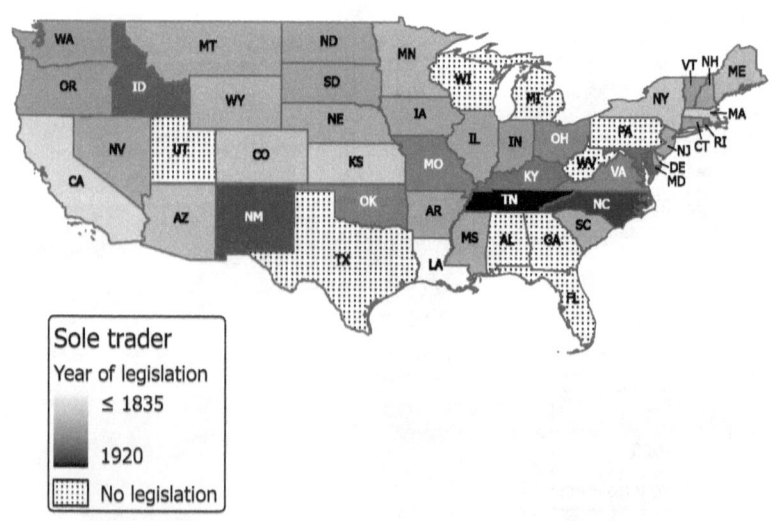

FIGURE 1.5. Passage of sole-trader rights reforms.

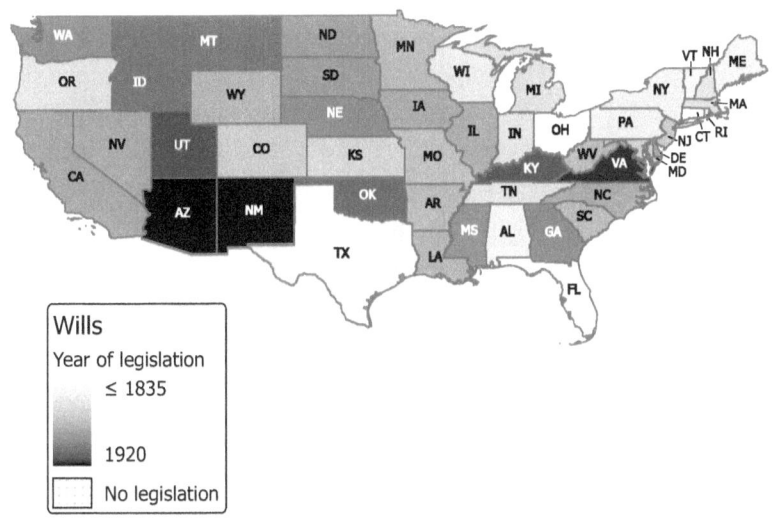

FIGURE 1.6. Passage of testamentary rights reforms.

Many studies of married women's economic rights have been case study driven and are characterized by rich, contextual historical work that typically examines one or a limited number of states. These studies come largely from scholars working in history or law, although some come from work in sociology and economic history. New York is probably the most frequently analyzed case because it was an early adopter of reforms that was used as a model in other states. But other work has examined different states and regions, and some research has sought to summarize knowledge within and across regions.

These studies frequently seek to identify and analyze the factors that contributed to the passage of a specific reform or set of reforms. They have uncovered a wide variety of such factors, some applicable to multiple cases and others highly specific to a particular time and place. For example, Mississippi historians cite the influence of an important state court case involving Chickasaw tribal law as partially inspiring Mississippi's early married women's property act, but Chickasaw property arrangements do not seem likely to have been influential elsewhere in the nation.[30]

Other influences on reforms do apply more widely, however, either regionally or nationally. As I discuss in more detail later, states and territories used married women's property law to define the "ideal citizen" of their state and to empower some women while disempowering others. The particulars of this process varied substantially by region. For example, states and territories on the frontier had different considerations than more settled areas when it came to married women and their property.[31] A major factor shaping women's rights on the frontier was gender imbalance in that the frontier tended to have many fewer women than men.[32] Politicians in these areas hoped to attract women to move west, and scholars have linked this desire specifically to broader goals of settler colonialism and the displacement of Native people.[33]

Another important regional influence was the existence of chattel slavery in the South. Antebellum southern married women's property rights laws often specifically listed enslaved human property as among the types of property "protected" by legislation (i.e., "protected" for the benefit only of white women slaveholders and their male descendants), and enslaved human property was sometimes treated differently than other types of property. Although not all analyses of southern reforms address enslaved human property in detail, some do, as in Joyce Broussard's discussion of how Mississippi's legislature of 1839 debated whether allowing married women to own and potentially manage enslaved human property would disrupt social, racial, and sexual hierarchies.[34]

Many historians also cite the importance of economic factors unrelated to gender in shaping the perceived need for these laws. A series of panics, economic upheavals, and financial crises took place in the United States throughout the 1800s and early 1900s, coinciding with the period when married women's economic rights were reformed. These crises were often precipitated by monetary policy, land and railroad speculation, and the disruption of financial markets—issues not inherently linked to married women's rights. Yet the economic consequences of these panics could be long lasting and affect the economy broadly, and the panics hit different states and territories with different levels of severity.

These crises had a variety of causes, including rampant speculation in land and railroads, crop failures, political and legal developments, an increasingly integrated international financial and commercial system, machinations in the financial community, and disasters such as fires and earthquakes in major cities.[35] These varied causes often led to bank runs and to a shortage of specie—gold and silver coins as opposed to notes or paper money—which could cause banks to close temporarily or even to fail entirely.[36] Regional effects varied, with, for example, the Panic of 1837 hitting the South and Northeast hardest, while the Panic of 1857 affected the West and Great Lakes regions the most.[37] In general, though, these crises and panics devastated many businesses, drove up unemployment, and led to foreclosures, creating an unstable economic situation for many ordinary Americans, even those who lived far from financial hubs or interacted little with international markets.

Compounding the impacts of a boom-and-bust economy was the changing role of debt in the economy and a growing middle class. Debtors increasingly came from all parts of the class structure, so that issues of debt relief began to matter to more and more people. The middle class was growing, thus increasing the number of people with family wealth that they wanted to protect.[38] Many historians studying married women's property rights reforms cite these economic conditions as crucial for understanding the passage of the acts. For laws that included debt-relief provisions, the goal was not primarily (or even at all) the empowerment of women but rather the protection of some portion of family property from creditors, responding to indebted men's demand to keep them from financial ruin.[39] In the case of broader grants of economic power to married women, scholars have argued that they were part of broader shifts toward commercialization, industrialization, and adjustment to market forces.[40] In using married women's property law as one tool in their toolbox to respond to these changing economic conditions, male state politicians were able to leverage laws that expanded married women's rights in order to advance the politicians' own economic interests and to help stabilize state economies.

Even the concept of property and the definition of its proper role in society were being transformed during this period. Gregory Alexander writes that in the years before the Civil War there was a growing understanding of property through the lens of economics, market forces, and exchange. A competing vision of property considered it to function primarily as "the material foundation for creating and maintaining the proper social order."[41] The development of married women's economic rights included both property as a commodity and property as a means of social control and order. Lawmakers and jurists struggled to balance the idea of women as independent economic actors whose property could be bought and sold on the market with the desire to protect women from dangerous market forces and even from their husbands, a balancing act that led to laws that combined both liberal and illiberal elements.

A number of scholars have emphasized legislators' paternalist or protective goals. This emphasis on protection sometimes concerned specific relationships—that is, fathers who wished to protect both their daughters and their family money from questionably responsible sons-in-law.[42] In other cases, these arguments were broader, seeking to protect married women generally through the use of state power. Married women were seen as in need of protection both from their husbands as well as from broader market forces and risky economic deals. These arguments sometimes mirrored those made by supporters of the temperance movement, pleading for the state to protect wives and children from drunken, dissolute husbands.[43]

Other work links the passage of married women's property acts to the broader codification movement that was active across the nation during this period. This movement aimed to rationalize and systematize state law with the creation of codes, which were typically written and compiled by experts and then adopted by a state legislature in an up-or-down vote. Codes would then replace judge-made common law. Rationalization of property law meant that married women's participation in economic interactions could not be treated according to special rules or exceptions. Thus, as part of the codification process, married women's economic powers were sometimes enlarged to better mirror those of single women. Even where wholesale codification efforts failed, these debates sometimes opened up discussion around married women's rights reforms.[44]

The literature is divided on the impact that women themselves, especially those working through organized groups, had as a primary or even a major force behind the passage of reforms. This may seem odd in that women are obviously the subject of these laws and did agitate for them in some cases. But some scholars point out that the self-interested motivations of male political actors outlined earlier provide a more accurate explanation for why these laws were passed and that the women's movement was either weak or nonexistent in some of the locations and times that reforms were enacted.[45] Reva Siegel argues that women did organize around property rights but that their more radical demands were roundly rejected by state legislatures. She writes that antebellum women organized around demands for joint property as opposed to separate property—that is, instead of women being able to hold and control property that they separately brought to a marriage, they would have joint rights to control all family property by right of the otherwise unpaid labor they contributed to the household.[46] State legislatures responded to these demands with a very clear negative, explicitly exempting household labor from married women's property rights laws.

Other scholars, however, argue that although women's voices were missing or ignored in the development and passage of some reforms, their organizational skill and strategic moves in other times and places did influence the speed, content, or progressiveness of reforms.[47] Petitions, for example, were a particularly important method for women to make demands on politicians despite the fact that women could not vote, and such petitions were exploding in number and organizational sophistication during this period.[48] The use of petitioning around both property and suffrage demands in state legislatures granted women access to legislative hearings, often for the first time in U.S. history.[49] Holly McCammon, Sandra C. Arch, and Erin M. Bergner emphasize that in the right context—in states with an active women's movement already mobilizing around suffrage issues—women were able to secure earlier passage of economic reforms by strategically framing these reforms as more "moderate" than radical suffrage rights.[50]

Finally, whereas many case study approaches to married women's property rights reform focus on the initial passage of statutes or constitutional provisions in specific states, other work has examined how state courts interpreted these reforms in the years after their passage. This work has largely highlighted the conservative nature of the state judiciary, arguing that courts limited a more liberal potential within married women's property acts and clung to common-law interpretations of the marriage relationship despite legislative interventions.[51] In contrast, I argue that although state court rulings were indeed not radical on women's rights issues, state court judges' approach was largely consistent with that of state legislatures and constitutional conventions, which also had ambivalent attitudes toward women's economic empowerment.

On the whole, these scholarly works are very valuable for understanding the mechanisms behind the passage of married women's economic rights reforms in particular historical contexts as well as, in some cases, the development of such reforms over time in a given state. This rich historical context can help us understand the historically specific forces that political actors were responding to within their geography and time. However, because there were significant differences between early and late laws, between different types of reforms, and between regions, these studies can make it hard to grasp an overall national story of reform and to create cumulative knowledge about the broader processes of reform. Findings can be very dependent on which states were selected for study, with different explanatory factors coming to the forefront depending on which specific locations and periods are being studied.

Taking a very different approach, a group of scholars largely within economics and economic history have worked to generalize our knowledge about married women's economic rights reforms by constructing and analyzing data sets that include the forty-seven territories and states in existence at the time these reforms were enacted. This work has examined both the predictors of reforms as well as the downstream impacts of reforms, largely with a focus on economic rather than political variables.

A major challenge for this literature has been accurate dating of reforms. Because deeper state-level context is reduced in such studies, and each state (or territory) is represented in the data with one or two reform dates and a limited number of additional covariates, accurate identification of the year reforms were enacted is clearly crucial. Early work tended to rely on contemporaneous legal treatises and commentaries to identify the dates of reform passage.[52] In more recent years, as state statute books have become more readily available online, scholars have begun to compile date lists based more directly on these primary sources. The most commonly used dating scheme was compiled by R. Richard Geddes and Sharon Tennyson, including dates for married women's property acts that granted married women control-and-management powers as well as for earnings acts.[53] These lists still contain some errors, though, and are limited in the number of reform types they cover. A fuller discussion of the dating issue and a comprehensive list of statute dates for all five reform types laid out in table 1.1 can be found in the "Methods Appendix."

Data limitations notwithstanding, economics research has examined several possible factors influencing the timing of reform passage in the states. Scholars have found that lower levels of fertility, higher levels of urbanization, and preexisting legal approaches to married women's property are associated with earlier passage of reforms, whereas findings on the impact of per capita wealth and girls' schooling are mixed.[54] There is also evidence that competition between states and territories to attract unmarried women to migrate was also an important factor affecting the timing of reforms, as Jayme Lemke shows using a variety of evidence from different regions and periods, including industrialization in the Northeast, the growth of transcontinental railroads, and the incentives of territorial government.[55]

Other work has focused on the impacts of married women's property rights reforms on women's lives and on the economy and society more broadly. Probably the most obvious potential impact of these reforms would have been on women's ownership of property, but even in this area there has been considerable debate in the literature. Some research has found that after the passage of various reforms, women were more likely to be included in wills, to will property to others, and to file for patents.[56] Other work, though, has found that the gender wealth gap began to narrow prior to the passage of married women's property acts in some parts of the country, largely among single and widowed women, thus calling some of the earlier findings into question.[57] Relatedly, Evan Roberts has found that the laws had no immediate impact on married women's labor-force participation.[58]

Although the direct impacts of economics rights reform on the wealth and labor of married women are ambiguous, economists have found that such reforms led to broader changes in family structure and choices, including greater investments in girls' schooling,[59] delayed age of marriage among young women,[60] higher divorce rates,[61] and a drop in the number of children born out of wedlock.[62] Married women's property rights reforms have also been linked to changes in financial and credit markets and to deepening industrialization.[63]

Ultimately, this set of studies is helpful for understanding the broader patterns and impacts of married women's economics rights reform. That

Life Under Coverture and How It Changed 31

being said, these studies can tend to flatten differences between cases and tend to be focused primarily on economic causes and impacts due to disciplinary priorities. This means they may miss important political and institutional factors that influenced both the timing of reforms as well as the form and extent of change but that are not easily captured in statistical models. These statistical approaches allow us to compare across states and show us specific historical junctures when multiple states passed reforms, but they can miss the importance of longer developmental processes in states. By focusing largely on economic factors, these studies can obscure the political messiness of state institutions and the important role of gradual, over-time change.

MARRIED WOMEN'S PROPERTY RIGHTS IN AMERICAN POLITICAL DEVELOPMENT

A perspective grounded in American political development can help bridge these two types of approaches, allowing us to identify big-picture patterns and implications but in ways that are more grounded in historical and political context. In particular, my approach to married women's economic rights focuses on the development and maintenance of state power. Although married women's property laws are important and interesting to study in their own right, they also played meaningful roles in supporting the slave economy in the South before the Civil War and in the settlement of western territories and the displacement of Native peoples.

A developmental approach also allows for a more nuanced approach to the way reforms developed over time both within *and between* states. Within each state, reforms cycled through multiple state-level institutions, typically over the course of many years. Throughout this process, changes in reforms were influenced not only by idiosyncratic state-level factors but also by institutional practices and larger national crises and developments. Moreover, states did not come up with new reforms from scratch. Political and legal elites actively sought out information about how other states were reforming their laws, and they debated successes and failures elsewhere in the nation. The borrowing of both ideas and language was common and had a substantial influence on reform processes.

CHAPTER TWO

Married Women's Rights Reforms in American Political Development

In this chapter, I identify institutional and political patterns that can help us understand important aspects of the reform process not fully captured by previous studies. Although married women's economic rights reform took place at the state level and without national-level coordination, there were connections between states and common patterns across states. I argue that married women's property rights reform occurred through a two-level process. On one level, policy developed within each state, cycling through different state-level institutions with their own institutional logics. On a second level, policies spread throughout the states, with institutional actors borrowing, copying, and learning from the successes and failures of other states in the nation.

This two-level process explains a number of important features of how married women's property rights evolved in the United States. First, it helps us understand how and why every U.S. state and territory passed some type of married women's economic rights reform during this period despite dramatically different political cultures and levels of women's organizing. States passed remarkably similar reforms due to the adaptability of reform policies to meet male state actors' varied goals and through diffusion processes. Social movements and other political actors with different purposes were able to mold rights reforms to their ends in different times and places, with the result of increasing state power, among other outcomes.

Second, this approach helps explain the distinctive roles of different state-level institutions in the development of women's economic rights. These institutions interacted to develop policies within states and became sources of diffusion as political actors in legislatures, courts, and constitutional conventions looked to other states as sources of information about reforms. Policies developed through an iterative process as they were taken up by these different institutions.

Finally, a focus on the self-interest of male political actors working through state institutions is important for understanding not only why rights were expanded but also how those expansions were limited. Rather than responding primarily to the demands of women organizers on their own terms, elites were responding to policy demands from a variety of sources. Depending on the time and place, politicians used married women's property acts to advance interests as diverse as limiting women's dependency on the state, protecting indebted men, and bolstering westward expansion. This interest-centered process led to reforms that were inherently limited in what they could ultimately accomplish and that affected different groups of women in conflicting ways.

INTRASTATE REFORM DEVELOPMENT

First, I consider the reform of married women's economic rights within an individual state. Although each state's path to reform varied in important ways, there were some commonalities that can help us understand why states decided to reform their marital-property laws when they did and how these reforms were shaped by their movement through state institutions.

Although the doctrine of coverture was strict and unforgiving in many ways, states did have various sources of information about other ways to envision marital property and the host of rights that went along with it. These sources included preexisting non-common-law legal arrangements and observations of how other states and territories organized their property laws. Women organizers, despite their lack of formal political power, could also be a source of new ideas for reform. Ultimately, though, information was not enough. Political actors needed reasons to actively push for and advocate for reforms. Reforms were enacted through the intersection of multiple social movements that found married women's property acts appealing, combined with secular trends that made reform of economic rights increasingly attractive. These intersections led to a convergence on married women's property reforms as a policy solution that could satisfy male political actors' multiple goals, at least partially. Male political actors across multiple political institutions needed to and did find the passage of married women's property rights to be in their own self-interest, for a variety of overlapping and sometimes conflicting reasons. These reasons included not only personal or group self-interest but also the development of state power for purposes such as colonization of the frontier and support for the institution of slavery.

Then, once these policies entered state politics through either a statute or new constitutional provision, they kicked off an iterative process in which the reforms were interpreted and updated by multiple state-level institutions over time. Rather than a one-and-done reform process in which a new policy was passed and then cleanly implemented, the most typical reform process was one that unfolded gradually over time and over multiple institutions. For example, a state constitutional provision might direct the state legislature to develop protections for married women's property; the legislature would then do so; and state courts would interpret these new rules in the context of specific cases. If legislators found the outcomes of those cases problematic—as they often did—they might then revise the reforms or adopt new ones. This iterative process most commonly led to an expansion of rights over time, though with important limits that ultimately link back to the state actors' interests.

SELF-INTEREST AND ADOPTION OF REFORM POLICIES BY MOVEMENTS

Married women's property acts were a sort of solution in search of a problem. We find this concept in the political scientist John Kingdon's work on agenda setting and policy making—some policy solutions exist that could be applied to multiple and potentially disparate political problems or issues.[1] Male political actors and social movement organizers of both genders seized on the "solution" of married women's economic rights reform for any number of problems depending on the actors' and organizers' geographic, political, and economic context. The expansion of married women's rights became a flexible policy tool that could be employed to achieve a number of diverse objectives. Some of these policy goals enhanced (some) women's power, but others were unrelated to women's empowerment. Some even aimed to and resulted in stripping economic power and property from particular groups of women—especially Black and Native women.

As I discuss in more detail in chapter 3, groups whose interests were not directly related to women's rights found that they could at least partially achieve their particular goals through these reforms, piggybacking on a policy trend that was increasingly gaining steam. That reforms of married women's economic rights could be used to respond to problems as varied as postbellum indebtedness, gender imbalances in the marriage market, and a rapidly changing class structure is indicative of how willing male legislators were to see these reforms as a ready solution.

The push for reform came, at least in large part, from the adaptability of married women's property rights reforms to meet the needs of multiple, often intersecting social movements and state developmental demands. For those who supported temperance, married women's property acts were a way to shield women's property from drunken husbands who became indebted from alcohol abuse. For the codification movement, married women's property laws were needed to rationalize and simplify the common law. Supporters of the homestead-exemption movement viewed married women's property law as a complementary policy that could accomplish the similar goal of protecting a portion of family property in a time of widespread indebtedness and speculation. Suffrage organizers saw property rights as part of their agenda of advancing the rights of women. Alongside these more organized movements were secular trends, such as industrialization; shifts in credit markets; economic panics and land speculation that led to economic instability and indebtedness; broad changes to people's understanding of certain types of property, such as wages; and even falling fertility rates. Each of these trends could at times put pressure on lawmakers to expand property and economic rights for married women.

But convention delegates and lawmakers reforming property rights faced a dilemma. Protecting women from their husbands necessarily entailed turning over some powers to wives, yet a complete end to coverture would mean women were left without any special protection under the law and thus vulnerable to exploitation not from their husbands but from business partners.[2] Around the country, many legislators were deeply ambivalent about how far married women's rights should extend. Although this book uses the term *married women's economic rights*, the rights in question were not inherently advancing either "prowoman" or "antiwoman" causes. Instead, the motivations for and effects of these reforms were much more ambiguous and contextual. At times, expansions of married women's economic rights did allow married women entry into the economy, while at other times they did not or were very limited in how they did. Moreover, the ways in which these rights benefited *other* groups—husbands, fathers, male children, suitors, capitalists, creditors, and debtors—is often obscured by this term. Of course, married women were the ones explicitly mentioned in these reforms. Nevertheless, these male beneficiaries were at least as important—if not more important—than married women in explaining why these reforms were so successful in spreading to every state in the nation.

Perhaps most importantly, though, political leaders could use married women's property rights reforms in service of state projects unrelated to women's empowerment. Priscilla Yamin writes in her work on marriage as a political institution that marriage "shapes notions of inclusion and civic belonging and it is a language through which we discuss and debate national identity and economic equality.... The American political system relies on marriage as a political tool and resource."[3] Extending married women's property rights was particularly useful as a political tool in the contexts of the antebellum South and the frontier. In slave states, giving white married women ownership of enslaved people that they brought into their marriage was one way to prop up the slave economy in a period of economic instability. The "protection" of wives' enslaved human property meant white families would be able to preserve some of their wealth even if they went into debt. On the frontier, granting expanded rights to women encouraged them to move west and colonize Native people's lands as part of family units, which was an important goal for male settlers who sought to establish statehood and increase the population of white women in areas that had extreme gender imbalances.

ITERATIVE INSTITUTIONAL CYCLE

The process of reforming married women's economic rights was slow, incremental, and iterative. Even though the earliest reforms in many states granted minimal rights to married women, these laws laid the foundation for the passage of later, more expansive reforms. This was especially true as these laws were implemented by state courts, which issued decisions in individual cases that interpreted new reforms in the context of specific disputes. This process often revealed contradictions and complications that were not necessarily apparent when the initial laws were passed.

Many married women's economic rights reforms, especially early reforms, included a mix of powers and protections for women. This mix translated into confusion in a variety of economic transactions. These contradictions were made most clear as state courts attempted to resolve disputes between creditors and debtors, and so state legislatures eventually responded with more legislation, often tipping the balance toward empowering reforms rather than protective reforms. Alongside these interactions between legislatures and courts, constitutional conventions sometimes chose to elevate married women's economic rights to constitutional guarantees. These provisions often included requirements for state legislatures to pass further reforms. To best understand these reforms, we must consider the larger, iterative, multibranch process that took place over decades rather than the passage of just one or two key statutes. Most often, economic rights reforms started in state legislatures, with the dynamics explained earlier, but legislative bodies were clearly not the only important venue for married women's rights reforms.

Nineteenth-century state constitutional conventions were called largely for two broad reasons that were not randomly distributed around the nation and did not include the purpose of advancing women's rights. Southern states were writing new constitutions in the years during and after the Civil War and Reconstruction, and frontier states were drafting founding documents as part of their bid for statehood. Nineteen states included a married women's property rights provision in their constitution. These provisions ranged from the extremely basic—such as

Maryland's provision of 1867 stating only that "the property of the wife shall be protected from the debts of her husband"—to much more expansive guarantees, as in Mississippi's Constitution of 1890, which stated, "The legislature shall never create by law any distinction between the rights of men and women to acquire, own, enjoy, and dispose of property of all kinds, or their power to contract in reference thereto."[4]

Besides the negative limits on state legislatures, some constitutions also included positive guarantees, requiring that legislators pass certain reforms or develop a registration system for married women's property. These rights were often packaged with or discussed alongside other constitutional provisions meant to hang an economic safety net for struggling families, such as homestead exemptions that allowed each family to protect a certain dollar value of land and sometimes to protect other property from seizure by creditors. By enshrining married women's property rights in constitutions, convention delegates signaled the importance of the policies to state politics and guaranteed that legislatures and courts would protect at least basic economic rights for married women.

As early laws and constitutional provisions with a variety of economic and paternalistic motivations proliferated, legal cases around these laws made their way to the courts for interpretation. State courts most often interpreted reforms to married women's economic rights cautiously, avoiding broad interpretations and sticking closely to the acts' text.[5] This cooperative, deferential approach among judges tried to balance legislators' conflicting motivations and to interpret exception-filled laws narrowly.

Although many legal historians have argued that state courts' narrow interpretations limited a more radical potential of legislative and constitutional reforms, these courts nevertheless played a crucial role as catalysts in pushing more expansive reforms forward.[6] Though not necessarily state judges' intention, the rulings they made often led to a cycle in which legislative actions were interpreted in ways that increased confusion and decreased predictability, which in turn spurred popular pressure for further reforms. Legislators then modified laws, gradually expanding the rights of married women in piecemeal fashion.

Cases brought under married women's property acts most often involved conflict between debtors and creditors rather than disputes between spouses. Granting partial rights to separate property for married women and combining those rights with elements meant to protect women created a complex legal situation. States quickly learned that providing married women with the right to, for example, own property but not to mortgage that property impeded the free flow of capital. Worse, many of the early statutes provided for partial-control rights that created unpredictable, unclear contracts. For example, a married woman might be able to mortgage her property for some purposes but not for others. Laws granting partial rights to married women created legal disputes in which creditors acting in good faith could not collect on debts because the legal structure around married women's economic rights was so uncertain. The legality of a debt could turn on minute details surrounding the exact nature of the woman's separate property and the purpose and type of the debt contracted, with little way for the average creditor to determine in advance whether the debt could be legally collected.

Once states provided limited rights to married women, pressure from business interests grew to liberalize women's place in the market. This pressure led to new reforms that further liberalized married women's economic rights. For example, at a South Carolina constitutional convention in 1895 where delegates debated a more expansive reform and ultimately passed it, one delegate argued that "the Acts of the Legislature tinkering with the laws relating to the property of married women had caused more litigation and expense to the people of the State than any other one thing."[7]

This iterative process illustrates the subtle role of courts in policy reforms. In the case of married women's economic rights, state courts (as opposed to federal courts) took the nearly exclusive lead in interpreting married women's property laws, and there was never a national landmark case that defined our understanding of courts' posture toward married women's economic rights. Nor do we see evidence of strategic litigants intentionally using the legal process to direct the course of policy or to bring attention to an important issue. Rather, most cases surrounding these issues were small-stakes claims involving the repayment of debt or the recovery of damages for accident victims. Nevertheless, the court system revealed the inherent contradictions in laws that attempted to expand rights by too little. Even when courts are not engaged in extensive, high-profile conflict with legislatures, they can still be an important player in the path of reforms. In handing down decisions that deferred to piecemeal legislation, state courts exposed a legal environment in which property rights were confused and inconsistent, prompting further reforms from elected bodies.

When political values and motives clash in the reform process, the resulting change is unlikely to be neat and tidy or to present clear beginnings and ends. Legislators at the beginning of the era at issue here wrote statutes with limited, modest expectations for how much the new laws would empower women. As specific cases worked their way through the court system, however, a piecemeal system of women's economic rights proved unworkable, so legislatures gradually expanded and liberalized these rights in an iterative cycle between judicial and legislative bodies over time. Constitutional conventions were venues for protecting rights from legislative backsliding and for directing legislators to pass further reforms. They also became important moments for delegates to debate the reforms made by other states and sometimes to adopt them word for word, which was part of the process of diffusing these reforms throughout the nation. It was this interaction between state institutions that transformed early debt-relief statutes into genuine rights-granting provisions over time.

Despite these meaningful changes in property law across a variety of reforms, women still faced a legal environment with meaningful illiberal elements that enforced a male–female hierarchy within the marriage relationship and limited women's ability to fully participate in the market, including by means of de jure and de facto limitations on entry into various careers and a lack of legal recognition for the economic value of work performed in the home. These limits were a direct result of women's lack of political power and men's political incentives. Reforms were designed to provide the sorts of extensions of married women's rights that served the male political actors' multiple interests, including making markets more stable and predictable, while also excluding reforms that women's groups fought for, such as statutory recognition of household labor.

INTERSTATE REFORM DEVELOPMENT: DIFFUSION OF RIGHTS REFORMS

Reforms to married women's economic rights did not take place in just one state or through a national process by which the federal government exerted control over the passage and development of new rights. Moreover, although each state and territory would go through its own reform process, these processes were not independent of one another. Rather, policy making was permeable, with ideas coming from the outside into each of the three venues—legislatures, constitutions, and courts. State institutions' permeability to outside ideas allowed for diffusion of reforms to occur across the nation.

Even without federal intervention, married women's property laws were commonplace by the 1870s and universal by 1920. Because these reforms dealt with property arrangements within marriage, they were part of family law and thus outside the bounds of congressional power. Unsurprisingly, Congress rarely passed legislation affecting married women's economic rights.[8] Although some cases on women's issues reached the U.S. Supreme Court during these years, there was no landmark case on married women's economic rights that influenced state policy. Family law was not constitutionalized until the 1960s,[9] and it was not until *Frontiero v. Richardson* (1973) that the Supreme Court afforded heightened scrutiny to laws discriminating on the basis of gender, and so it is probably not until this point that federal courts would have potentially struck down state policies prohibiting married women from holding separate property or making legal contracts. Of course, by that point, the liberalization of married women's property rights had largely already been worked out in the states. In his opinion in *Frontiero*, Justice William J. Brennan discussed coverture as being firmly in the past, alongside slavery and the lack of franchise, writing that "throughout much of the 19th century, the position of women in our society was, in many respects, comparable to that of blacks under the pre–Civil War slave codes. Neither slaves nor women could hold office, serve on juries, or bring suit in their own names, and married women traditionally were denied the legal capacity to hold or convey property or to serve as legal guardians of their own children."[10]

The adaptability of married women's economic rights to serve multiple policy goals meant that states frequently borrowed reform language from one another. Laws did not develop independently but spread among the states. Some states copied language from reforms passed elsewhere; others passed these laws to stay competitive; and still others adopted reforms because they faced similar economic and demographic conditions and problems. The drafters of legal codes and constitutions looked to the content and wording of reforms around the nation in drafting their own reforms. Lawmakers sometimes had firsthand experience with reforms elsewhere in the nation, which they had gained before a move west. They also consulted compilations and other resources to learn about how other areas of the country were treating the law of married women's property. This engagement with out-of-state policies could lead to either the copying of successful reforms or the rejection of specific reforms that had worked poorly in other states.

But it is consequential that there was no national "big bang" moment as it meant that the timing and level of liberalization varied. Southern states tended to pass the most expansive versions of married women's economic rights reform later than other regions. One state was an extreme laggard. Florida passed an initial debt-relief law protecting married women in 1845 but took almost one hundred years after that to extend more significant management rights to married women (which it eventually did in 1943). Because there was no major federal-level liberalization of married women's property rights, each state took a different path at constitutional conventions, in the legislature, and in the courthouse, and advocates for the passage of these laws varied.

METHODOLOGICAL APPROACH

Although this theory has many moving parts, a number of specific empirical observations have allowed me to explore and elaborate specific pieces of the argument. An understanding of the intrastate reform process leads to observing the presence of multiple, conflicting arguments for why property rights should be expanded, drawing on the language of multiple social movements and the development of state power. The process of rights expansion was iterative and took place both over time and with cycling between multiple institutions rather than within a single state-level institution. Limitations on reforms connected directly to the politically empowered male actors' incentives. With respect to the interstate reform process, the adaptability of married women's economic rights to serve multiple and conflicting policy goals led to widespread reform adoption, *even among states with few other similarities*, as states copied from and competed with other states. Diffusion occurred across all three state-level institutions as convention delegates, judges, and legislators all had the opportunity to look to other states for models of reform.

I deployed a multimethod research design that employs both qualitative and quantitative data and analyses. I collected data on five types of reforms in all forty-seven states and territories from 1835 to 1920 as well as the full text of these reforms, which allowed me to look at broad patterns and to analyze the text of reforms nationwide. These data are described in more detail at the beginning of chapter 1 and analyzed primarily in chapter 5.

I also conducted a closer analysis of eight case study states (Mississippi, South Carolina, Florida, New York, Ohio, California, Colorado, and Nevada), distributed around the nation, which I use as my primary source of evidence in chapters 3, 4, and 6. These case studies allow for a more nuanced portrayal of reform pathways that traces reforms in greater detail than the five broad categories identified for all territories and states. The eight case study states provide a cross-section of the experience of U.S. states because they are states from multiple regions; states that passed their first married women's property reforms in state legislatures and those that did so in constitutional conventions; states that passed reforms earlier or later; and, finally, states with both conservative and liberal political cultures and different experiences with women's organizing and activism. In the remainder of this chapter, I provide brief sketches of the pathways of reform in each region of the United States. As the book proceeds, I draw on these case study states particularly in illustrating the motivations of political actors and the roles of legislatures, courts, and constitutional conventions as institutional sites of reform. These case studies illustrate the multiple pathways by which states came to pass initial reforms of married women's economic rights and then to liberalize them over time.

Table 2.1 provides an overview of the eight case studies, and tables 2.2–2.4 outline the key legislative and constitutional reforms enacted in each of these states or territories. Each of the five reform categories is represented across the case studies, as are a variety of intermediate reforms that either built up to or expanded upon the core reforms. Some reforms were statutory, whereas others were constitutional.

Southern states, including early and late adopters, took a variety of pathways to reform. Before 1920, southern states typically lacked a strong, organized women's movement pushing for reforms. In terms of liberalism, other policies affecting married women in the South, such as those centering on divorce, tended to lag behind policies produced by the rest of the nation. Despite this seemingly unfriendly cultural environment, Mississippi was the first state to pass married women's property reforms, with a law that focused primarily on enslaved human property owned by white married women. Both Mississippi and South Carolina ultimately passed relatively expansive reforms, including constitutional guarantees. Even Florida, which was very late to allow married women control and management of their property, did enact some reforms before 1920. These southern states demonstrate how the logics of male politicians' self-interest played out to the benefit of property-regime liberalization even in places without a pro-feminist culture and highlight the importance of racial hierarchies in understanding these reforms.

In contrast, women's organizations were more active in the North and Midwest in lobbying for married women's economic rights. These areas had political cultures more open to women's demands. And women made up a significant portion of these areas' population, in contrast to their scant presence in many western territories—especially those that enacted married women's property rights early. New York was the first state to pass a married women's property act that included meaningful management-and-control rights, as well as an early state in allowing married women to write wills, own and control their earnings, and conduct business as sole traders. In Ohio, married women gained testamentary rights very early, and the state was also on the earlier edge in enacting other economic rights. In both states, women organized significant campaigns that engaged with both constitutional conventions and state legislatures around property rights. Yet even these reforms were ultimately still limited in important ways.

TABLE 2.1
Case Study Overview

	Dates of Major Reforms	Constitutional Action	Date Territorial Legislature First Met; Statehood	Common Law Versus Civil Law/Community Property
Southern Territories and States				
Mississippi	Debt free: 1839 Control/management: 1880 Earnings: 1871 Sole trader: 1871 Wills: 1880	Married women's rights protected in both 1869 and 1890 constitutions.	Statehood before 1835	Common law
South Carolina	Debt free: 1868 Control/management: 1868 Earnings: 1887 Sole trader: 1870 Wills: 1868	Married women's rights protected in both 1868 and 1895 constitutions.	Statehood before 1835	Common law
Florida	Debt free: 1845 Control/management: 1943 Earnings: 1892 Sole trader: N/A Wills: 1823	Constitution of 1861 prohibits legislature from extending management rights to married women; married women's rights protected in 1868 and 1887 constitutions.	Territorial legislature first meets in 1822; statehood in 1845	Civil law under Spanish control; common law adopted in 1822

Northern/Midwestern States

New York	Debt free: 1848 Control/management: 1848 Earnings: 1860 Sole trader: 1860 Wills: 1849	Delegates at 1846 convention debate but do not approve protections for married women.	Statehood before 1835	Common law
Ohio	Debt free: 1846 Control/management: 1861 Earnings: 1861 Sole trader: 1887 Wills: 1808	Delegates at 1851 convention debate but do not approve protections for married women.	Statehood before 1835	Common law

Western Territories and States

California	Debt free: 1850 Control/management: 1872 Earnings: N/A Sole trader: 1852 Wills: 1874	Married women's rights protected in both 1849 and 1879 constitutions.	No territorial legislature meets; statehood in 1850	Civil law under Spanish control; common law adopted generally in 1850 but with community-property exemption for married women

(continued)

TABLE 2.1
Case Study Overview (*continued*)

	Dates of Major Reforms	Constitutional Action	Date Territorial Legislature First Met; Statehood	Common Law Versus Civil Law/Community Property
Colorado	Debt free: 1861 Control/management: 1861 Earnings: 1861 Sole trader: 1861 Wills: 1861	Delegates at 1876 convention debate but do not approve protections for married women.	Territorial legislature meets in 1859; statehood in 1876	Common law
Nevada	Debt free: 1865 Control/management: 1873 Earnings: N/A Sole trader: 1873 Wills: 1873	Married women's rights protected in 1864 constitution.	Territorial legislature first meets in 1861; statehood in 1864	Community property

TABLE 2.2
Southern Case Study Timelines

Mississippi	South Carolina	Florida
		1821–1824: United States signs a treaty with Spain acquiring Florida Territory; as part of this process, women who married before the treaty's signing could hold separate property as under Spanish law, and all married women could write wills.
1839: Married women may own separate estates; enslaved human property is exempted from husband's debts, but control, management, and profits remain with the husband.		
1846: Free married women gain ownership of rents and profits from their lands and enslaved human property and can make some contracts. Separate property must be registered.		1845: Debt-free separate-estates law extends separate-property rights to all married women; husbands retain management rights.
1857: Free married women can purchase property, manage enslaved human property, rent lands, and make loans. They can contract for expanded but still limited purposes.		*1861: Constitutional provision prohibits legislature from allowing married women to manage property.
*1869: Constitutional protection is extended to married women's separate property.	*1868: Constitution establishes debt-free separate estates, control-and-management rights, and testamentary rights.	*1868: Constitutional provision reaffirms debt-free separate-estates statute.

(continued)

TABLE 2.2
Southern Case Study Timelines (*continued*)

Mississippi	South Carolina	Florida
	1870: Statute carries out constitutional mandate and includes a right to contract.	
1871: A married woman's earnings and damages to her person become part of her separate property. Married women can be employed in trade or business as *femme sole*.		
1873: Married women are allowed to control their wages.		
		1879: Married women may become sole traders by court order.
1880: All disabilities of coverture are removed with regard to property, and married women are allowed to write wills as if they are unmarried.	1882: Statute limits a married woman's right to contract and sue to cases directly involving her separate property and to suits against her husband.	
		*1886: Constitutional provision reaffirms debt-free estates law and grants limited management rights to married women.
	1887: Married women may convey or mortgage their property without restriction. Earnings and income are part of the separate estate and treated like other separate property.	
*1890: Constitutional provision prohibits the state legislature from ever creating a legal distinction between men and women in their rights of property or contract, except between husband and wife.	1891: Married women may purchase and convey property and make legal contracts as if unmarried but may not be a guarantor or otherwise liable for the debts of any other person.	1892: Broad earnings act is passed.

Mississippi	South Carolina	Florida
	*1895: Constitution guarantees married women unrestricted contract rights and all other rights with regard to their separate property that a single woman or man would have.	
		1943: Control-and-management rights are granted by statute.

* The asterisk indicates a constitutional reform.

Finally, frontier territories and states—as later adopters by nature of their later governmental organization—were frequent borrowers of reform language and concepts from the eastern part of the nation. They were also the most motivated by settler colonialism as a state interest. Territories typically had fewer women, and lawmakers desired to attract single women and families to their land. Convincing white women to move to territories was a crucial part of the settler project. The presence of families was necessary for permanent, sustainable settlement, and white women were thought to bring a "civilizing" influence to the frontier. Frontier states were also most likely to be influenced by Spanish civil law, which had different and arguably more expansive property arrangements for married women.

The combination of case study evidence and statistical analysis of nationwide trends allows me to explore different facets of the theory outlined in this chapter. Although no one piece of evidence is conclusive, all pieces together tell a compelling story of how married women's economic rights advanced in fits and starts through a patchwork and decentralized process that nonetheless had national consequences. This story has important implications for understanding the role of political power in democratizing rights reforms. Despite the complexity of multiple iterations of reforms happening in each of the forty-seven states and

TABLE 2.3

Northern/Midwestern Case Study Timelines

New York	Ohio
	1808: Wives are given the right to make a will as if unmarried.
1836: Statute limits use of trusts in equity courts, making it more difficult for married women to use trusts as a mechanism for protecting their rights.	
1845: Married women gain ownership and control over patents for their inventions.	
*1846: Constitutional convention abolishes equity courts.	1846: Debt-free separate estates are established.
	1846: Married women may petition court to protect their property from a husband in cases of the husband's intemperance.
1848: Both debt-free separate estates and control-and-management rights are established by statute.	
1849: The 1848 act is amended to explicitly allow women to convey their separate property and bequeath it in a will.	1857: A husband is prohibited from disposing of his wife's personal property without her consent; married women can control earnings in cases of a husband's intemperance or desertion.
1860: Earnings act is passed, and women are given the right to carry on a trade or business as a sole trader and the right to sue and be sued. But the husband's consent or a court order is now required for women to convey or contract real estate.	1861: All married women gain control and management of separate property with some limitations, including earnings.

New York	Ohio
1862: Earnings act from 1860 is amended such that married women may now bargain, sell, and convey real estate without the consent of a husband or a court order, as if they are unmarried.	1866: Revisions to the 1861 act allow married women to make contracts to improve their separate property.
1878: A married woman age twenty-one and older may "execute, acknowledge, and deliver her power over attorney" as if unmarried.	1874: Married women are extended rights to sue and be sued as well as expanded management and control rights.
1884: Married women are granted a general right to contract, except with their husbands.	1885: Some limits on married women's ability to control their real estate are restored.
1887: Husbands and wives are permitted to convey property directly to each other.	1887: Sole-trader rights are extended to all married women.
1890: Married women gain a right of action for injuries to their property, person, character as well as for injuries "arising out of the marital relation," the same as for a single woman or a married man.	

* The asterisk indicates a constitutional reform.

TABLE 2.4
Western Case Study Timelines

California	Nevada	Colorado
*1849: Statehood constitution provides for separate property for married women and directs the state legislature to enact legislation protecting it.		
1850: Debt-free separate estates and a registration system for married women's separate property are created. The husband has management-and-control rights over separate property.		
1852: Married women may transact business as sole traders.		
		1861: Comprehensive reform statute includes all five key reforms. A ban on imprisonment for debt is also passed in this year.
1862: 1852 act is amended to impose some additional limits on sole-trader status for married women.	*1863: Statehood constitution provides for separate property for married women and directs the state legislature to enact legislation protecting it.	

California	Nevada	Colorado
	1865: Statute provides for registration of married women's separate property and exempts a wife's registered property and money in specie from being seized for her husband's debts.	
1870: A married woman's earnings are protected from her husband's debts, but only become part of her separate property if they are living separately or if she is registered as a sole trader. Wives are allowed to sue and convey property when living separately from their husband.	1867: Married women can become sole traders with court approval.	1868: New code adopted that limits married women's rights to convey real estate independently of their husband.
1872: All married women may convey their separate property and may contract regarding that property. 1872: Married women may dispose of separate property by will, without consent of a husband.		1872: A married woman may take out loans to benefit her separate estate, and said estate will be liable.

(continued)

TABLE 2.4

Western Case Study Timelines (*continued*)

California	Nevada	Colorado
	1873: Married women gain control-and-management rights to convey and encumber separate property without their husband's consent. Married women may enter into contracts regarding their property as if unmarried. A wife's earnings are not liable for her husband's debts but are controlled by him unless they are living separately. Married women may sue and be sued alone only when living separately from their husband. 1873: Married women may make wills.	1874: A married woman may form a business partnership with her husband or other people and sign legal contracts as part of that partnership. 1874: Married women are granted general rights to contract, sue, and convey as if unmarried.
*1879: New constitution contains simplified version of married women's protections granted in 1849.		

* The asterisk indicates a constitutional reform.

territories over multiple decades, the ultimate result of these reforms was the accumulation of power to elite interests. The intersection of marital and property law proved to be a useful vehicle for politicians to provide economic benefits to some social groups but not to others and to advance projects such as settler colonialism and slavery.

CHAPTER THREE

Social Movements and State Power
Reform in State Legislatures

Scholars have provided evidence for an almost dizzying array of possible causes for the democratization of married women's economic rights.[1] Ranging from women's activism to the anticourt codification movement to economic panics to western expansion, this work does not provide a clear, systematic story of how all these different movements and causes could ultimately lead to similar policy outcomes. As we have seen, although all states enacted married women's economic rights reforms in some form, they took remarkably different paths to get there. In this chapter, I explore the ways that political and economic actors coming from different motivations could all see married women's economic rights reforms as a potential solution to their goals. Although at times this mix of goals and interests can seem highly contingent and almost random, a key takeaway here is that what resulted from marital-property law being so adaptable to these different projects was its use to consolidate and expand state power.

Women did advocate for reform to economic rights in some states, but organized feminist activity was entirely absent in other parts of the country at the time these reforms were enacted. That being said, group mobilization is still central to understanding the development of married women's property rights. Alongside women's groups, multiple other groups were able to utilize property rights to further their own interests— interests that were often far removed from advancing women's interests specifically. Married women's property acts proved to be extremely malleable, able to serve a wide variety of ends. These ends included the varying goals of social movements with differing degrees of connection to the women's movement, responses to economic changes and crises, and the bolstering of state power and development along multiple dimensions. Each of these interests was able to use married women's property rights reforms to their ends, sometimes in ways that produced expansions to women's rights as a by-product or unintended consequence instead of the direct goal. Thus, although group mobilization clearly mattered, the ways it mattered are not direct and obvious. Rather than women's interests being *the* central force behind reforms, the interests of multiple groups, of male political actors, and of the state are crucial to understanding the reform process as well as the ultimate outcomes of who systematically benefited and who lost out from the laws.

I highlight evidence of how seemingly different "causes"—social movements, organized elite interests, economic shocks, and male actors' interests in their own economic status and in the building of state power—could all lead to similar reforms of married women's economic rights. I explore how these reforms were adaptable to serve a variety of different ends, some linked to women's empowerment and others not. Even with all this complexity, state power *did* expand in meaningful and systematic ways. Marriage, as an institution sitting at the intersection of public and private and with a central role in defining citizenship, proved to be a powerful vehicle for these expansions. Because of the confused, contradictory purposes of married women's property acts, in which women's interests were often not central in the decision-making process, the reforms had built-in limits to their potential for women's empowerment. Especially in a political context where rights claimants did not have the ability to organize electorally, rights arose from more powerful political actors' responses to a range of demands and from their shaping of reforms to their own purposes.

THE ROLE OF MOVEMENTS AND ACTIVISM

Elizabeth Bowles Warbasse writes that "any investigation of one nineteenth century American reform finds that it intertwines with others. This is especially true of the early women's rights agitation, which originally was appended to other more vigorous reforms."[2] The movement for married women's property rights reforms was part of the broader women's movement, which had close ties to other contemporaneous movements, such as abolition and temperance. These movements did have different time spans, goals, and tactics, but the overlap and connections among them were considerable.[3]

Previous research has disagreed substantially as to the importance and impact of the women's movement on the enactment of married women's property legislation.[4] Of course, women did advocate for their own economic rights, using a variety of strategies, such as speaking tours, petitioning drives, and testimony before state legislatures. But in many locations and periods where states enacted reforms, such advocacy was either absent, as in states where there was not much of an organized women's movement at all, much less one around property rights specifically, or impossible, as in territories and states where very few women lived. Figure 3.1 shows a box plot of the percentage of the population that was female in each state or territory at the time that jurisdiction first adopted a married women's property rights reform. This plot indicates that the percentage of women in an area varied dramatically when reforms were first passed: in some places, women at least had the numerical potential or opportunity to organize, but in others they did not. The population of eight states or territories was composed of less than 30 percent women at the time their first reform was enacted, all of them located in the West: Arizona, California, Colorado, Idaho, Montana, Nevada, Washington, and Wyoming. For example, in 1861, the year the Colorado Legislature passed a comprehensive married women's property rights package, the governor addressed the body: "The predominance in numbers of male citizens over females and children, is a fact so remarkable as to have no recorded precedent in any new society voluntarily planted and perpetuated in the wilderness."[5]

If we were to take the women's movement as being the major factor driving economic reforms, we would expect to see bifurcated outcomes, in which states with different levels of women's organizing activity would experience dramatically different levels of legal reform. Yet this is not the pattern we observe. As discussed in more detail in chapter 5, the presence of an organized women's movement in a state was related to earlier passage of some types of reforms, although not all, and significant reforms

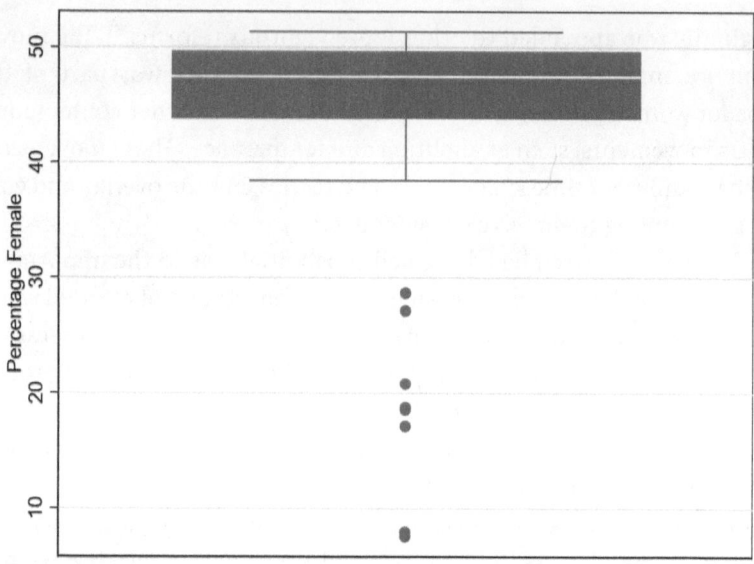

FIGURE 3.1. Box plot of the percentage of women in the population of each state/territory in the year of passage of its first married women's property rights reform. Three states adopted a reform prior to 1835, so the percentage of women in 1835 is indicated here. Data are linearly interpolated between census years.

were frequently enacted without this type of activism. Table 3.1 illustrates this finding by highlighting the states (or territories) that enacted the five major categories of reform during a period that a state-level woman suffrage organization was active. Although there are many ways to measure state-level women's activism, the rough measure illustrated in the table allows us to see that although women were actively organizing in some states at the time that rights expansions were implemented, these organizations had not yet formed in many other states.

In states where women did petition legislatures or take other actions to advocate for property-law liberalization, these efforts were often individual and local rather than coordinated through broad-based women's organizations.[6] Particularly after the Civil War, women's organizations focused their legislative efforts on suffrage. To the extent property rights reform was part of feminist groups' agenda, it was often used as a recruiting tactic to convince potential members that suffrage was a crucial next step before women could enjoy broader economic rights, or women sought more radical reforms such as joint property rights (as opposed

TABLE 3.1
Timing of Married Women's Property Reforms and Woman Suffrage Organizations

Reform Type	States Passing Reform While State-Level Woman Suffrage Organization Active (Total Number)*
Debt-free separate estates	N/A
Control-and-management rights	California, Connecticut, Iowa, Indiana, Kentucky, Louisiana, Missouri, Nebraska, Rhode Island, Tennessee, Texas, Vermont (12)
Earnings	Connecticut, Iowa, Illinois, Indiana, Michigan, Missouri, North Carolina, Nebraska, Oregon, Pennsylvania, Rhode Island, Tennessee, Texas, Vermont (14)
Sole-trader status	Connecticut, Iowa, Illinois, Indiana, Kentucky, Maryland, Missouri, Nebraska, New Hampshire, Ohio, Oregon, Rhode Island, South Carolina, Tennessee (14)
Wills	Arizona, California, Iowa, Illinois, Kentucky, Nebraska, New Mexico (7)

Note: Holly McCammon generously shared data on state-level suffrage organizations. This data set includes any suffrage organization with the state name in its title. States that enacted woman suffrage before the passage of a given reform are not included in this table but can be located in table 3.2.

separate property rights) that would compensate wives for household labor.[7] In the legal arena, women's organizations' strategic efforts were also focused on suffrage; in the late 1860s and early 1870s, the National Woman Suffrage Association launched a legal campaign challenging bans on woman suffrage.[8]

This is not to say that women's organizations were completely silent on issues of property rights, but in some ways asking whether women's organizations worked toward property rights reform is the wrong question. Women's organizations could and did engage in multiple forms of activism around economic rights, but in most states they lacked a key resource: the vote. This point is illustrated in table 3.2, which summarizes the timing of state-level woman suffrage compared to the timing of the passage of economic reforms focused on married women.

It makes sense that women's groups after the Civil War were so focused on the suffrage goal because without the vote any reforms that passed had first and foremost to satisfy male legislators and male voters. Although some male politicians and voters undoubtedly did have feminist motivations, many were responding to other movements, economic developments, and state goals, some of which had connections to women's rights but many of which did not. Ultimately, women's organizations were one of many movements providing input to state legislatures around the issue of married women's property, and although they could be pivotal in some times and places, they often were not in other times and places.

In addition to being part the women's movement, advocates of property-law reform for married women had close ties to other contemporaneous

TABLE 3.2

Timing of Married Women's Property Reforms and Woman Suffrage

Reform Type	States Passing Reform After Full State-Level Suffrage	Number of States or Territories Passing Reform by 1920
Debt-free separate estates	Utah, Wyoming*	46
Control-and-management rights	Idaho, Utah, Wyoming*	45
Earnings	Arizona, Idaho, Utah, Wyoming*	41
Sole-trader status	Idaho, Wyoming*	38
Wills	Utah, Wyoming*	47

Note: This table includes both statutory and constitutional changes

* States indicated with an asterisk passed state-level suffrage and a given reform in the same year.

movements, including abolition and temperance. These ties encompassed common organizers among different movements, linked arguments and analogies, and shared strategies. Women organizers during the period were often part of multiple, interlocking movements and saw themselves as "universal reformers," pursuing multiple social issues simultaneously and with closely connected arguments.[9] Writing about the connections among feminism, abolition, and temperance, Blanche Glassman Hersh notes that "the arguments for the three causes often meshed so closely as to be practically indistinguishable. The radical social reformers of the day viewed all three crusades as part of the broader effort to elevate all of humanity."[10] Many of the leaders of the early women's movement began public organizing around abolition and through that movement learned both practical tactics as well as a broadly emancipatory agenda that could be applied to other issues going forward.[11]

The rhetoric of the temperance movement was used frequently as a defense of the need for wives to have greater control over economic resources, yet whereas arguments for temperance focused on the need to restrict the availability of alcohol, those arguing for married women's economic rights tried to tackle the problems of alcoholism from a different angle. Joseph Ranney writes, "Husbands who succumbed to drink often descended into poverty; in the process, they expended their wives' assets to satisfy creditors and eventually left their families destitute."[12] Activists argued that if married women were provided with ownership and control of property and wages, they would be able to support themselves and their children when their husbands could not as a result of alcoholism, thus reducing the family's potential for dependence on state resources. Elizabeth Cady Stanton, speaking in 1854, argued: "If by unwearied industry and perseverance she can earn for herself and children a patch of ground and a shed to cover them, the husband can strip her of all her hard earnings, turn her and her little ones out in the cold northern blast, take the clothes from their backs, the bread from their mouths; all this by your laws may he do, and has he done oft and again, to satisfy the rapacity of that monster in human form, the rumseller."[13] Similarly, Mary Livermore argued that the Illinois Earnings Act of 1869 was needed primarily "for the poor and down-trodden women, the wives of drunkards and wife-beaters."[14]

Male political actors readily picked up these arguments, at least sometimes as justification for limiting the reach of married women's new rights. Judge Nott, in a DC Court of Claims ruling that denied Belva Lockwood admission to the bar, outlined his explanation for the passage of married women's property acts—namely, "the unhappy recurrence of drunken or profligate or spendthrift husbands with patient and industrious wives"—not the inherent rights or liberation of married women.[15] As is clear from this passage, while temperance-based justifications for married women's property rights reforms could be successful in achieving specific policy outcomes—for example, they do seem to have influenced lawmakers in New York, Massachusetts, and Illinois—they did not necessarily translate into broader-based rights that some women's organizers demanded.[16]

Outside of movements with close ties to women's rights organizers, other movements with less clear links to women's empowerment also saw this expansion of women's economic rights to be in their own interests. One was the codification movement. Multiple states embarked upon codification starting in the early nineteenth century and continued it over several decades. The movement was anticourt and antilawyer and sought to broadly rationalize, simplify, and systematize laws through the legislature, thus taking power away from the judiciary.[17] Reformers working on state codes sought to replace judicial common-law rules around a variety of property arrangements with legislative codes intended to be more appropriate for a growing commercial economy, not just those codes specific to women or wives.[18] As applied to married women, however, the codification movement saw the various exceptions to the common law carved out through equity and other means as overly complex and limited to the wealthy and connected. Rationalization of property law meant that for creditor–debtor interactions to operate smoothly, married women's participation in these interactions could not be treated according to special rules.[19] Thus, codifiers sought to create general, simple rules for married women's property that would be defined through legislative codes.

The creation of new codes was often delegated to experts, and then the new codes were adopted (or not) as part of an up-or-down vote by the state legislature. This means that the reform process was quite different from the passing of laws as individual bills. Instead of requiring a sponsor, committee work, debate, and a legislative vote on issues specific to married women's property, reforms through codification were simply included in detailed legal codes rather than individually considered by legislative bodies, thus giving significant power to the individual or commission designated to prepare the code.

Table 3.3 separates out the reforms from each of the case study states or territories into those that were passed as stand-alone statutes and those that were passed as part of larger codes. As is evident from this table, the use of codification to advance married women's economic rights was uneven across states but meaningful in some places. I describe here three reforms in Mississippi, California, and New York that demonstrate

TABLE 3.3
Reforms Found in Codes Versus Stand-Alone Statutes

State	Dates of Reforms Passed as Stand-Alone Statutes	Dates of Reforms Passed as Part of Codes
Mississippi	1839, 1846	1857, 1871, 1873, 1880
South Carolina	1870, 1887, 1891	1882
Florida	1823, 1824, 1835, 1845, 1879, 1881	1892
New York	1845, 1848, 1849, 1860, 1862, 1878, 1884, 1887, 1890, 1902	
Ohio	1808, 1846, 1857, 1861, 1866, 1871, 1884, 1885, 1887	
California	1850, 1852, 1862, 1870, 1874	1872
Nevada	1865, 1867, 1873	
Colorado	1861, 1872, 1874	1868

different ways that codification affected married women's property rights reforms.

In 1880, Mississippi's Democratic-dominated legislature enacted a reform of married women's property rights that the *Chicago Daily Tribune* deemed "the most radical legislation yet had on the subject."[20] The new act was sweeping in its annulment of the common law as it applied to married women's property rights, reading in part: "The common law, as to the disabilities of married women, and its effect on the rights of property of the wife, is totally abrogated, and marriage shall not be held to impose any disability or incapacity on a woman, as to the ownership, acquisition or disposition of property of any sort, or as to her capacity to make contracts, and do all acts in reference to property, which she could lawfully do, if she was not married."[21]

The adoption of this "radical" reform was part of a codification effort in the state. Codification was placed in the hands of Josiah A. P. Campbell, a justice of the Mississippi Supreme Court.[22] The state legislature appointed him to write a new code of statutes for the State of Mississippi in 1878, and Dunbar Rowland described this endeavor in a history of judges and courts in Mississippi published in 1935: "[The code] was adopted with but little change by the legislature of 1880. The Code of 1880 abounds in reformatory laws which have proved of great value to the people. It contains nearly two hundred sections written solely by Judge Campbell, which were adopted as written."[23] Although Campbell's motivations behind including substantial changes to married women's rights in the 1880 code are unknown, he was widely known as a reformer. In a message to the Mississippi Legislature upon delivering the draft code, Campbell did not explicitly mention the married women's provision in the code but did outline his general approach to the task, insisting that he had attempted to leave the code unaltered except as required "to be [easily] understood by those for whom they are designed as rules of action ... [and] to meet the suggestions of experience in the practical operation of the statutes."[24] Earlier married women's property acts in the state had granted married women partial rights in ways that resulted in substantial legal confusion, a situation that would have been familiar to Campbell as a Mississippi Supreme Court justice.[25]

About twenty years earlier, through the late 1860s and early 1870s, California embarked on its own process of codification. Much of the code, particularly the civil code, was drawn from the Field Code, a collection of provisions developed in New York by David Dudley Field, who was commissioned to write a systematic code for the state.[26] Field's efforts covered all aspects of law, from civil to criminal to political, but he also wrote about women's rights reform specifically. Peggy Rabkin writes that Field "blamed the common law for its retention of 'feudal tenures with all their burdensome incidents...and [for] wives...[having] only the rights which a barbarous age conceded them.'"[27]

Accordingly, the Field Code contained a substantial number of sections dealing with married women's economic rights; for instance, the Code provided that a husband had no legal-economic interest in his wife's property, that she had the right to contract with regard to property as if she were single, and that she had the power to mortgage or otherwise deal with her property as if she were single.[28] Yet the Field Code also contained sections that called a married woman's economic status as an equal partner into question, naming the husband the head of the household, responsible for the financial support of his wife. Nonetheless, Field noted that in his proposed code "the disability of coverture is completely taken away, and a married woman may execute during coverture any power which may be lawfully conferred upon any person."[29]

Although New York largely failed to adopt significant portions of the codes Field prepared, the codes had considerably more influence in the western states.[30] Numerous states adopted at least some portion of the Field Code, and five states adopted Field's civil code in large part.[31] California was one of the latter, adopting significant portions of the Field Code, including elements of its approach to married women's property.

Henry Field's brother, Stephen J. Field (later a U.S. Supreme Court justice), moved to California and became a member of the state legislature and then a justice on the California Supreme Court. As a member of the California Legislature, he sat on the judiciary committee and was responsible for drafting various codes for the state in the 1850s, which he based largely upon his brother's work.[32] Stephen Field was not a member of the commission in 1871 that drafted the California Codes and included major revisions to married women's property rights, but this commission also based the California Codes in large part on the Field Code, and Stephen Field oversaw an examination of the draft codes for the governor, in which he recommended them strongly.[33]

The provisions in California's new code concerning married women's property rights included passages taken directly from the Field Code, combined with elements from California's Constitution of 1849 and married women's property act of 1850.[34] Like the Field Code, the California Code extended to married women the right to sell and mortgage their separate property without spousal permission and the right to contract as if they were single. Husbands retained management and control of community property, but married women still made significant gains in terms of their separate property and their rights to contract with third parties. The legislative committee that reviewed the prepared code approved of the document as a whole, with no debate or revision of any specific sections, including those dealing with married women's property; both houses of the legislature then approved the code without debate.[35] As Donna Schuele writes, "One of the most significant advances in equalizing California's marital property law was achieved more obliquely than any other reform during this period. Although the organized women's rights movement had called for this reform, activists appeared to play no direct role in actually gaining it."[36] Women had petitioned the legislature extensively on property rights, testified before a legislative committee, and even contributed to getting a married women's property rights bill passed through the legislature, only to see it vetoed by the governor.[37] Reform was instead achieved through a new code that did not directly involve these activist women.

Even where codification did not specifically address married women and their rights, as in New York, the creation of codes could still open up discussion about and activism for the passage of married women's rights reforms.[38] The New York Revised Statutes of 1836 significantly limited the use of trusts in courts of equity. These sections of the code were not directly aimed at married women's separate equitable estates but were instead part of a more general effort to simplify the legal code and prevent fraud. However, the effect on married women was to turn equitable estates (which women could hold separately from their husbands) into legal estates (which were the sole property of the husband under the doctrine of coverture), a situation that became even more problematic when the New York Constitution of 1846 completely abolished chancery (equity) courts.[39] Together, these changes inspired by the codification movement meant that a law specifying married women's property rights was needed simply to restore women's economic rights to the status they had before 1836, which the New York Legislature did by passing the state's first married women's property act in 1848.[40]

The homestead-exemption movement was another nineteenth-century social movement that shared connections with multiple other movements of the time, including abolition, temperance, and married women's property rights.[41] Paul Goodman writes that advocates of homestead exemptions "aimed at providing a measure of security in an increasingly insecure, volatile economy ... [promising] to shield at least homes so that families no longer need worry that the breadwinner's bad luck or incompetence would plunge an entire household into destitution."[42] Beginning in Texas in 1839, states began to enact exemption laws that protected certain amounts of land—indicated by acres, dollar value, or lots—from seizure by creditors; the policy ultimately spread to all but three states.[43] Like married women's property acts, homestead exemptions set aside a portion of family property for protection, and the laws shared many similar justifications and goals. Both types of policies were part of broader debt-relief efforts enacted by states.[44] The two policies were often included together in state constitutions, and the passage of homestead-exemption laws was associated with earlier passage of laws granting debt-free separate estates to married women.[45] Missouri's debt-free estates law of 1849 was even an amendment to an earlier homestead act.[46] Goodman writes that "the movement for homestead exemption converged with the reform of married women's property law. Both recognized that the market revolution had weakened the traditional assumption that wives and children could rely on male household heads as breadwinners. The ups and downs of the economy, failure in business, or loss of jobs left families destitute."[47]

Wives typically gained new rights as part of homestead-exemption acts, specifically through rules that required their consent to the sale or mortgage of a designated homestead.[48] In practical terms, however, there is little evidence of women being able to take advantage of these rights for the purpose of increasing their bargaining position or leverage within marriages, and more evidence points to homestead exemptions materially benefiting married men rather than women.[49] Thus, as in the case of married women's property acts, male political actors had clear personal incentives to include rights for women in the laws: both personal gain and the reduction of dependency on the state.

A NOTE ON PARTISANSHIP

It is also important to note briefly the role of partisan politics in married women's economic rights reforms. Many issues in American politics have been sharply divided along party lines, whereas other issues have been championed by both parties or by neither of them. Because the passage of married women's reforms had an economic component, we might expect to see Republicans and Democrats taking opposing positions on this issue.[50] Yet because these reforms were so adaptable to different goals and because the parties themselves were changing dramatically during this time, we might also expect to see both parties (or neither) supporting these policies. I examined national party platforms from 1840 to 1920 to look for evidence of party attention to married women's economic rights.[51] Both Republicans and Democrats during this period included planks that made gestures toward acknowledging women's role in the economy and in public life, occasionally touching specifically on married women and their economic rights.

In its platform for 1872, the Republican Party included a plank expressing general support for women's employment and the women's movement, writing: "[Women's] admission to wider fields of usefulness is viewed with satisfaction, and the honest demand of any class of citizens for additional rights should be treated with respectful consideration."[52] Its platform for 1876 was even more specific and spoke explicitly to the passage of economic reforms for married women in the states: "The Republican party recognizes with approval the substantial advances recently made toward the establishment of equal rights for women, by the many important amendments effected by Republican legislatures in the laws which concern the personal and property relations of wives, mothers, and widows.... The honest demands of this class of citizens for additional rights, privileges, and immunities should be treated with respectful consideration."[53]

The Republican Party was then silent on women's issues for twenty years, until 1896, when its platform again included a plank referencing women's rights quite expansively: "The Republican party . . . believes that [women] should be accorded equal opportunities, equal pay for equal work, and protection to the home. We favor the admission of women to wider spheres of usefulness." In 1908, the party called for an investigation into the working conditions of women and children, and in 1912 it called for labor protections for women and children. By 1916, the Republicans were calling for an extension of suffrage to women, a call that was repeated in 1920. In the latter year, the party also included a plank titled "Women in Industry," calling for equal pay in federal jobs, legislation on limited hours for women, and closer study of the particular issues women faced in the working world.[54]

The Democratic Party paid less attention to women's work in its national platform but included it starting in the early 1900s. Its platform in 1908 referenced "millions of working men and women" in calling for a reduction in government spending. In 1916, the Democratic Party called for labor laws providing for "decency, comfort and health in the employment of women as should be accorded the mothers of the race." In 1920, the platform continued to advocate protections for women in the working world, alongside other provisions aimed to benefit women's welfare, but Democrats never called specifically for married women's property acts in these documents. They did call for women's suffrage in 1916 and 1920.[55] Thus, both parties spoke favorably of women's economic rights when they mentioned them at all, but married women's property rights rarely reached the level of salience needed to be mentioned in a national party platform.

At the state level, married women's property rights were more salient but remained bipartisan in terms of support. Table 3.4 indicates party control for each case study state in each year that the state enacted a stand-alone reform granting at least some new rights to married women. As is evident, depending on the state and period, multiple parties were involved in the passage of married women's rights reforms, even as parties themselves were shifting dramatically on numerous issues and priorities. A similar pattern is evident in constitutional conventions, whereby conventions dominated by either Republicans or Democrats included constitutional provisions protective of married

TABLE 3.4

Stand-Alone Rights-Expanding Married Women's Property Acts and State Party Control

State	Year	Party Control of State Legislature	Party of Governor
Mississippi	1839	Democratic	Democratic
	1846	Democratic	Democratic
South Carolina	1870	Republican	Republican
	1887	Democratic	Democratic
	1891	Democratic	Democratic
Florida	1823	Territory, appointed	Territory, appointed
	1824	Territory, appointed	Territory, appointed
	1835	Territory, elected	Territory, appointed
	1845	Democratic	Democratic
	1879	Democratic	Democratic
	1881	Democratic	Democratic
New York	1845	Democratic	Democratic
	1848	Whig	Whig
	1849	Whig	Whig
	1860	Republican	Republican
	1862	Union	Republican
	1878	Republican	Democratic
	1884	Republican	Democratic
	1887	Republican	Democratic
	1890	Republican	Democratic
	1902	Republican	Republican

State	Year	Party Control of State Legislature	Party of Governor
Ohio	1808	Democratic–Republican	Democratic–Republican
	1846	Whig	Whig
	1857	Democratic	Republican
	1861	Republican	Republican
	1866	Republican	Republican
	1871	Republican	Republican
	1884	Democratic	Democratic
	1887	Republican	Republican
California	1850	Nonpartisan	Democratic
	1852	Democratic	Democratic
	1870	Democratic	Democratic
	1874	Split	Republican
Nevada	1865	Republican	Republican
	1867	Republican	Republican
	1873	Republican	Democratic
Colorado	1861	Territory, nonpartisan	Republican
	1872	Territory, nonpartisan	Republican
	1874	Territory, nonpartisan	Republican

Note: Data for this table were compiled from Michael J. Dubin, *Party Affiliations in the State Legislatures: A Year by Year Summary, 1796–2006* (Jefferson, NC: McFarland, 2007); *Gubernatorial Elections: 1787–1997* (Washington, DC: Congressional Quarterly, 1998); Jerrold G. Rusk, *A Statistical History of the American Electorate* (Washington, DC: CQ Press, 2001). The adoption of codes is not included here because these votes covered so many issues. In a few cases, a bill advanced married women's rights in some areas but limited them in others; these bills are still included in the chart. The only bills excluded are those that solely restricted rights.

women's economic rights, even when the parties were sharply divided on other issues.[56] Overall, the evidence suggests that support for married women's property rights was bipartisan (and sometimes nonpartisan) and that both parties saw benefits to these policies when they were in power.

ECONOMIC FORCES

In addition to the intersecting movements that saw married women's property rights reform to be in their favor, dramatic changes in the economy were also taking place during the 1800s and early 1900s. They included economic crises, changes to credit markets, and industrialization and commercialization. Both the fundamentals of the economy and the nature of economic threats were transformed over the period of study. These changes to the economy provided another source of motivation for male political actors to expand married women's rights and reduce the potential for women's and children's dependence on the state.

The 1800s and early 1900s were a time of boom and bust in the economy, marked by crises, panics, and widespread indebtedness. Economic historians have identified a large number of financial panics and crises during the period under study. For example, Elmus Wicker highlights banking panics in 1837, 1857, 1860, 1861, 1873, 1884, 1893, and 1907.[57] Edward Balleisen describes the antebellum economy as "a chaotic economy in which almost all business owners found themselves entangled in complex webs of credit, at once debtors to suppliers and creditors to customers, [and in which] insolvency constituted an omnipresent counterpart to the narratives of economic achievement so often lauded by the era's pundits and politicians. No sector ... was immune from bankruptcy."[58] This unstable economy and the growing ranks of debtors became a backdrop against which legislators considered policies such as debt relief for families and women.

The homestead-exemption movement, discussed earlier, was one response to a changing economy that intersected with married women's property rights; beyond this movement, however, economic protection for debtors in an unstable economy was a key motivation for passing debt-protection-focused married women's property laws. Nancy Cott writes: "The laws aimed mainly to keep ordinary families solvent, at a time when most farmers operated in a dangerous cycle of borrowing and amassed dangerous levels of debt."[59] Despite coverture's hierarchical definition of the marriage relationship, a rapidly changing economy produced countervailing forces in favor of a new role for legislatures in defining married women's economic rights and responsibilities. Legislators hoped to keep women and children from becoming dependent on the government. Economic upheaval was connected to increasing numbers of debtors from an increasingly broad spectrum of the class structure, which left legislatures searching for ways to protect family assets—in practice, ways that often protected wives' assets specifically.[60] Legislators argued for the economic necessity of such laws for protecting the assets of indebted families amid the economic crises caused by the Panic of 1837, the Civil War, and rampant land speculation in the West.

Mississippi's debt-relief reform in 1839 provides a good example of this type of motivation. Along with other early married women's property acts in the South, this reform was passed "during and in the wake of the panics of the late 1830s and the severe depression that followed."[61] Sandra Moncrief describes Mississippi in the 1830s as being in a state of rapid political and economic change. In the early years of the decade, the combination of a high number of immigrants, the opening of Native American lands to settlers, and access to easy, largely unsupervised credit led to an economic boom. The economic fortunes of the state quickly shifted with the passage in Congress of both the Coinage Act in 1834 and the Distribution Act in 1836 as well as the resulting Panic of 1837.[62] Mississippi was among the hardest hit by the panic, and as Reginald Charles McGrane points out, "[by] 1839 extensive plantations were thrown out of cultivation and lying waste for want of hands to till them, the slaves having been seized under execution and carried off by the sheriff."[63] The Panic of 1837 created a recession that lasted until the mid-1840s, and Mississippi lawmakers extended debt relief to the state's citizens through both a married women's property act in 1839 and a homestead-exemption act in 1841.[64]

Senator Thomas Hadley introduced the married women's property law and another related law to the Mississippi Senate.[65] Hadley was in serious financial trouble and sought both direct debt relief for himself through a bill providing him personal relief as well as debt relief more generally through the protection of married women's property. Sources vary on Hadley's marital status at the time he proposed the bill, but all agree he stood to benefit financially if his wealthy wife (or fiancée) could keep her property separate from his.[66] A personal motivation for debt relief, in particular debt relief through the protection of married women's assets, played a significant role in the introduction of the bill.

Debate over the married women's bill included substantial discussion of debt relief and the economy, with particular concern over whether the bill would tilt power too much in the direction of debtors. Senator Grayson, for example, argued that if the bill passed, married men would simply transfer the titles of their land over to their wives to fraudulently avoid repaying their debts.[67] Once an amendment to the bill was offered that addressed this issue, providing that any property married women obtained from their husbands would not be exempt from debt collection, the bill passed handily by a margin of nineteen to nine.[68] Megan Benson explains: "A great many legally adroit, masculine, southern minds found that by granting their wives a separate legal identity by law, they could shelter assets—primarily slave property—from hungry creditors."[69]

The passage of partial economic rights for married women like those in this reform interacted with an economy that was rapidly becoming more commercialized and industrialized. As the simple logic of coverture—all property in a marriage belonged to the husband absolutely—gave way to piecemeal reforms that gradually granted married women more control over their property and their place in the business and working world, the logic of liberalism took over, and pressure from business and other capitalist interests grew to liberalize women's place in the market. Partial rights, however, led to an exceedingly complicated legal environment and often to perverse outcomes in disputes between creditors and debtors, as discussed in more detail in chapter 6. Further, as women were increasingly incorporated into the wider economy, restrictions on economic rights such as the ability to sign legal contracts (and have them enforced) placed an increasing burden on economic activity.[70] As the economy became more commercialized and industrialized, giving women more opportunities to take on work outside the home, coverture created incentives against economic growth. Women who could not claim ownership to wages earned or business profits would have had less incentive to engage in market labor.[71]

MARRIED WOMEN'S ECONOMIC RIGHTS AND STATE POWER

Finally, state legislators were motivated by both race and gender hierarchies in drafting married women's property laws, especially to the extent that these reforms could bolster state power in reinforcing these hierarchies. Racial hierarchies entered into the calculus of the design and passage of reform through three regionally specific pathways: the explicit inclusion of slavery in pre–Civil War southern reforms; the passage of reforms in the context of wider sets of property and domestic-relations law that racialized property rights; and the use of married women's property rights reforms to support settler colonialism and consequently the stripping of property from Native people on the frontier. Reforms also reinforced gender hierarchies even as they expanded women's rights, often emphasizing patriarchal state protection of women rather than their economic independence. On the whole, these patterns indicate that whereas some women benefited from married women's property rights reforms and gained greater economic power as a result of them, other women were excluded or actively harmed by this legislation—an outcome that was welcomed by state legislatures, which used the reforms to identify and extend rights to the "ideal" (white, propertied) female citizen.

In their discussion of the impact of married women's property acts on credit and investment, Peter Koudijs and Laura Salisbury write that "slaves were the most valuable form of property in the South."[72] According to the U.S. censuses of 1850 and 1860, almost half the wealth in the South was in the form of enslaved human property.[73] Beyond the dollar value assigned to them, enslaved humans were especially valuable as collateral for loans because they were easily seized and sold and were highly sought after in the southern economy.[74] As such, the "protection" of enslaved humans as property became a major goal of married women's property acts in the antebellum South.

At least five slave states—Mississippi, Maryland, Kentucky, Arkansas, and Texas—explicitly listed enslaved people as married women's property that would be exempted from a husband's debts.[75] Most of these states treated enslaved human property differently than other sorts of property—for instance, by ensuring that the husband would have management and control of his wife's enslaved human property. For example, the married women's property law enacted in Mississippi in 1839 had five sections, four of which were specific to enslaved human property. Enslaved people were to be the separate property of married women and exempt from the husband's debts, but "control and management of all such slaves, the direction of their labor, and the receipt for the productions thereof, shall remain to the husband."[76] Thus, for slaveholding families, married women's property rights reforms provided a continuing revenue stream. Even where slave states did not explicitly list enslaved human property in married women's property acts, the laws still had important implications for slavery.

In thinking about these implications, there are two important considerations. First, southern women were especially likely to hold enslaved people as property as compared to other types of property. Second, in a period when many states were passing married women's property laws that operated largely as debt-relief bills, the role of enslaved human property was central to the southern credit market.

Stephanie Jones-Rogers argues that slaveholding by women in the South was "fundamental to the nation's economic growth and to American capitalism."[77] Even before the passage of married women's property acts, wealthy slaveholding families gifted and bequeathed enslaved people to their daughters and used a variety of legal mechanisms to retain control over the enslaved people that women brought into their marriages. Enslaved people were perceived as easier to control than land or other forms of property, and formal legal protections that came from married women's property acts only solidified women's ownership rights.[78] Jones-Rogers argues that parents were especially likely to give enslaved people to their daughters rather than other types of property, such as land.[79] This argument is corroborated by state-specific evidence gathered by other scholars. Michael Dougan analyzed records from four Arkansas counties that included schedules in which married women recorded their separate property. He found that before the Civil War enslaved people were the most common type of separate property listed by these Arkansas wives, appearing on 77 percent of property lists.[80] Similarly, Laurel Clark indicates that enslaved human property was the most common form of property noted in Florida court records dealing with married women's property rights.[81] It is clear that enslaved people were central not only to the southern economy but also specifically to married white women's place in that economy.

In addition to being perhaps the most significant form of property brought to marriages by married white women, enslaved people also played critical roles in southern credit markets. In the antebellum South, most married women's property rights reforms that state legislatures passed were focused on debt relief, which had specific implications for enslaved people. For slave owners, using enslaved people as collateral for loans had benefits: enslaved people were "valuable and highly liquid"—in contrast to assets such as land, they could be more easily sold in small units and moved to other locations.[82] But for the enslaved people themselves, the consequences of this system were severe: "financial risks were ... transmuted for slaves into particular risks of loss and displacement, even as these individuals were denied any claim to the profits."[83] Edward Baptist writes that "human flesh ... proved a liquid resource in times of trouble for many a white person."[84] In discussing Mississippi's married women's property rights reform of 1839, Elizabeth Warbasse draws explicit connection to the use of enslaved people as credit: "Newspapers were filled with advertisements of Negroes and lands for sale in satisfaction of debts. ... As a result to the passage of the married women's act, however, an indebted husband might avoid the forced sale of his wife's slaves, thus retaining the income they produced and escaping bankruptcy."[85] By exempting the enslaved human property held by a married woman from her husband's debts, married women's property acts provided economic stability to white families during turbulent times.

Beyond the preservation of slavery, married women's economic rights reforms were part of broader sets of laws relating to domestic relations and property rights that allowed state legislators to maintain and strengthen racial hierarchies in their states. On a basic level, laws protecting the property of married women were beneficial only to women who had property to protect. State laws relating to property, land, and marriage around the country differed, but in general white women were most likely to bring property to their marriages, and thus they were the most likely to benefit from the new reforms.

So-called Black codes in southern states sometimes either prohibited Black citizens from purchasing farmland or prohibited landowners from selling to them.[86] This restriction extended to informal practices as well, where in many areas white landowners chose to take a loss rather than sell to a Black purchaser.[87] Although racial politics were different in the North and West, property law and its intersection with married women's rights in these regions were not friendly to nonwhites, either. Some nonsouthern states passed "Black laws" entirely barring entry or settlement to Black migrants or making settlement more difficult for Black migrants.[88] Although the federal Homestead Act of 1862 did not explicitly mention race, in practical terms it primarily benefited white settlers at enormous cost to Native people, whose lands were stripped from them.[89] State-level homestead acts sometimes were explicitly racial in nature, limiting full homestead rights to whites, as in California laws passed in 1851 and 1860.[90] Even when Black citizens could migrate, settle, and purchase land, some states limited their right to testify against whites in courts, which of course made legally defending claims relating to land, wages, or contracts against whites impossible.[91]

As Emily Zackin and Chloe Thurston discuss in their research on homestead exemptions, because of racial patterns in property ownership, any policy "designed to keep land in the hands of their current owners" would have the effect of making it more difficult for Black people to purchase land.[92] This same principle applies to the debt-relief versions of married women's property laws, which similarly kept property, including land, off the market. Though the particulars differed between states and regions, this constellation of state laws and policies added up to a system in which white married women were granted substantially greater protection for their property by state governments than were Black and Native married women.

In addition to the ways that married women's property acts hardened Black/white racial hierarchies, they also had substantial connections to colonization and the dispossession of Native people, including women, of their property. Tonia Compton writes that "the American empire in the West can best be understood as an enterprise of settler colonialism. Settler colonies were built through an imperial process, but, unlike extractive colonies where the focus was obtaining resources through the enforced labor of natives or imported enslaved workers, the invading forces arrived with the intent of staying put and reproducing the society from which they originated."[93]

The settler quality of American empire meant that single men moving to the frontier was not sufficient to achieve the goals of state expansion. Families—which required women—were needed as a critical component of settlement. Because (white) women were essential for the project of settlement, men on the frontier had an interest in granting them increased rights to incentivize them to move west. Mari Matsuda writes: "The wives, school-teachers, and mothers of the West were seen as civilizers. Women meant families, permanence, and care for the community[, and so the] scarcity of white women was of serious concern to Western political leaders."[94] Tonia Compton adds that in addition to bearing children who would increase the white population in the West, white women settlers aided the colonial project through the "establishment of families, churches, schools, social organizations, and expectations for proper behavior."[95] Thus, economic citizenship was extended to (some) women to expand colonial power.

Multiple scholars have noted that western territories and states were early adopters of state-level woman suffrage, and in doing so some were at least partially motivated by the same desire to attract women settlers with the promise of greater rights.[96] Yet we don't see similar temporal patterns in the case of married women's economic rights, with western territories and states enacting these reforms before the eastern part of the nation did. A major reason for this difference is the timing of westward expansion and statehood—reforms around married women's economic rights simply happened earlier than those for suffrage, often being passed in eastern states before western areas had even become organized territories. But once western territories had the opportunity to pass legislation, they often did so quickly and with more comprehensive packages. For example, Wyoming became a territory in 1869 and passed a married women's property law that included all five economic policies (separate estates, control and management, earnings, sole-trader status, wills) in one bill. This sweeping legislation was passed as soon as legislators met and in the same year as woman suffrage was passed in the territory. The married women's property act was approved on December 4, 1869, and woman suffrage was enacted just a few days later, on December 10.[97]

Of the states, twenty-three were either territories or had an active legislature before attaining statehood during the period covered in this study (1835–1920). All of these territories would become states before the end of this period. Many passed at least some married women's property rights reforms prior to statehood: fifteen territorial legislatures passed debt-free separate-estate laws and wills statutes, with smaller numbers passing the more expansive reforms (see table 3.5).

Finally, states around the nation passed antimiscegenation laws, many after the Civil War, that also worked in favor of white men and women and to the detriment of racialized women and their children. In

TABLE 3.5
Territorial Reforms to Married Women's Economic Rights

Reform Type	Territories Adopting the Reform	Number of Territories (Percentage of Total Number)
Debt-free separate property	AR, AZ, CO, ID, IA, KS, MT, Dakota Territory, NE, NM, OK, OR, UT, WA, WY	15 (65%)
Control and management	AZ, CO, KS, MT, Dakota Territory, NM, OK, UT, WA, WY	10 (43%)
Earnings	CO, KS, MT, WA, WY	5 (22%)
Sole trader	AZ, CO, KS, LA, MT, Dakota Territory, NM, OK, WA, WY	10 (43%)
Wills	AZ, CO, FL, ID, KS, MT, Dakota Territory, NM, OK, OR, TX, UT, WA, WY	14 (61%)

Note: Twenty-three states were territories or otherwise held legislative sessions prior to statehood during the period defined in this study (1835–1920): Arkansas, Arizona, California, Colorado, Florida, Iowa, Idaho, Kansas, Michigan, Minnesota, Montana, Dakota Territory (later North and South Dakota), Nebraska, New Mexico, Nevada, Oklahoma, Oregon, Texas, Utah, Washington, Wisconsin, West Virginia, and Wyoming. Iowa passed a debt-free separate-estates law in the same year it entered the Union as a state. The statute was passed by Iowa's final territorial legislature on January 2, 1846, and Iowa statehood was granted later that year, on December 28, 1846.

discussing Texas's antimiscegenation statute, Mark Carroll writes that with the nullification of interracial marriages "free black or manumitted slaves who actually exchanged wedding vows with whites thus had no matrimonial rights whatsoever, including those to community property. By the same token, children born of attempted marriages between blacks and whites could assert no legal claims to patrimonial inheritance."[98] Similarly, Peggy Pascoe writes that western territories' and states' attitudes against marriages between white men and Native women were motivated, at least in part, by a desire to keep newly settled hands in the ownership of "lawful [white] settlers" and not their "Indian wives."[99]

Although some states initially allowed the surviving spouse of an interracial couple to inherit, state courts were beginning to uphold criminal convictions of and to eliminate inheritance rights for Black–white interracial couples by the mid-1870s.[100] By the 1890s, western state courts regularly invalidated marriages between white men and Native women, transferring the husband's property to white relatives after his death.[101] Thus, just as states were passing laws to protect the property of white married women, they stripped Black and Native women who had married white men of their property rights.

Peter Bardaglio defines state paternalism as the "intrusion of the state into ... the private lives" of citizens, with both state legislatures and state courts "taking over patriarchal control from individual fathers."[102] The focus of his work is the South, but the concept of "a paternalistic state that granted dependents certain legal interests and rights" is relevant throughout the country, although of course with regional variation.[103] Legislators in many states saw married women's property acts as a way to protect women by using state power when private relationships broke down.

Concerns for the protection of married women and the property they brought into marriage were especially important for wealthy fathers. Joseph Ranney discusses the importance of antenuptial agreements in equity courts and later in married women's property acts throughout the South, writing that these policies were necessary to "preserve stable property ownership and social order. In the South, daughters of the planter class remained a part of their original families after they married and retention of family land holdings was a key to preserving family wealth and power."[104] Writing about the passage of Mississippi's reform in early 1839, one contemporaneous newspaper commentator wrote:

> There should certainly be some legislative enactment to prevent some unscrupulous husbands, from wantonly squandering the estate vested in them by marriage and bring virtuous wives and helpless children from want and wretchedness. There are also such people in the world as "fortune hunters"—men without morality—without hearts, who are ever prone to deceive and divest women of wealth, that their prodigal hands may be furnished with the pecuniary means of continuing a life of splendid dissipation and degrading indolence. The licentiousness of such men should be checked. They not only disgrace the name of man—they not only sport with the holiest feelings of a woman's heart—but they prey upon their victim and their children, the countless miseries of poverty.[105]

Meanwhile in New York, fathers expressed similar concerns about protecting family wealth from irresponsible husbands. In *History of Woman Suffrage* (1881), women's rights activists noted that "among the Dutch aristocracy of the State [New York] there was a fast amount of dissipation; and as married women could hold neither property nor children under the common law, solid, thrifty Dutch fathers were daily confronted with the fact that the inheritance of their daughters, carefully accumulated, would at marriage pass into the hands of dissipated, impecunious husbands, reducing them and their children to poverty and dependence."[106] Geoffrey Geddes, a supporter of the law, later wrote that he supported the New York law of 1848 because "I had a young daughter, who, in the then condition of my health, was quite likely to be left in tender years without a father, and I very much desired to protect her in the little property I might be able to leave."[107]

A final example comes from the constitutional context in Indiana. In 1850, arguing in favor of a married women's rights provision in the Indiana Constitution, one delegate expressed the idea of state paternalism as such: "The lawgiver is, or should be, dispassionate and experienced; the young betrothed is usually neither one nor the other. The law, therefore, interposing its protecting shield, should, by general enactment, create those checks and guards which she is not likely, even though she has the right while yet single, to provide in her individual case for herself."[108]

In each of these debates around the passage of married women's property rights reforms, state lawmakers described a need for state power to protect women and prevent dependency on the government or private charity. Women in this view were not independent economic actors operating in a free-market framework but rather potential victims who remained embedded in a gender hierarchy—but now with the state at the top instead of a husband or father.

LIMITS AND IMPACTS OF REFORMS

Ultimately, the goal of this chapter is not to try and identify one specific cause of married women's property rights reforms—such a thing does not exist. Rather, this set of reforms is characterized by a political context in which numerous overlapping and sometimes conflicting causes ended up pointing toward a particular policy solution. In some times and places, women's organizing had significant impacts, but reforms were often passed by legislatures that were otherwise hostile or indifferent to women's rights. Overall, the driver of reform was not group mobilization in the traditional sense but rather male legislators and judges whose motivations were often anything but feminist and were instead focused on responding to both women-led and non-women-led movements, economic crises, and attempts to prop up the power of the state to enforce racial and gender hierarchies. These legislators pursued expansions of married women's property rights in a piecemeal fashion, granting additional rights as early laws proved unworkable or inefficient, but not necessarily with an end goal of freeing women from all the disabilities of coverture. Unsurprisingly, though the reforms made during this period meaningfully changed the economic citizenship of (some) married women, they did not completely eliminate these disabilities.[109] Paternalistic views of women placed real limits on how far economic reforms could proceed.

Legislators carefully wrote reform laws to ensure that the marriage relationship as it was defined at that time was unsettled as little as possible. Although married women gained a new foothold in the market vis-à-vis third parties and were now able to make contracts and appear in court without being joined by their husbands, this new legal status often did not penetrate the marriage relationship. Married women's property acts had many shortcomings with regard to women's rights broadly, but one specific characteristic of these laws is especially useful in demonstrating the ways that male political actors circumscribed rights narrowly to achieve their purposes while failing to grant the broader rights that women's activists demanded.

Women's organizations in the antebellum period had sometimes demanded joint property rights that would give married women an equal stake in family assets, but legislation and court rulings made it clear that husbands would remain in control of the bulk of family assets, and a married woman would gain control only over property she alone brought into the marriage and that she specifically elected to keep in a separate account.[110] For example, in a proposal based on the idea of community property but focusing on equal control of community property by husbands and wives, a plank from the First National Woman's Rights Convention in 1850 stated: "Resolved, That the laws of property, as affecting married parties, demand a thorough revisal, so that all rights may be equal between them;—that the wife may have, during life, an equal control over the property gained by their mutual toil and sacrifices."[111] Rather than granting wives control simply over the separate property they brought into a marriage, such a proposal would have ensured them an equal say in managing *all* marital property. No state adopted such a proposal.

Through earnings acts, women eventually gained control over the wages they earned from work done for employers outside the family, but legislators and courts clearly delineated this work from labor performed within the home for the support of the family, which remained under the husband's control. When reforms addressed housework and child care at all, legislators and judges specifically exempted these types of labor under the doctrine of marital service, which stated that women owed domestic service to their husbands as part of the marriage contract.[112] For example, the Maine Earnings Act of 1857 stated that married women "may demand and receive the wages of her personal labor, performed other than for her own family."[113]

Even as reforms contained both new rights and limits on those rights, they also resulted in meaningful changes in state power that disempowered some women, especially Native women and Black women. This is not to say that there was a planned, national strategy to use married women's property acts for the purposes of supporting slavery or divesting Native people of their lands. As we have seen throughout this chapter, these laws were often responses to local, contingent problems and concerns. Nonetheless, the ultimate impact was that state power was expanded and consolidated because of the way that all these different motivations and movements were channeled through state institutions and power structures.

CHAPTER FOUR

Constitutional Conventions as Key Reform Moments

Between 1835 and 1920, forty-three states ratified new constitutions. State-level constitutional conventions were called for various reasons, most commonly as part of the process of admitting new states to the Union and in association with the Civil War, Reconstruction, and the end of Reconstruction. As a result, the drafting of these documents was typically focused on establishing basic rules of governance and on including or excluding African Americans and Native people from state-level politics. Although conventions were not called for the purpose of addressing married women's economic rights, delegates nonetheless did debate these issues and often included various forms of protections for these rights in their state's foundational documents.

Constitutional conventions became focusing moments when political actors were particularly engaged in discussions about rights for multiple groups and may have been more inclined to consider changes to major legal principles, such as the common-law principle of coverture. Other conventions did not do much to change married women's economic rights but rather enshrined in constitutional text protections that had already been extended through statute. Even the latter type of constitutional provision was important for married women in protecting their newly gained rights from a change of heart in a state's legislature. With only one exception, state constitutions were protective of married women's rights. Conventions with dramatically different partisan and racial composition and policy goals often passed very similar rights reforms, demonstrating the malleability of this policy to suite diverse political goals.

Ultimately, state constitutional conventions became important sites for introducing or enshrining reform. They were also critical moments when political leaders laid out a vision of what their state's ideal citizenry should look like. The inclusion of married women's property rights was part of the process of establishing that ideal citizenry. Constitution drafting was deeply racialized for states in both the South and the West as delegates sought to protect and attract certain types of women.

Constitutional conventions illustrate three important themes. First, married women's property rights occupied a liminal space between positive and negative rights. Especially in constitutions, these rights operated as a sort of rudimentary social safety net, often explicitly packaged with other protections for indebted families.[1] Second, borrowing and copying were frequent practices among states as convention delegates actively surveyed the landscape of married women's rights in other states and weighed which provisions would be best suited to their state and would place them, the male delegates, at a competitive advantage. Finally, there was a broader context of exclusion at work even as married women saw their rights expanded in nineteenth-century constitutional conventions.

OVERVIEW OF MARRIED WOMEN'S PROPERTY RIGHTS IN STATE CONSTITUTIONS

Nineteen U.S. states include a statement about married women's property rights either in their current constitution or in a historical constitution.[2] Because many of these states revised these constitutional provisions over time, the constitutions of these nineteen states have included fifty-one total provisions passed at various points in their history. Most of these provisions were ratified during the main period under study in this book (1835–1920), although seventeen were ratified afterward (sometimes with substantive changes but often more focused on removing gender-specific language, such as a Georgia constitutional provision in 1983 that changed the word *wife* to *spouse*[3]). All but one provision were positive statements affirming economic rights for married women (to varying degrees), with the exception being a Florida constitutional provision in 1861 prohibiting the state legislature from passing legislation "allowing married women . . . to contract or manage their estates."[4] This provision was removed from the Florida Constitution of 1868, so that prohibition was ultimately short-lived.

As compared to statutes, constitutional provisions tended to be shorter and contain less policy detail. Some were simply statements that married women could own separate property or that their separate property should be protected, with the details left to future legislatures to work out. The text of provisions ratified between 1835 and 1920 can be found in tables 4.1, 4.2, and 4.3, which are separated into southern-state constitutions, statehood constitutions, and all other constitutional conventions and amendments, discussed further in later sections.

Most of these provisions (forty-one of fifty-one) were the result of constitutional conventions that drafted whole or partial new documents but that generally considered a variety of issues, including but not limited to married women's property rights; ten were amendments to pre-existing constitutions.[5] Constitutional conventions were mainly called for two particular reasons: southern states were ratifying new constitutions at the start of the Civil War, during Reconstruction, and at the end of Reconstruction; and Western states were writing their first state constitutions as part of the statehood process. I consider southern constitutions and statehood constitutions separately in this chapter because they were obviously quite different processes. What these conventions share, however, is that they were called for reasons unrelated to the question of married women's economic rights; that is, the delegates gathered for reasons other than intense demands for expanded women's rights. Nonetheless, delegates did find married women's economic rights salient enough to the politics and governing of their state to include these rights in their founding or foundational documents.

STATE CONSTITUTIONAL RIGHTS IN U.S. HISTORY

In contrast to the U.S. Constitution, state constitutions have proved to be much more "malleable," with an average of one hundred constitutional amendments per state accomplished through state constitutional conventions (more than two hundred and counting), direct democracy, and

TABLE 4.1
Married Women's Rights Provisions in Southern Constitutions

State	Secession	Restoration/Reconstruction	End of Reconstruction/Reassertion of White Supremacy
South Carolina		1868: Article 14, section 8. "The real and personal property of a woman, held at the time of her marriage, or that which she may thereafter acquire, either by gift, grant, inheritance, devise or otherwise, shall not be subject to levy and sale for her husband's debts, but shall be held as her separate property, and may be bequeathed, devised or alienated by her the same as if she were unmarried: Provided, That no gift or grant from the husband to the wife shall be detrimental to the just claims of his creditors."	1895: Article 17, section 9. "The real and personal property of a woman held at the time of her marriage, or that which she may thereafter acquire, either by gift, grant, inheritance, devise or otherwise, shall be her separate property, and she shall have all the rights incident to the same to which an unmarried woman or a man is entitled. She shall have the power to contract and be contracted with in the same manner as if she were unmarried."
Mississippi		1869: Article 1, section 16. "The rights of married women shall be protected by law in property owned previous to marriage; and also in all property acquired in good faith by	1890: Article 3, section 94. "The legislature shall never create by law any distinction between the rights of men and women to acquire, own, enjoy, and dispose of property of all

(*continued*)

TABLE 4.1
Married Women's Rights Provisions in Southern Constitutions (*continued*)

State	Secession	Restoration/Reconstruction	End of Reconstruction/Reassertion of White Supremacy
		purchase, gift, devise, or bequest after marriage; Provided, That nothing herein contained shall be so construed as to protect said property from being applied to the payment of their lawful debts."	kinds, or their power to contract in reference thereto. Married women are hereby fully emancipated from all disability on account of coverture. But this shall not prevent the legislature from regulating contracts between husband and wife; nor shall the legislature be prevented from regulating the sale of homesteads."
Florida	1861: Article 4, section 21. "The General Assembly shall pass a general law prescribing the manner in which names of persons may be changed, but no special law for such purpose shall be passed; and *no law shall be made allowing married women or minors to contract or to manage their estates, or to legitimate bastards.*"	1868: Article 4, section 26. "All property, both real and personal, of the wife, owned by her before marriage, or acquired afterward by gift, devise, descent, or purchase, shall be her separate property, and not liable for the debts of her husband."	1886: Article 11, section 1. "All property, real and personal, of a wife owned by her before marriage, or lawfully acquired afterward by gift, devise, bequest, descent or purchase, shall be her separate property, and the same shall not be liable for the debts of her husband without her consent given by some instrument in writing executed according to the law respecting conveyances by married women."

Section 2.

"A married woman's separate real or personal property may be charged in equity and sold, or the uses, rents and profits thereof sequestrated for the purchase money thereof; or for money or thing due upon any agreement made by her in writing for the benefit of her separate property; or for the price of any property purchased by her, or for labor any material used with her knowledge or assent in the construction of buildings, or repairs, or improvements upon her property, or for agricultural or other labor bestowed thereon, with her knowledge and consent."

Section 3:

"The Legislature shall enact such laws as shall be necessary to carry into effect this Article."

(continued)

TABLE 4.1
Married Women's Rights Provisions in Southern Constitutions (*continued*)

State	Secession	Restoration/Reconstruction	End of Reconstruction/Reassertion of White Supremacy
Alabama		1868: Article 14, section 6. "The real and personal property of any female in this state, acquired before marriage, and all property, real and personal, to which she may afterwards be entitled by gift, grant, inheritance, or devise, shall be and remain the separate estate and property of such female, and shall not be liable for any debts, obligations, and engagements of her husband, and may be devised or bequeathed by her, the same as if she were a femme sole."	1875: Article 10, section 6. 1901: Article 10, section 209. "The real and personal property of any female in this state, acquired before marriage, and all property, real and personal, to which she may afterwards be entitled by gift, grant, inheritance, or devise, shall be and remain the separate estate and property of such female, and shall not be liable for any debts, obligations, and engagements of her husband, and may be devised or bequeathed by her, the same as if she were a femme sole."
Georgia		1868: Article 7, section 2. "All property of the wife, in her possession at the time of her marriage, and all property given to, inherited, or acquired by her, shall remain her separate property, and not liable for the debts of the husband."	1877: Article 3, section 11. "All property of the wife at the time of her marriage, and all property given to, inherited, or acquired by her, shall remain her separate property, and not be liable for the debts of her husband."

Louisiana 1868: Title 6, article 123.

"The general assembly shall provide for the protection of the rights of married women to their dotal and paraphernal property, and for the registration of the same; but no mortgage or privilege shall hereafter affect third parties, unless recorded in the parish where the property to be affected is situated. The tacit mortgages and privileges now existing in this state shall cease to have effect against third persons after the first of January, 1870, unless duly recorded. The general assembly shall provide by law for the registration of all mortgages and privileges."

(continued)

TABLE 4.1
Married Women's Rights Provisions in Southern Constitutions (*continued*)

State	Secession	Restoration/Reconstruction	End of Reconstruction/Reassertion of White Supremacy
Texas		1866: Article 7, section 19. "All property, both real and personal, of the wife, owned or claimed by her before marriage, and that acquired afterward by gift, devise, or descent, shall be her separate property; and laws shall be passed more clearly defining the rights of the wife in relation as well to her separate property as that held in common with her husband. Laws shall also be passed providing for the registration of the wife's separate property." 1869: Article 12, section 14. "The rights of married women to their separate property, real and personal, and the increase of the same, shall be protected by law; and married women, infants, and insane persons shall not be barred of their rights of property by adverse possession, or law of limitation, of less than seven years from and after the removal of each and all of their respective legal disabilities."	1876: Article 16, section 15. "All property, both real and personal, of the wife, owned or claimed by her before marriage, and that acquired afterward by gift, devise, or descent, shall be her separate property; and laws shall be passed more clearly defining the rights of the wife in relation as well to her separate property as that held in common with her husband. Laws shall also be passed providing for the registration of the wife's separate property."

Virginia		
Arkansas	1868: Article 12, section 6. "The real and personal property of any female in this state, acquired either before or after marriage, whether by gift, grant, inheritance, devise or otherwise, shall, so long as she may choose, be and remain the separate estate and property of such female, and may be devised or bequeathed by her the same as she were a femme sole. Laws shall be passed providing for the registration of the wife's separate property, and when so registered, and so long as it is not entrusted to the management or control of her husband, otherwise than as an agent, it shall not be liable for any of his debts, engagements, or obligations."	1874: Article 9, section 7. "The real and personal property of any femme covert in this state, acquired either before or after marriage, whether by gift, grant, inheritance, devise or otherwise, shall, so long as she may choose, be and remain her separate estate and property, and may be devised, bequeathed or conveyed by her the same as if she were a femme sole; and the same shall not be subject to the debts of her husband." Section 8: "The general assembly shall provide for the time and mode of scheduling the separate personal property of married women."

(continued)

TABLE 4.1
Married Women's Rights Provisions in Southern Constitutions (*continued*)

State	Secession	Restoration/Reconstruction	End of Reconstruction/Reassertion of White Supremacy
Tennessee			
North Carolina		1868: Article 10, section 6. "The real and personal property of any female in this State, acquired before marriage, and all property, real and personal, to which she may after marriage, become in any manner entitled, shall be and remain the sole and separate estate and property of such female, and shall not be liable for any debts, obligations, or engagements of her husband, and may be devised or bequeathed, and, with the written assent of her husband, conveyed, by her, as if she were unmarried."	

Note: States are listed in order of secession. The sole example of an "anti–married women's property rights" constitutional provision is in Florida's Constitution of 1861, written upon the state's secession from the United States. This provision is given in italics in the table.

Table 4.2

Married Women's Property Rights Provisions in Statehood Constitutions, 1835–1920

State	Date Admitted to Union	Constitutional Text
Arkansas	June 15, 1836	
Michigan	January 26, 1837	
Florida	March 3, 1845	
Texas	December 29, 1845	Article 7, section 19. "All property, both real and personal, of the wife, owned or claimed by her before marriage, and that acquired afterwards by gift, devise, or descent, shall be her separate property; and laws shall be passed more clearly defining the rights of the wife in relation as well to her separate property as that held in common with her husband. Laws shall also be passed providing for the registration of the wife's separate property."
Iowa	December 28, 1846	
Wisconsin	May 29, 1848	
California	September 9, 1850	Article 11, section 14. "All property, both real and personal, of the wife, owned or claimed by marriage, and that acquired afterwards by gift, devise, or descent, shall be her separate property; and laws shall be passed more clearly defining the rights of the wife, in relation as well to her separate property, as to that held in common with her husband. Laws shall also be passed providing for the registration of the wife's separate property."
Minnesota	May 11, 1858	

(*continued*)

Table 4.2

Married Women's Property Rights Provisions in Statehood Constitutions, 1835–1920 (*continued*)

State	Date Admitted to Union	Constitutional Text
Oregon	February 14, 1859	Article 15, section 5. "The property and pecuniary rights of every married woman, at the time of marriage or afterwards, acquired by gift, devise, or inheritance shall not be subject to the debts, or contracts of the husband; and laws shall be passed providing for the registration of the wife's separate property."
Kansas	January 29, 1861	Article 15, section 6. "The Legislature shall provide for the protection of the rights of women, in acquiring and possessing property, real, personal and mixed, separate and apart from the husband; and shall also provide for their equal rights in the possession of their children."
West Virginia	June 20, 1863	
Nevada	October 31, 1864	Article 3, section 31. "All property, both real and personal, of the wife, owned or claimed by her before marriage, and that acquired afterward by gift, devise or descent, shall be her separate property; and laws shall be passed more clearly defining the rights of the wife, in relation as well to her separate property, as to that held in common with her husband. Laws shall also be passed providing for the registration of the wife's separate property."
Nebraska	March 1, 1867	

State	Date Admitted to Union	Constitutional Text
Colorado	August 1, 1876	
North Dakota	November 2, 1889	Article 17, section 213. "The real and personal property of any woman in this state, acquired before marriage, and all property to which she may after marriage become in any manner rightfully entitled, shall be her separate property and shall not be liable for the debts of her husband."
South Dakota	November 2, 1889	Article 21, section 5. "Rights of married women. The real and personal property of any women in this state acquired before marriage, and all property to which she may after marriage become in any manner rightfully entitled, shall be her separate property, and shall not be liable for the debts of her husband."
Montana	November 8, 1889	
Washington	November 11, 1889	
Idaho	July 3, 1890	
Wyoming	July 10, 1890	
Utah	January 4, 1896	Article 22, section 2. "Real and personal estate of every female, acquired before marriage, and all property to which she may afterwards become entitled by purchase, gift, grant, inheritance or devise, shall be and remain the estate and property of such female, and shall not be liable for the debts, obligations or engagements of her husband, and may be conveyed, devised or bequeathed by her as if she were unmarried."

(continued)

Table 4.2

Married Women's Property Rights Provisions in Statehood Constitutions, 1835–1920 (*continued*)

State	Date Admitted to Union	Constitutional Text
Oklahoma	November 16, 1907	
New Mexico	January 6, 1912	
Arizona	February 14, 1912	

other methods of amendment. Both constitutional conventions and the adoption of new constitutions were more common practices in the nineteenth century than they are today.[6] As compared to the federal constitution, state constitutions also tend to be long and contain numerous "legislative"-style provisions specifying state policy in particular areas as opposed to general principles. The legal scholar Christian Fritz explains that delegates to state constitutional conventions in the nineteenth century believed that politics and economics had become more complex since the time of the country's founding. Delegates saw constitutional legislation as a way to constrain the otherwise plenary power of state legislatures and sometimes to direct legislatures' actions in ways that state courts could not easily contest.[7]

Emily Zackin has written on the importance of state constitutions as a major source of positive rights (as defined later in this section). She argues that in contrast to the U.S. Constitution, which is focused primarily on negative rights, state constitutions tend to be filled with positive rights similar to those found in the constitutions of other nations. In Zackin's account, positive constitutional rights were meant to form a sort of "social safety net of heartier stuff than mere statutes."[8] We see a similar approach with the inclusion of married women's economic rights in state constitutions in that these provisions were often included even where legislatures had already passed comprehensive statutes on the subject; creating constitutional guarantees ensured that state legislatures could not so easily change their minds. The new constitutional rights

TABLE 4.3
Other State Constitutional Married Women's Property Rights Provisions and Amendments, 1835–1920

State	Year	Constitutional Text
Michigan	1850	Article 16, section 5. "The real and personal estate of every female, acquired before marriage, and all property to which she may afterwards become entitled, by gift, grant, inheritance, or devise, shall be and remain the estate and property of such female, and shall not be liable for the debts, obligations, or engagements of her husband; and may be devised or bequeathed by her as if she were unmarried."
Maryland	1851	Article 3, section 38. "The general assembly shall pass laws necessary to protect the property of the wife from the debts of the husband during her life, and for securing the same to her issue after her death."
Maryland	1864	Article 3, section 42. "The general assembly shall pass laws necessary to protect the property of the wife from the debts of the husband during her life, and for securing the same to her issue after her death."
Maryland	1867	Article 3, section 2. "The property of the wife shall be protected from the debts of her husband."
West Virginia	1872	Article 6, section 49. "The Legislature shall pass such laws as may be necessary to protect the property of married women from the debts, liabilities and control of their husbands."
California	1879	Article 20, section 8. "All property, real and personal, owned by either husband or wife, before marriage, and that acquired by either of them afterward by gift, devise, or descent, shall be their separate property."

(continued)

Table 4.3

Other State Constitutional Married Women's Property Rights Provisions and Amendments, 1835–1920 (*continued*)

State	Year	Constitutional Text
Michigan	1909	Article 16, section 8. "The real and personal estate of every woman, acquired before marriage, and all property to which she may afterwards become entitled by gift, grant, inheritance or devise shall be and remain the estate and property of such woman, and shall not be liable for the debts, obligations or engagements of her husband, and may be devised or bequeathed by her as if she were unmarried."

Zackin studies often involved forcing state legislatures to intervene in state economies for the protection of citizens, such as by means of debtor protections and homestead exemptions.[9] Similarly, the protection of indebted families was an important motivation behind the push for married women's separate-property rights in many states. Along with other protections for debtors, such as constitutional provisions exempting homesteads from being seized by creditors, married women's property rights provided a sort of rudimentary social safety net by placing some portion of a family's property in a protected category that could not be taken for repayment of debts.

Zackin's book examines the inclusion in state constitutions of positive rights requiring state governments to take action around issues such as education and labor. Married women's economic rights, examined here, occupy a more liminal state. Zackin identifies two key dimensions distinguishing positive from negative rights.[10] First, negative rights protect individuals from governmental threats, whereas positive rights protect individuals from nongovernmental actors. On the second dimension, negative rights require the government to restrain itself from acting, while positive rights require the government to take action or intervene to protect or help individuals. The placement of married women's economic rights in this matrix is not immediately clear.

Property rights have traditionally been categorized as negative rights. A number of scholars have challenged the clean distinction between negative and positive rights, arguing that most negative rights can be recast as requiring some sort of government action.[11] In the case of property rights specifically, for a right to own property to be meaningful, the state must invest in passing relevant laws to protect property and must then enforce those rights with police, bureaucrats, courts, and so on.[12] As the legal scholars Stephen Holmes and Cass Sunstein write, "Without legislation and adjudication there can be no property rights in the way Americans understand that term. Government lays down the rules of ownership specifying who owns what and how particular individuals acquire specific ownership rights."[13]

Even if we are to accept the distinction between positive and negative rights as a general matter, married women's property rights seem to fill a different space than the property rights found in the U.S. Constitution. Writing about the U.S. Constitution, the legal scholar Frank Cross argues that the property rights guaranteed therein are negative because the text references only government restraint, not government action: "The Fifth Amendment's property right is 'not a right to possess property,' but an opportunity to acquire it and a prohibition upon its being taken by the government."[14] In contrast, the married women's economic rights guaranteed in state constitutions do not primarily protect married women's property from government seizure but rather from their husbands and from private creditors. Some constitutions even required state governments to establish a system by which married women could register their property with the state to guarantee protection (for example, see the Arkansas Constitution of 1874, which provided that "the general assembly shall provide for the time and mode of scheduling the separate personal property of married women"[15]). These constitutions seem to envision a more active role for state governments in ensuring that married women's property would be protected *by* the state, not merely protected *from* the state.

Finally, although married women's property rights included in state constitutions were technically race neutral—no post–Civil War constitutional married women's provisions explicitly mentioned enslaved human property, as did many statutes before the war—the constitutions they were part of were not always inclusive documents (some, such as

Reconstruction constitutions in the South, were more inclusive). It is important to consider which women the constitutional convention delegates had in mind as deserving of protection in their promotion of expanded rights for women. To start with, of course, reforms by definition were limited to women in possession of property—without it, they had nothing to protect under these laws. Further, for many constitutions, white women were the beneficiaries of these policies, as in constitutions that ended Reconstruction and sharply limited the rights of African American women and men. Statehood constitutions also protected married women's property even as they engaged in a colonial project that stripped Native people of their property rights—though the latter intent was not stated explicitly in said constitutions because tribes dealt directly with the national government. As the historian Laurel Clark Shire argues in her analysis of married women's property laws in Florida, these new rights for married women "enlisted white women in colonization in order to replicate the settlement process unfolding in other territories, realizing that war and removal alone could not accomplish the same colonial goal: permanent settlement."[16] Attracting white families—not just white men—was central to this goal.

SOUTHERN CONSTITUTIONS: RECONSTRUCTION AND POST-RECONSTRUCTION

Southern constitutions ratified around the Civil War, Reconstruction, and the end of Reconstruction demonstrate both the importance of constitutional conventions for pushing married women's economic rights forward and the bipartisan nature of these measures. During this period, southern states ratified at least two (and sometimes more) new constitutions.[17] Immediately after the Civil War, most states were forced to accept military-imposed constitutions in order to be readmitted to the Union. These typically brief documents dealt only with the basics. Then during Reconstruction, conventions met to lay out new constitutions on much broader terms. These conventions were filled with Republican delegates and included many African Americans. The resulting constitutions typically included comprehensive bills of rights that "guaranteed the political and civil rights of all citizens, both black and white; declared the national Union to be perpetual; and prohibited religious or property qualifications for voting or holding public office."[18] Of eleven states that seceded from the Union, all but two (Virginia and Tennessee) incorporated married women's economic rights in their new Reconstruction constitutions. Over the subsequent decades, however, almost every southern state ratified yet another constitution. With the abandonment of Reconstruction in the South, white southern Democrats met to debate and pass constitutional provisions that sharply limited the civil rights of African Americans and rolled back many more progressive measures written into Reconstruction constitutions. These white-supremacist documents did not roll back married women's economic rights, however.

Table 4.1 outlines the married women's rights provisions in southern constitutions during the Reconstruction and post-Reconstruction periods. Nine of eleven states included protections for married women's property in at least one of these documents, and seven states included reforms in both their Reconstruction and post-Reconstruction constitutions.[19] Of those seven states, four expanded married women's economic rights further in their post-Reconstruction constitutions (South Carolina, Mississippi, Florida, and Arkansas), while three included identical or near-identical provisions (Alabama, Georgia, and Texas). This record confirms evidence from state legislatures that married women's economic rights were not a partisan issue on the whole; both parties were willing to advance these policies when they were in power. Reconstruction and post-Reconstruction constitutional conventions approached their work from opposite ends of the political spectrum, but married women's property rights were one area where they were apparently in consensus. Moreover, it was not only the constitutional provisions of Republicans and Democrats that looked similar but also the judicial interpretations of married women's property provisions, with southern judges from both parties tending to interpret these provisions relatively narrowly—that is, neither striking them down nor giving them radical, feminist interpretations.[20]

The bipartisan nature of support for reforms is particularly interesting when considering that the parties were sharply divided on other issues related to marriage and property. For example, in his analysis of miscegenation laws in the United States, the historian Peter Wallenstein discusses the role of courts in recognizing interracial marriages for the purposes of inheritance by nonwhite spouses and mixed-race children.

Although Republican judges in some southern states during Reconstruction were willing to acknowledge interracial marriages for the purposes of property inheritance, courts in the South quickly reversed course after Reconstruction ended.[21] Post-Reconstruction judges overruled prior case law legitimating relationships between white men and Black women, thus limiting the rights of Black widows in interracial relationships.[22]

The inclusion of married women's economic rights was apparently relatively uncontroversial in many states, likely at least in part because most southern states had at least some experience with reforming married women's property rights before the post–Civil War conventions. Only one state, South Carolina, passed its first reform of married women's property rights after the war, as part of the Constitution of 1868; the other southern states had passed statutory reforms in earlier years. Thus, many southern states were engaged in a process of elevating married women's economic rights to constitutional guarantee, not necessarily changing the policy on the ground. For instance, at the Arkansas constitutional convention in 1868 the main objection to including married women's rights in the document was that exemption laws in general (both homestead exemptions and exemptions for married women's property) were legislative matters rather than constitutional ones.[23] The substantive debates around women's rights instead centered on whether to include a provision providing for woman suffrage in the constitution, a much more controversial matter. The convention leadership determined Mr. Langley, the primary supporter of this measure, to be out of order for even trying to introduce a suffrage provision, as they did an attempt by another delegate to debate the matter.[24] When the woman suffrage clause was eventually debated, the discussion was apparently heated, with interruptions from both sides.[25] Langley was openly mocked, with one delegate proposing a substitute amendment that would have denied men the right to vote if they permitted their wives to go to the polls.[26] Ultimately, the woman suffrage amendment died without ever getting a formal vote.[27] This treatment stands in stark contrast to the uncontroversial manner in which the delegates treated married women's property rights—no extended debate and no laughter, just disagreement over whether these rights were best protected by statutory or constitutional law.

Southern constitutions also offer an important window into another aspect of reform: the transmission of text and content among states. Throughout the South, delegates often used similar language to describe married women's new economic rights and included similar types of protections in their constitutions. Six states inserted a constitutional debt-free provision ensuring that married women's separate property could not be seized by their husbands' creditors. Five included language guaranteeing a married woman the right to make at least some decisions about her property "as if she were unmarried" or "as if she were a *feme sole*."

Both Mississippi and South Carolina included married women's property protections in their Reconstruction and post-Reconstruction constitutions, and the debates in these states are illustrative of broader processes in the South. These debates demonstrate the ways in which both Republicans and Democrats championed reforms, the political discourse around the protection of women, the connection of married women's rights to broader concerns around family debt relief, and the dynamics of inclusion and exclusion surrounding these provisions.

In 1869, in the midst of Reconstruction, delegates met to write a new constitution for Mississippi. In addition to the significant post–Civil War changes to the document, delegates included a brief provision that gave married women's property rights constitutional protection (see table 4.1). The convention's delegates passed this measure as part of the new bill of rights by a vote of thirty-nine to twenty.[28] The convention journal records no debates specific to the married women's provision, likely because the provision was a brief, generic version of laws that had been in existence for quite a few years and made no substantial changes to these laws. The historian Suzanne Lebsock argues that married women's property rights reforms passed by Radical Republicans as part of Reconstruction constitutions, including in Mississippi, "continued an established southern tradition of legislation, a tradition of progressive expansion of the property rights of married women for utterly nonfeminist purposes"—namely, the protection of women from irresponsible men, the protection of daughters by fathers who were concerned with passing on property to their grandchildren via those daughters, and the protection of indebted families in a period when debt was a widespread and serious problem—motives that were reflected in Mississippi's earlier statutory reforms as well.[29]

Despite the lack of lengthy debate over Mississippi's constitutional married women's property rights provision, there were significant debates on issues surrounding debtor protection that are relevant to understanding the context of married women's property rights reforms. For instance, one delegate, Mr. S. Johnson, argued that almost all exemptions (here referring largely to homestead exemptions) should be eliminated with the exception of married women's inheritances.[30] Although this provision failed, the proposal indicates two important issues. First, women's separate-property rights were at least to some extent still seen as an "exemption" allowed to debtors alongside their right to keep exempt some amount of housing, farming implements, and necessities from their creditors' claims; although some delegates may have seen married women's reforms as a proactive extension of women's rights, others classified them alongside other exemptions that were based on family-level protection and unrelated to gender. Johnson's justifications for the proposed provision also provide a window into concerns over debtor–creditor politics at the time. He argued that excessive exemptions actually hurt debtors as much as creditors, noting that poor families often could not obtain needed medical treatment on credit because homestead and other exemptions were so generous that it would be too easy to escape repayment.[31] Although Johnson did not extend this discussion to married women's property, it seems likely that married women would have faced similar issues with obtaining needed credit because of the fact that their right to mortgage and more generally to contract was limited in various ways.

Even as some delegates argued for more creditor-friendly exemption laws, others argued for increased debtor protection. The latter approach seems to be in response at least in part to the nationwide trend of a growing number of debtors across the class structure, in particular debtors whose economic problems were seen as beyond their personal control and responsibility. Rather than being seen as personal moral failings, debts became viewed as an integral part of the commercial economy, for which both creditors and debtors had to take on some level of risk.[32] For instance, Mr. Railsback argued that "a large portion of the planters and businessmen of the State of Mississippi are grievously oppressed by unliquidated liabilities" in large part due to the economic devastation of the Civil War.[33] Although Railsback's proposed solution, a suspension of all debt collection within the state, was not adopted, these economic circumstances do help explain why the convention incorporated a variety of provisions that benefited debtors. These provisions included banning imprisonment for debt, granting the legislature the power to pass homestead-exemption laws as well as "any and every act deemed necessary for the relief of debtors," and protecting married women's property rights.[34]

Two decades later, in 1890, a convention dominated by white southern Democrats wrote a new constitution for Mississippi that gave the state's statutory reform of 1880 the weight of constitutional provision. The married women's reform of 1890 was a dramatic expansion of the provision of 1869, providing that married women be "fully emancipated from all disability on account of coverture" and prohibiting the state legislature from passing any law that treated men and women differently when it came to property or contract power.[35] The convention, however, was by no means a progressive one; it introduced literacy tests and poll taxes that would prevent most African Americans from voting and required racial segregation in public schools. Yet the married women's property rights reform included in the constitution passed with apparently little controversy. One delegate bragged, for example, that Mississippi "was among the first of the political bodies of the world" to grant rights to married women, such that "to-day a married woman is as good as a married man in Mississippi."[36] This attitude toward women went only so far, however—one delegate proposed extending the vote to some women (those who met the property and education requirements), but this proposal never made it out of committee.[37]

The context had also changed with regard to concern for debtors and debt relief. Although the Mississippi Constitution of 1890 did include a prohibition on imprisonment for debt (carried over from the Constitution of 1868), there were no other provisions relating to debt relief, and the issue was not a major point of debate at the constitutional convention.[38] The energy around homestead exemptions had largely faded in the South by this point as delegates saw property owners' ability to obtain credit as more important than exemptions.[39] The married women's property rights provision, introduced by the Democrat R. H.

Thompson, was stated in terms that did not reference debt and instead provided sweeping guarantees for equal economic rights for women in the realm of property, which prohibited the state legislature from enacting any law treating men and women differently with regard to property ownership and explicitly eliminated the disabilities of coverture.[40]

South Carolina also included married women's property rights in both its Reconstruction and post-Reconstruction constitutions. South Carolina passed its first reform of married women's property rights in the wake of the Civil War as part of its new state constitution in 1868 (see table 4.1). This constitution was focused on equal opportunity and was written largely by Radical Republicans.[41] At two points, delegates raised the issue of women's property rights specifically. Early in the convention, on the fifth day that delegates met, delegates debated a variety of debt-relief proposals aimed in particular at wartime debts. For instance, one delegate proposed a resolution directing the military to suspend collection of debts for three months, until the economy was in less chaos.[42] The convention did not move forward with this proposal, and another delegate then proposed a series of resolutions aimed at debt relief: a provision exempting $1,000 from debt collection per resident, a homestead exemption of up to $2,500 worth of property and housing, a homestead exemption specifically benefiting widows or women who had been abandoned by their husbands, and a separate-estates provision exempting the separate property of wives from liability for the debts of their husbands.[43] Clearly, these proposals, which ultimately did not pass as a unified debt-relief policy, were aimed primarily at relieving war debt rather than at advancing the interests of married women specifically, even though women were listed as specific beneficiaries in some cases. The proposals responded to the massive economic disruption of the Civil War and aimed to protect wealth and to prevent indebted families, women, and children from falling back on state dependency.

When the South Carolina convention's delegates next took up the topic of married women's property rights, the debate focused more specifically on the women themselves, this time with an eye toward the protection of married women from irresponsible and unscrupulous husbands. One delegate argued: "I appeal to you who have lived here all your lives, and seen women suffer from the hands of the fortune hunters; the plausible villains, who, after securing the property of their wives, have squandered it in gambling and drinking; a class of men who are still going about the country boasting that they intend to marry a plantation, and take the woman as an incumbrance [sic]."[44]

The debate continued in a similar fashion, with another delegate accusing those who opposed a married women's property rights provision of being "unmarried members of the Convention who may be looking for rich wives" and arguing that delegates with female relatives should be concerned with looking out for their protection.[45] The provision ultimately passed eighty-eight to eight, with twenty-five delegates abstaining.[46] It gave married women the right to separate estates not subject to their husband's debts.[47]

The particular concern for female family members and the protection of family property was discussed, with delegate B. F. Randolf arguing: "[There] are those here . . . who have mothers, sisters and daughters, all of whom may come into possession of property; and I ask if it is just that those who are so near and dear to us, shall be left in a position where a man without principle may, by marriage, take possession of their property, and leave them dependent upon the cold charities of the world?"[48]

This interest in protecting female family members and their property was particularly acute in the years immediately after the Civil War. With the South experiencing military deaths three times that of the North (approximately one-fifth of military-age white men in the Confederacy died in the war), single white women with property often either remained unmarried longer or had to turn to "less desirable" classes for marriage prospects.[49] The historians J. David Hacker, Libra Hilde, and James Holland Jones note that "after the war, wealth became less important in the economically devastated South when contracting marriages, and many women married below their social class."[50] With wealthy women now facing the prospect of marrying men from lower classes who could bring little of their own property to the marriage, it was now more important than ever for wealthy fathers to ensure that family property passed on to daughters would be protected.

Ultimately, the language in the South Carolina Constitution did give married women broad control over their separate property. But it is important to note here that despite the seemingly expansive language of the constitutional text—providing a married woman rights over her property "as if she were unmarried"[51]—the delegates were concerned largely with protecting victimized women, in particular relatives, or protecting the property interests of indebted men, not in putting forward a liberal view of married women as full, equal citizens. When the convention raised the issue of women's suffrage, it was only to criticize a proponent of the provision for being too liberal, a charge he quickly denied.[52]

The major opposition to including a married woman's property rights provision at the convention was that the reforms opened the door to fraud, abuse, and legal uncertainty over exactly what property was owned by a wife (and thus was exempt from debts) versus what property was owned by her husband.[53] In fact, over the next few decades, this is precisely the legal situation that would develop around married women's property in South Carolina, with a confusing legal system in which married women could own property but under which it was never exactly clear what they could legally do with that property or what potential creditors could expect when demanding repayment. Indeed, the legal problems arising from partial property rights for married women was a major motivator of expanded married women's property rights at South Carolina's constitutional convention in 1895, a topic discussed in greater detail in chapter 6.

Constitutional conventions were important moments when state-level elites were involved in the process of considering the political system as a whole and the citizens that made up that system. In the South as elsewhere, women's rights were clearly not the reason these conventions were called; rather, the conventions were a response to the Civil War and the end of Reconstruction. Yet they provided a political opening for elites to consider how best to define married women's property rights. Many states that already had reforms on the books elevated them to constitutional status, thus protecting these rights from possible legislative reversals.

Votes from Mississippi's and South Carolina's conventions confirm that there were no clear partisan or racial patterns among those in support of married women's economic rights. At Mississippi's convention in 1869, the married women's property rights provision was approved by a vote of thirty-seven to twenty, with Black delegates making up about 24 percent of the "yea" votes (nine of thirty-seven) and 30 percent of the "nay" votes (six of twenty). Conservatives were somewhat more likely to support the measure than Radical Republicans, although a majority of both factions supported the measure—Conservatives voted to support married women's economic rights seven to two, versus Radicals at twenty-three to sixteen.[54] At the Mississippi convention in 1890, the vote on the married women's property rights provision was not recorded, but the convention delegates were overwhelmingly Democratic, and the provision could not have been adopted without Democratic support.[55]

Similar patterns can be found in South Carolina. That state's convention in 1868 was dominated by Radical Republicans, with little Conservative opposition and many lopsided votes, including the vote for the married women's property rights provision.[56] It passed by a vote of eighty-eight to eight, with a majority of both Black and white delegates supporting the measure. About 60 percent of the "yea" votes came from Black delegates (fifty-three of eighty-eight), versus around 63 percent of the "nay" votes (five of eight) coming from Black delegates.[57] Three decades later, the married women's property rights provision at the South Carolina convention in 1895 passed without a recorded vote. But by that time all but six delegates were white Democrats, with the remaining six being Black Republicans.[58] So, despite the lack of a recorded vote, it is clear that this measure must have been supported by Democrats.

In addition to illustrating the bipartisan and often uncontroversial nature of including married women's property rights in southern constitutions, these conventions reveal other important themes. Debates often focused on the need to protect women from both men and the economy more broadly. Connections to debt relief were central, especially in Reconstruction constitutions. In post-Reconstruction conventions, expansive protections for married women were combined with severe restrictions on the rights of African American women and men, demonstrating that white Democratic delegates in the 1890s saw these protections for women as primarily benefiting white women despite the use of race-neutral language in the provisions.

STATEHOOD CONSTITUTIONS

Between 1835 and 1920, twenty-four states entered the Union, and all had to draft a constitution as part of this process. Of these twenty-four, eight included a married women's property rights provision as part of that first constitution (see table 4.2). Thus, for territories becoming states, the inclusion of these protections at the constitutional level was not as universal as in the case of post–Civil War southern constitutions, although it was still a fairly common practice. Of the eight constitutions with a married women's property rights provision, half included debt-free separate-estates clauses; half provided for the registration of married women's property; half directed the state legislature to pass further reforms; and one guaranteed wives control rights over their separate property "as if [they] were unmarried."

Amy Bridges writes that western statehood conventions were distinctive from territorial (and later state) legislatures. Despite including many provisions that might be considered legislative in nature, these conventions did not simply reproduce legislative dynamics. They tended to be more representative of territorial constituents, and delegates paid more attention to popular opinion—both because constitutions needed to be ratified by popular vote and because territorial newspapers covered conventions to a much greater extent than they covered legislative activity.[59]

Delegates at western statehood constitutional conventions were intentional about assessing the constitutions of other states and selecting text to include in the new documents they were drafting. Instead of simply unthinkingly copying text, delegates carefully weighed the successes and failures of other states' experiences and saw such assessment as crucial for successful constitution writing.[60] In addition, western conventions that incorporated married women's economic rights were conscious of attracting women to their territory. Thus, attending to the constitutions of other states might allow them not only to craft the best policies but also to gain a competitive advantage. Here, I examine debates from the California and Nevada statehood conventions to explore the major arguments made by delegates, with special attention to the ways in which delegates viewed their approach to married women's property rights in comparison to the approaches taken by other states.

At California's statehood constitutional convention in 1849, borrowing from other states was a significant part of the process. Iowa's and New York's constitutions were the major sources of inspiration, with 66 of the

136 sections in the California Constitution coming from the Iowa Constitution and 19 from the New York Constitution.[61] The provision on married women's economic rights was no exception to the rule of borrowing and was taken verbatim from the Texas Constitution (see table 4.2).

Although this provision provided for a married woman's ownership of separate property, it did not specify whether she could control or manage that property or whether it might be liable for some or all of her husband's debts. The text was introduced by William Shannon, a delegate originally elected to the convention because of his strong antislavery positions.[62] Shannon may also have been inspired by his home state, New York, which never included a married women's property provision in its constitution but was seen as a national leader on the issue of married women's economic rights more generally.[63] The Texas Constitution was not specifically mentioned by delegates in debating the married women's property provision but did come up at other times during the convention. For example, Mr. Gwin defended copying a provision on taxation from the Texas Constitution by stating that "Texas is very similarly situated to this country"; he also defended the model of a biennial legislature, with the argument that Texas was "a Territory somewhat similar in the character of its population to this."[64]

In the case of married women's rights, Texas had a background similar to California's, having based its entire property system on the Spanish civil code prior to statehood. For married women, this meant a community-property system that was not based on the "civic death" of women upon marriage but instead allowed them at least somewhat of a legal identity after marriage. The debates surrounding the inclusion of married women's property rights in the California Constitution involved both proponents of the old Spanish community-property system and proponents of the English common-law system.[65]

Delegates at the convention praised the experience of other states in passing reforms for married women's economic rights. For instance, Mr. Tefft argued: "This very section [of the proposed constitution] not only stands upon the statute books of many of the old States, but is inserted in the Constitution of some of them."[66] Another delegate, Mr. Jones, agreed, arguing that the common law, as judge-made law, was too complicated and that a provision clarifying the rights of married women was needed:

State after State has adopted this principle. . . . For forty or fifty years the States of the American Union have been trying to modify and simplify this principle of the common law. . . . [Californians] want a code of simple laws which they can understand; no common law, full of exploded principles, . . . they want something that the people can comprehend. The gentleman forgets that the law is the will of the people properly expressed, and that the people have a right to understand their own will and derive the advantage of it, without going to a lawyer to have it expounded. It is absurd to require them to apply for legal advice to learn how they are to collect a debt of fifty dollars.[67]

In addition to these appeals to other states' experiences, the delegates made arguments both for and against the new married women's property rights provision that echoed those made at southern conventions. Some opponents emphasized the potential for fraud, arguing that dishonest male debtors would simply pretend their property belonged to their wives.[68] Mr. Botts argued that the provision would benefit only "the fraudulent husband and the colluding wife," who would take advantage of creditors and "leave us pennyless while they revel in luxury."[69] Other opponents argued that the new rights were "a dangerous subject of experiment" likely to destroy the marital relationship, cause "dissension and strife in families," and turn men into "Prince Albert's [sic]" (husband of Queen Victoria).[70] Meanwhile, supporters of the provision largely stressed the need to protect women from husbands who were "idle, dissipated, visionary, or impractical," with one delegate arguing that it was only fair that the constitution "protect frail and lovely woman."[71] Still, feminist arguments were not entirely absent, such as Mr. Dimmick's statement in support of reform: "The time was, sir, when woman was considered an inferior being; but as knowledge has become more generally diffused, as the world has become more enlightened, as the influence of free and liberal principles has extended among the nations of the earth, the rights of woman have become generally recognized."[72]

Delegates also argued that California and other western states had particular concerns not present in northeastern and southern states. "Wild and hazardous speculations" on the frontier were commonplace and brought with them great risk of family ruin, which protections of married women's property would help mitigate.[73] The state's gender imbalance and the desire to attract white female settlers of a particular sort—wives, not prostitutes or independent single women—also played an important role both in the abstract and for individual delegates. Mr. Halleck stated:

> I am not wedded either to the common law or the civil law, nor as yet, to a woman; but having some hopes that some time or other I may be wedded, and wishing to avoid the fate of my friend from San Francisco, (Mr. Lippitt [a delegate who opposed the provision]), I shall advocate this section in the Constitution, and I would call upon all the bachelors in this Convention to vote for it. I do not think we can offer a greater inducement for women of fortune to come to California. It is the very best provision to get us wives that we can introduce into the Constitution.[74]

Finally, it was clear that in California's case a failure to include any sort of protection for married women's property rights would alter the rights of married women currently living in California under the community-property system.[75] Because the common law would be adopted in the state as a general rule when it gained statehood, any exceptions to this system based on civil law would need to be expressly spelled out in the constitution. Ultimately, the married women's property rights provision passed and was included as part of the new state constitution.

At Nevada's statehood constitutional convention in 1864, delegates considered two provisions regarding married women's economic rights, one of which passed and the other voted down. The successful provision was a standard protection of married women's property rights written with language very similar to that in both the Texas and California constitutions (see table 4.2). This provision received little debate before being approved by the delegates without a recorded vote, raising only one objection from a Mr. Johnson, who said only: "I do not like he-women."[76]

Garnering much more debate was a provision that would have prohibited married women from acting as sole traders: "No law shall be passed authorizing married women to carry on business as sole traders."[77] Much of the debate over this provision focused on explicit comparison to the failures and successes of sole-trader laws in California, especially around the issue of fraud. Mr. Wetherill spoke out in support of the ban: "We have seen the evils of the system of 'sole traders' in California, in divers [sic] instances. It has led to abuses throughout the State. Dishonesty is practiced under it in every shape."[78] Another delegate, Mr. Brosnan, further argued that women engaged in sole trading were employed in "the most unbecoming occupations . . . that female modesty would blush at."[79]

Opponents of the prohibition on sole trading by women, however, pointed to arguments similar to those used in favor of married women's economic rights more generally, focusing in particular on connections to temperance and the avoidance of dependency on the state. For example, Mr. Chapin argued on behalf of the "many wives in this Territory . . . now suffering from having miserable, intemperate husbands who are incapable of transacting business" and believed that allowing for sole trading by women would decrease the high divorce rate.[80] Mr. DeLong gave an impassioned speech on the need to protect women from drunken and wasteful husbands:

> I have also seen hundreds of instances, where the profligate husband not only refused to pay anything for the support of his family, but even wrung from the wife and mother her hard earnings, and prostituted them to the gratification of his own base appetite, leaving her and her children to suffer and starve. I have even seen the whiskey-seller bring suit to recover the wife's wages, and take the fruits of her toil, to pay the debts which her dissolute husband had incurred for bad liquor, in his vile hell. I have seen these things until it has made my blood almost curdle, and my soul rebel against the thought of this sort of thing being tolerated—against any law which will allow such things to be done.[81]

DeLong went on to say that most of the fraud taking place in California had been under an older sole-trader law, since repealed, and that the state had improved the law and seen a decrease in fraud, an argument repeated later by another delegate.[82] Ultimately, the prohibition of women acting as sole traders was voted down, twenty-four to six.[83] All members of the convention recorded their current politics as pro-Union, and based on their presidential preferences in the election of 1860 (thirteen supported

Abraham Lincoln; nine supported a Democratic candidate, either Stephen Douglas or John Breckinridge; two supported John Bell of the Constitutional Union Party), sole trading clearly drew wide support.[84]

The use of California's reforms as both a positive and a negative model is not surprising given the makeup of the Nevada constitutional convention. Of the thirty-five delegates present at the convention, thirty-three of them had come to Nevada Territory from California.[85] Thus, these delegates would have been intimately aware of the ways that California's reforms were both successful and unsuccessful.

Like convention delegates in the South, Western delegates emphasized the protection of women as a key motivator behind constitutional provisions around married women's property. There was also significant emphasis on explicitly borrowing from successful models in other states as well as on attracting women to the West. The western constitutions considered here are not as infamously and explicitly racist as the post-Reconstruction constitutions of the South, which ushered in an era of Jim Crow. Nonetheless, these documents still include evidence of exclusion even as they extended property rights for married women. Oregon's statehood constitution includes the clearest provision indicating whom delegates thought property rights were "for." This provision guaranteed that only white immigrants to the state would be granted equal property rights to "native born citizens."[86] Five of the other western states that extended property rights to married women in their statehood constitutions simultaneously limited voting rights to white men or explicitly limited the voting rights of Native Americans and/or African Americans.[87]

To complete the picture and provide points of comparison, table 4.3 outlines women's property rights provisions written into the constitutions and amendments of states other than the ones covered in more detail here.

HOMESTEAD EXEMPTIONS, MARRIED WOMEN'S PROPERTY, AND A SAFETY NET FOR FAMILIES

Married women's property rights in state constitutions were closely tied to another aspect of economic protection, the homestead exemption.

As discussed in chapter 3, homestead exemptions typically exempted from the collection of debts land and personal property up to a certain value owned by a head of household (who was most often male, although sometimes women could qualify as heads as well, especially if they were single, abandoned, or widowed). As with married women's economic rights, statutory homestead exemptions were near universal by the end of the nineteenth century.[88] But, also as in the case of married women's property rights, only some states elevated homestead exemptions to constitutional guarantees. Twenty-five states gave homestead provisions constitutional status, either requiring legislatures to pass homestead-exemption laws or regulating the details of those exemptions or, as in Mississippi's case, simply empowering the legislature to act on the subject.[89]

The states that included homestead exemptions in their constitutions were concentrated in the South and West and were especially likely to

TABLE 4.4

Homestead Exemptions and Married Women's Economic Rights in State Constitutions

	No Constitutional Protection for Married Women's Economic Rights	Constitutional Protection for Married Women's Economic Rights
No constitutional homestead exemption	Twenty-one states: AZ, CT, DE, IA, ID, IN, KY, MA, ME, MN, MO, NE, NH, NJ, NM, NY, OH, PA, RI, VT, WI	Two states: MD, OR
Constitutional homestead exemption	Eight states: CO, IL, MT, OK, TN, VA, WA, WY	Seventeen states: AL, AR, CA, FL, GA, KS, LA, MI, MS, NC, ND, NV, SC, SD, TX, UT, WV

Source: Data on constitutional homestead exemptions come from "State Homestead Exemption Laws," *Yale Law Journal* 46, no. 6 (1937): 1023–41.

include married women's property rights as well (see table 4.4). Susan Lebsock notes that to the extent both homestead protections and married women's property protections focused on protecting a certain subset of property from creditors' claims, they were "functionally similar" in that they provided protection from financial ruin to families.[90] In the South, these provisions first appeared in Reconstruction constitutions, where Radical Republicans championed generous homestead exemptions with a goal of expanding their base and attracting poor whites to the party.[91] Even after Republicans lost power, Democrats in some states continued to support scaled-back exemptions as a means to promote economic recovery.[92]

In both the South and the West, delegates drew clear parallels between homestead exemptions and family protection.[93] Several states—Texas, Wisconsin, Michigan, Alabama, Arkansas, Georgia, North Carolina, and South Carolina—even combined homestead exemptions and married women's property rights into one article or committee.[94] At Nevada's convention in 1864, one delegate argued that a homestead exemption would be "a protection to the wives and children in this Territory[;] . . . the wife and children shall retain a rallying place, which shall be entitled to the sacred name of home, and of which no action of the husband and father can deprive them."[95] Another delegate described the homestead as "that household altar . . . where [a man's] wife and children are to reside when he has gone from them."[96] Yet another referred to the homestead as "an angel of mercy to hover over and bless the families of our nation."[97] Similarly, in Illinois in 1870 a delegate advocated in favor of a homestead exemption, arguing that "families are entitled to the protection of the government from the improvidence of heads of families . . . [because the] wife and children are frequently impoverished by the improvidence and recklessness of the husband."[98] Throughout the debate in Illinois, delegates made it clear that the goal of the homestead exemption, as for statutory protections, was to protect not only debtors as a general class but specifically "women, widows, and children."[99] In California, the debate over homesteads took place immediately after a lengthy debate over married women's property rights. After a discussion of what amount and type of property should be covered by the exemption, the provision that was agreed upon allowed homestead exemptions only for "heads of families."[100]

Several homestead provisions also contained explicit protections for wives, requiring that married men could not sell a homestead or waive the protections of homestead laws without their wives' written permission.[101] Although loopholes allowed husbands to avoid this requirement in practice,[102] it seems clear that convention delegates at least saw homestead exemptions as part of a social safety net for *families*, by which married women—not just men—would receive legal protection, as with married women's property protections.

BORROWING CONSTITUTIONAL TEXT

Multiple scholars of state constitutions emphasize the importance of copying and borrowing in the drafting process at conventions. Zackin writes: "This coordination among state constitutions is, in part, a result of the efforts of their framers to study the latest state constitutional practices, and to apply the lessons that other states offered as they designed their own fundamental laws."[103] Christian Fritz's analysis of state constitution drafting in the nineteenth century also highlights the important role of borrowing and copying from previous state constitutions. He writes that delegates were frequently "open and self-conscious about incorporating constitutional language" from other states and often approached the process carefully, weighing which provisions would work best in their particular state context.[104] The borrowing of constitutional provisions was aided by the circulation of compilations of existing state constitutions, of which more than seventy were published before 1894. These compilations allowed delegates to easily consult and compare multiple models.[105] Amy Bridges writes that the convention delegates' borrowing at western statehood conventions was careful and deliberative as delegates sought to identify not just successful practices but states that faced problems similar to their own, a review process resulting in "a far-flung and constructive conversation among the states."[106]

This process is clearly evident in the specific case of married women's economic rights. In his analysis of Reconstruction constitutions in the South, Paul Herron writes that the timing of many states' writing of new constitutions during the span of a few years and under similar postwar conditions led to a number of similarities among their constitutions, only one of which was the inclusion of married women's property rights.[107] The case studies presented in this chapter indicate clear references by both southern and nonsouthern delegates to the passage of married women's economic rights in other states in advocating for or against the practice in their own state, and a look at the constitutional language presented in tables 4.1–4.3 indicates many linguistic and substantive similarities in constitutional provisions across states.

In addition to this qualitative evidence, copying is also made clear by a quantitative analysis of constitutional texts.[108] I analyzed constitutional provisions dealing with married women's economic rights using software originally developed to detect plagiarism, WCopyfind.[109] Scholars have used this software to identify text reuse in political contexts, such as the inclusion of text from lower-court opinions and briefs in U.S. Supreme Court opinions, the borrowing of statute text between states, and the influence of presidential rhetoric and congressional press releases on news coverage.[110] Further details on the software and settings used can be found in the "Methods Appendix."

For an example of what this analysis means in practice, consider the constitutional provisions from Texas (1845) and California (1849). California's constitutional text is an overall 100 percent match to Texas's constitution despite some slight changes in wording. Matching words from the two constitutions are highlighted in italics in the following excerpts:

> Texas (1845): *All property, both real and personal, of the wife, owned or claimed* by her *before marriage, and that acquired afterwards by gift, devise, or descent, shall be her separate property; and laws shall be passed more clearly defining the rights of the wife in relation as well to her separate property as* that *held in common with her husband. Laws shall also be passed providing for the registration of the wife's separate property.*[111]

> California (1849): *All property, both real and personal, of the wife, owned or claimed by* marriage, *and that acquired afterwards by gift, devise, or descent, shall be her separate property; and laws shall be passed more clearly defining the rights of the wife, in relation as well to her separate property,* as to *that held in common with her husband. Laws shall also be passed providing for the registration of the wife's separate property.*[112]

In contrast, a 50 percent match can be found between the Michigan Constitution of 1850 and the North Carolina Constitution of 1868:

> Michigan (1850): The real and personal estate of every female, *acquired before marriage, and all property* to which she may afterwards become entitled, by gift, grant, inheritance, or devise, shall be *and* remain the *estate and property of such female, and shall not be liable for* the *debts, obligations, or engagements of her husband; and may be devised or bequeathed by her as if she were unmarried.*[113]

> North Carolina (1868): The real and personal property of any female in this State, *acquired before marriage, and all property,* real and personal, to which she may after marriage, become in any manner entitled, shall be and remain the sole *and* separate *estate and property of such female, and shall not be liable for* any *debts, obligations, or engagements of her husband, and may be devised or bequeathed,* and, with the written assent of her husband, conveyed, *by her, as if she were unmarried.*[114]

There are forty-two unique pairs of states with matching constitutional language. The percentage of matching language between constitutional provisions ranges from a low of 11 percent to a high of 100 percent, with an average match of 45.7 percent. Of the states that included a married women's economic rights provision in their constitution during this period (nineteen states), only three did not have overlapping text with the constitutions of any other state: Mississippi, Maryland, and West Virginia. In addition, Kansas and Louisiana matched only one another, and the match percentage was small (15 percent). Thus, just less than 74 percent of states that included this type of provision had substantial overlapping text—and thus likely borrowing—from other states.

Figures 4.1 and 4.2 illustrate borrowing patterns for states with above-average (i.e., greater than 45.7 percent) overlapping text. As is clear from these figures, there are two clusters of states borrowing constitutional text from one another. One cluster is made up largely of western states and is heavily influenced by the Texas Constitution of 1845. The other cluster contains states from multiple regions, with Michigan,

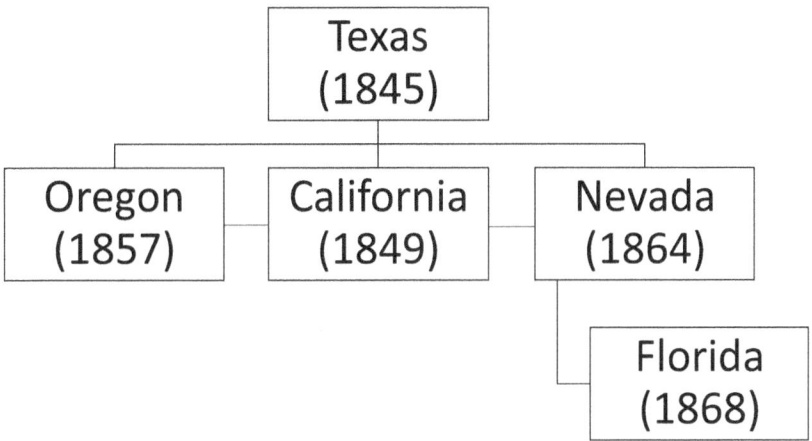

FIGURE 4.1. States sharing constitutional text, starting with Texas (1845). Solid lines between two states indicate that the later-adopting state borrowed more than 45.7 percent of the text of its married women's property provision from the earlier-adopting state.

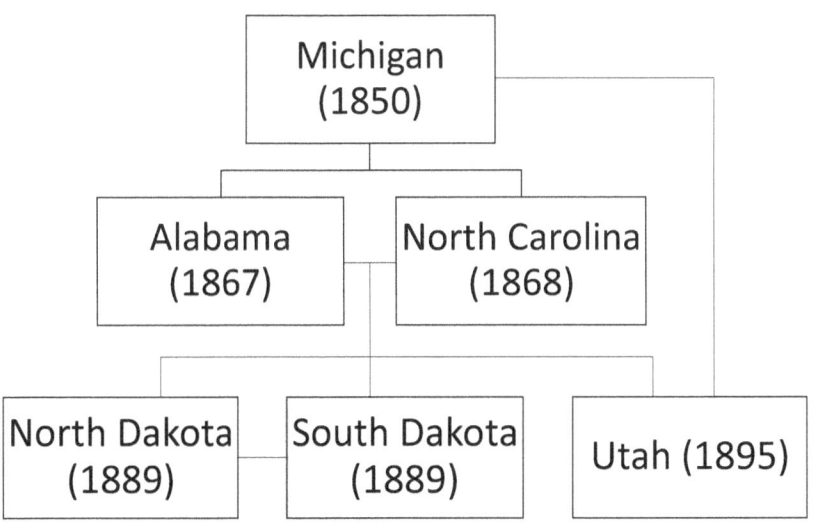

FIGURE 4.2. States sharing constitutional text, starting with Michigan (1850). Solid lines between two states indicate that the later-adopting state borrowed more than 45.7 percent of the text of its married women's property provision from the earlier-adopting state.

Alabama, and North Carolina seeming to play leading roles in creating earlier constitutions that multiple states borrowed from.

The copying of language by convention delegates is important for understanding how reforms spread across the nation without national-level coordination. Policy diffusion as a more general matter is discussed in more detail in chapter 5, where, using similar methods, I examine the copying of statutory language. For the purposes of understanding constitutional development, however, two major factors must be considered. First, modeling married women's economic rights reforms on other states' provisions was part of a broader process of constitutional borrowing and copying. This practice was common across multiple types of state constitutional provisions during this period. Second, although there were regional elements to these practices, borrowing did not take place only between neighboring states. Some studies of policy diffusion look primarily at geographic transmission of policies, but the data here indicate that states sometimes copied language from distant states as well as from those nearby. This finding is not surprising given the context of westward expansion—delegates to western conventions in particular had often moved to western territories from other states.

CONSTITUTIONS IN THE REFORM PROCESS

State constitutions are important rights-granting documents, and married women's property rights are no exception. Delegates in some states used constitutional conventions to grant new rights to married women, while others elevated these rights to constitutional status and prevented repeal by state legislatures. Married women's property rights occupied a status between positive and negative rights, with constitutions often requiring positive action on the part of state legislatures, such as requiring legislators to pass further reforms or to provide for the registration of wives' separate property. Although convention delegates had a variety of reasons for supporting the inclusion of married women's rights in their foundational documents, these reforms were commonly viewed as a form of government protection for families in economic distress and were closely associated with homestead exemptions. They were also part of a process by which delegates, especially on the frontier, aimed to attract certain women to settle the West.

Constitutional conventions were also an important venue for delegates to examine and debate the successes and failures of married women's property rights provisions in other states and often to borrow text from earlier constitutions, aided by popular compilations. This process meant that many constitutions from this period share substantial amounts of language and content. State constitutional conventions were a major pathway for the spread of married women's economic rights reform around the country despite the absence of coordination from national institutions.

CHAPTER FIVE

Decentralized Reform and Policy Diffusion

At South Carolina's state constitutional convention in 1868, one delegate, James Allen, discussed married women's property rights in other states: "Nearly all the States of the Union have passed laws for the protection of women's property; and shall we, when we have passed page after page of enactments, explaining the rights of man, stop here and make a wry face at a single clause?"[1] I have focused so far largely on the process of married women's economic rights reform within individual states. But as I began to discuss at the end of chapter 4, this process did not happen in each state in isolation. State actors knew about and responded to the sweep of marital rights reforms across the nation.

States in the nineteenth century faced common regional or national problems, and legislators, constitutional convention delegates, and code drafters communicated and looked to each other for examples and for language to borrow. We can see this communication in the similar—sometimes even identical—language across the statute books and constitutions of various states and territories. Even where states faced common problems, there was no guarantee that they would reach common solutions, yet, ultimately, most states *did* reach common solutions in the passing of married women's economic rights reform.

Even though there was never a federal law or court decision mandating married women's economic rights reform, every state passed at least one piece of legislation in this area and typically many more than that. This is not to say that diffusion of married women's economic rights reform among the states was uniform, though. In many ways, it was uneven—timing varied by decades, and whereas some states passed very expansive provisions, others passed limited reforms. Some states modeled their marital-property regimes on the common law, and some modeled it on civil law based on community property. Legislators also used married women's property rights reforms to solve a wide variety of societal problems, many that were unique to their region or time. Nevertheless, the similarities across states as well as the connections across states in this policy area are notable.

This chapter examines the pathways for the diffusion of married women's economic rights reform, identifying patterns and explanatory factors that can be commonly observed among all forty-seven states and territories.[2] Of course, many different types of provisions were included in married women's economic rights reforms, ranging from extremely limited measures that merely exempted wives' separate property from the debts of their husbands all the way to laws that granted them complete control over that property. It is not possible to capture all this diversity in a quantitative analysis. For example, some statutes made only very minor updates, such as the Mississippi law in 1857 that added a few additional types of purposes for which married women could mortgage their property.

To simplify, as explained in chapter 1 and shown in the "Methods Appendix," I have classified reforms into five different policies that fell under the umbrella of married women's rights reform, which in any individual state might be passed as five separate laws or bundled together, and I have analyzed the first time any given state or territory passed each of these policies. To recap, these reforms are: (1) the ability to own separate property exempt from the husband's debts, (2) broad control-and-management rights over separate property, (3) the treatment of married women's earnings and wages as separate property, (4) the ability of all married women—not just those whose husband was disabled or absent—to engage in business and sign contracts without her husband's permission, and (5) the right to write a will concerning that separate property without restrictions that did not apply to married men.

This chapter draws on what political scientists call "policy diffusion." Because the spread of reforms could take place through either geographic pathways—for example, borrowing from neighboring states—or nongeographic pathways, the best way to study this diffusion is through two types of analysis. The first analysis uses logit models to examine whether states tended to copy different reforms from their geographic neighbors. These models also allow me to capture other common factors that may explain early or late adoption of each reform. To examine diffusion not dependent on geographic proximity, I also use the plagiarism analysis described in chapter 4 to examine the text of reform statutes and how states adopted similar or identical statutory text. I conclude with a broader discussion of the importance of decentralization and diffusion in the development of married women's economic rights.

POLICY DIFFUSION AND MECHANISMS

Scholars of policy diffusion within the disciplines of political science and public policy have examined various methods of policy transmission in considering the passage of state laws and other policies. Virginia Gray defines diffusion as "the process by which [a policy] innovation spreads; it consists of the communication of a new idea in a social system over time ... [as] decisionmakers emulate or take cues from legislation passed by other states."[3] Subsequent research has delineated, especially through the use of formal models, multiple possible mechanisms by which diffusion may occur. These mechanisms include copying or taking cues from other states, learning from other states which policies work well and are popular (or, conversely, are failures), and competing.[4]

All three mechanisms were plausibly present in the case of married women's property rights reform. Of course, in some states simple copying or emulation may have been at work, as when constitutional convention delegates consulted compilations of constitutions from other states. But as the evidence from Nevada's constitutional convention discussed in chapter 4 shows, delegates also sometimes discussed in great detail the merits and drawbacks of reforms in other states, clearly demonstrating a desire to learn from these places' successes and failures. Competition could translate into both defensive actions—avoiding a loss from residents leaving for other states—or offensive actions—attempting to proactively attract residents.[5] In the case of women relocating, states and territories might pursue attractive property regimes that would allow women more freedom and control either to attract women to move West or to encourage them to stay in the East. In her research on married women's property acts, the economist Jayme Lemke examines the role of competition and finds that areas with higher competitive pressures—particularly with regard to the benefits of attracting unmarried women to the state or territory—were more likely to pass certain reforms earlier.[6]

Alternately, the political scientists Craig Volden, Michael Ting, and Daniel Carpenter have argued that "much of the evidence of diffusion could instead arise through a process of similar governments responding to a common policy problem independently, without learning from one another's experiences."[7] That is, rather than policy innovations actively spreading among states—through mechanisms such as learning, copying, and competing—states might instead make similar policy choices completely independently from one another. This could be especially true in cases where states faced similar political and economic problems. Although it is possible this mechanism operated in some states in the case of married women's economic rights reforms, the direct copying of language and the fact that states were actually responding to many *different* problems with the policy solution of rights reform make this explanation less plausible in this case.

Many studies model diffusion geographically by including a variable for the number or proportion of neighboring states that have adopted a particular policy.[8] The logic here is that states might be most likely to borrow policies from their neighboring states. These nearby states might not only be the most direct competition but also share similar characteristics and policy concerns, and politicians might be most aware of political innovations in their own region.

But policy diffusion is not necessarily geographic—instead of borrowing from neighboring states, states might choose to borrow policies based on other state-level similarities, such as political, budgetary, or demographic connections to other states, or they might select particularly successful or effective policies from anywhere in the nation.[9] Examining more than 180 different policies, the political scientists Bruce Desmarais, Jeffrey Harden, and Frederick Boehmke find that states may look to neighboring states when adopting new policies but that geography is not the only—or even the primary—pathway of diffusion. Regardless of geography, some states, especially those that are more populous and wealthier, are particularly innovative and take on roles as policy leaders, lending their policy expertise to numerous other states.[10] Therefore, I examine both geographic and nongeographic pathways for the diffusion of married women's economic rights reform and highlight states that played the role of policy leaders with respect to married women's rights.

EVENT HISTORY ANALYSIS

Event history analysis is a way to study how events play out over time and space. How and why did some states pass married women's economic reforms earlier than others? Although the case study evidence presented in this book digs more deeply into the mechanisms and motivations involved in the reform process, statistical analyses can reveal a broader view of the forces playing out around the nation by including all states and territories.

I use logit models to estimate the likelihood of a particular reform being enacted over time. Each of the five reform types are considered separately as outcome variables. I analyze explanatory variables in three categories: women's political organizing and power; state- or territory-level political context; and geographic diffusion. Table 5.1 summarizes these variables, and the "Methods Appendix" describes both the models and the variables in greater detail.

The results presented in table 5.2 estimate the likelihood of a particular reform being enacted over time. A positive and significant coefficient for an explanatory variable indicates that the risk of earlier enactment is increasing with that variable—in other words, the variable is associated with earlier reform enactment. In contrast, a negative and significant coefficient indicates that risk is decreasing with the explanatory variable, and so higher values of the variable are associated with later (or no) reforms.

As is clear from table 5.2, no one variable is associated with all five types of reforms. Although there are some common factors across

TABLE 5.1
Explanatory Variables for the Enactment of Women's Property Rights Reforms

Explanatory Variable Category	Specific Variables
Women's political organizing and power	Woman suffrage at the territorial or state level; existence of a state-level woman suffrage organization
State- or territory-level political context	Percentage of population that is female; existence of a homestead-exemption law; community-property regime; territorial status
Geographic diffusion	Indicator for whether a neighboring state has previously passed a specific reform

multiple reforms, there is overall a diverse set of predictors for each reform type. This finding is not unexpected given that the reforms accomplished different things and were sometimes passed decades apart. The most consistent predictor of early passage is gender imbalance, where higher levels of gender imbalance in a state's population predicts the earlier passage of three reform types. Other independent variables are important predictors only of those reforms where there is a clear theoretical reason to expect this relationship; for example, women's organizing power predicts earlier passage only of some reforms that gave women more meaningful economic power, and homestead-exemption acts predict earlier passage only of debt-free estate laws.

First, considering the role of women's political power, state-level woman suffrage is not a significant predictor of the timing of passage for any of the five statute types. This is not surprising given how few states or territories extended the vote to women prior to passing married women's property rights reforms. The organizing power of women is, however, a significant predictor of earlier passage of two types of reforms that were especially important for granting power to married women—control-and-management laws and earnings acts. These coefficients are easier to interpret when exponentiated, which results in the predicted increase in odds when the coefficient increases by one unit. Here, using

TABLE 5.2
Discrete Event History (Logit) Models for Married Women's Property Rights Reform

	Debt-Free Separate Estates	Control-and-Management Laws	Earnings Acts	Sole-Trader Statutes	Testamentary Rights
State-level suffrage	2.00 (1.44)	1.35 (0.75)	1.29 (0.84)	0.30 (0.83)	0.73 (0.92)
State-level suffrage organization	-1.01 (1.51)	0.99 (0.44)*	0.88 (0.42)*	0.58 (0.43)	0.19 (0.51)
Percentage of population that is female	-0.08 (0.02)***	-0.03 (0.02)	-0.07 (0.03)*	-0.08 (0.02)**	-0.01 (0.02)
Homestead exemption	0.96 (0.45)*	0.17 (0.48)	-0.30 (0.57)	0.23 (0.54)	0.27 (0.53)
Community property	-1.29 (0.60)*	-0.50 (0.48)	-3.16 (0.97)**	-0.69 (0.55)	-0.09 (0.50)
Territorial status	-0.45 (0.50)	0.13 (0.54)	-1.76 (0.82)*	-0.43 (0.57)	-0.36 (0.47)
Neighbors with reforms	0.04 (0.54)	1.50 (0.45)**	-0.40 (0.52)	0.75 (0.46)	-1.10 (0.54)*
Total subjects (failures)	47 (46)	47 (44)	47 (40)	47 (37)	47 (47)

Note: Standard errors are given in parentheses, and significance is indicated as follows: *** significant at the $p < 0.001$ level, ** significant at the $p < 0.01$ level, * significant at the $p < 0.05$ level. All territories/states are included in models. Territories/states enter the data set in 1835 or the first year that a territorial legislature meets and exit in the year after a particular reform is enacted. At the bottom of each column, the total numbers of subjects (i.e., states or territories) and failures (i.e., states or territories that enacted a given reform during the period of analysis) are listed. All models also control for duration, duration squared, and duration cubed.

the existence of a state-level woman suffrage organization as a proxy for women's organizing power in states, I find that states or territories had an approximately two-and-a-half times increase in the odds of passing both control-and-management reforms and earnings acts in a given year if a woman suffrage organization existed.[11]

What about the political context in states and territories? It seems that gender imbalance is the most common predictor of reform passage: states with more men than women tended to pass reforms earlier. For debt-free separate estates, earnings acts, and sole-trader statutes, greater gender imbalance in a state or territory predicts earlier passage. This finding is not surprising given that Western politicians cited gender imbalances and discussed the need to attract women to their area by granting them expanded rights. As found in other research, community-property states were also later to enact economic reforms for some but not all categories of reform.[12]

Finally, the passage of homestead exemptions was associated only with the earlier passage of debt-free separate-estates statutes, which aligns with the fact that both laws were aimed at family-level debt relief. The existence of a homestead exemption in a state is associated with a 2.6-times increase in the odds of passing a debt-relief married women's property act as compared to states that had not passed a homestead-exemption act.

Interestingly, territorial status is not strongly associated with the timing of reforms for most reform types. It is a statistically significant predictor only for the timing of earnings acts, where territorial status actually predicts later passage of this reform.

Geographic closeness—measured as whether a neighboring state has previously passed a given reform—is also not a consistent predictor of reform enactment. As can be seen in table 5.2, the coefficient "neighbors with reforms" is statistically significant for only two reform types, and the effect runs in opposite directions. Thus, although there is clear evidence that states did copy and learn from one another in drafting reforms to married women's economic rights, this practice was largely *not* about learning from immediate neighbors. In the following sections of this chapter, I explore the nongeographic pathways for the diffusion of reforms.

ANALYZING STATUTE TEXT

We can see how married women's economic rights spread through the states through nongeographic pathways by considering similarities in the texts of state statutes. This analysis mirrors the analysis of constitutional text in chapter 4, and details on the method can be found in the "Methods Appendix." I conducted this analysis separately for each type of reform, using the text of the first reform in each state as the comparison text. Because I collected only the first statute in each state that granted each separate reform, these estimates can be considered a lower bound of copying because it is possible that later statutes copied text from other states, but the latter copying is not included in the analysis.

An example of an overall 100 percent match can be found between Idaho's married women's property act of 1863 and Montana's statute of 1864. Both laws provided for debt-free separate estates but did not allow married women to control this separate property. Matching text is italicized in the samples given.

> Idaho (1863): *All real and personal estate belonging to any married woman at the time of her marriage, and all which she may have acquired subsequently to such marriage, or to which she shall have after become entitled in her own right, and all her personal earnings, and all the issues, rents and profits of such real estate, shall not be liable to attachment for or execution upon any liability or judgment against the husband,* so long as she or any minor child of her body shall *be living: Provided, That her separate property shall be liable for debts owing by her at the time of her marriage.*[13]

> Montana (1864): *All real and personal estate belonging to any married woman at the time of her marriage, and all which she may have acquired subsequently to such marriage, or to which she shall have after become entitled in her own right, and all her personal earnings, and all the issues, rents and profits of such real estate, shall not be liable to attachment for or execution upon any liability or judgment against the husband* so long as she or any minor child of her body be living: *Provided, that her separate property shall be liable for debts owing by her at the time of her marriage.*[14]

In comparison, the Dakota Territory's debt-free estates statute of 1862 copied 52 percent of its text from Nebraska's law of 1855 (again, matching text is indicated with italics):

Nebraska (1855): *The property owned by a married woman before her marriage, and that which she may acquire after marriage, by descent, gift, grant, devise or otherwise, and the use and profits thereof shall be exempt from all debts and liabilities of her husband* contracted or incurred by him previous to their marriage, or subsequently thereto, *unless for necessary articles for the use and benefit of the family,* or previous to the time the wife came into the possession of such property.

The property owned by a woman before her marriage and that which she may acquire after her marriage by descent, gift, grant or devise shall be exempt from levy and sale to pay any debt contracted as security, or liability incurred as security by her husband at any time or under any circumstances whatever, and such property shall be exempt from levy and sale for any fine or costs imposed on the husband by any court or in any criminal case whatever.[15]

Dakota Territory (1862): That *the property owned by any married woman, before her marriage, and that which she may acquire after marriage, by descent, gift, grant, devise, or otherwise, and the* increase, use, *and profits thereof, shall be exempt from all debts and liabilities of the husband, unless for necessary articles for the use and benefit of the family.* Provided, however, That the provisions of this act shall extend only to such property as shall be mentioned in a list of the property of such married woman as is on record in the office of the register of deeds of the county in which such married woman resides.[16]

Here, the first section of the law specifying which types of property may be exempted and when that property will be exempted is nearly identical, but Nebraska added a separate section extending additional protections to married women's property, while the legislature of Dakota Territory added a provision for the registration of married women's separate property. Thus, these two statutes share significant language but also diverge on important matters in specific clauses.

TABLE 5.3
Results of Plagiarism Text Analysis: The Language of Married Women's Property Rights Reforms in Constitutions and Statutes

	Constitutional Provisions	Debt-Free Separate Estates	Control and Management	Earnings	Sole Trader	Wills
Unique matches (total number)	42.0	176.0	125.0	42.0	61.0	33.0
Unique matches (total number, > 40 percent)	22.0	21.0	18.0	22.0	31.0	17.0
Average percentage match	45.7	16.6	19.3	47.5	50.5	53.6
N (number of states/territories in analysis)	19.0	44.0*	43.0**	40.0	38.0***	44.0****

* Forty-seven of forty-eight states/territories protected married women's separate property from their husbands' debts. Two of these states (Oregon and South Carolina) first included such protections as constitutional provisions, so they are analyzed separately with the constitutions data. Dakota Territory passed its debt-free estates statute before statehood and thus is counted only once in the analysis.

** Forty-five of forty-eight states/territories extended control-and-management rights to married women. One state (South Carolina) first included such protections as a constitutional provision, so it is analyzed separately with the constitutions data. Dakota Territory passed its control-and-management statute before statehood and thus is counted only once in the analysis.

*** Thirty-nine of forty-eight states/territories extended sole-trader rights to married women. Dakota Territory passed its sole-trader statute before statehood and thus is counted only once in the analysis.

**** Forty-eight states/territories extended testamentary rights to married women. Two states (Arkansas and Utah) first included these rights as constitutional provisions, so they are analyzed separately with the constitutions data. In Georgia, testamentary rights were first extended to married women by a court ruling. Dakota Territory passed its wills statute before statehood and thus is counted only once in the analysis.

In table 5.3, I list the total number of matching statutes in which the later statute matches 40 percent or more of the language from the earlier statute and the average percentage of matches for each type of reform.[17] I have included the comparable numbers for constitutional provisions as a point of comparison.

Table 5.3 demonstrates a few important findings about the copying of statute text among states. Debt-free statutes and control-and-management statutes were by far the most copied. They had 176 and 125 unique matches, respectively. However, many of these matches were of smaller snippets of text—stock phrases that were common across many states' statutes. Regarding matches that share more significant language and are more likely to indicate direct knowledge and copying of statute language between states, the numbers are more comparable among reform types. Depending on the reform type, there were between eighteen to twenty-six unique matches between states, indicating fairly extensive copying of provisions.

Figures 5.1–5.5 indicate clusters of states that shared statutory language, with each cluster containing states that borrowed at least 40 percent of statute language from at least one other state in the cluster for that particular reform type. In the "Methods Appendix," table A.3 lists the

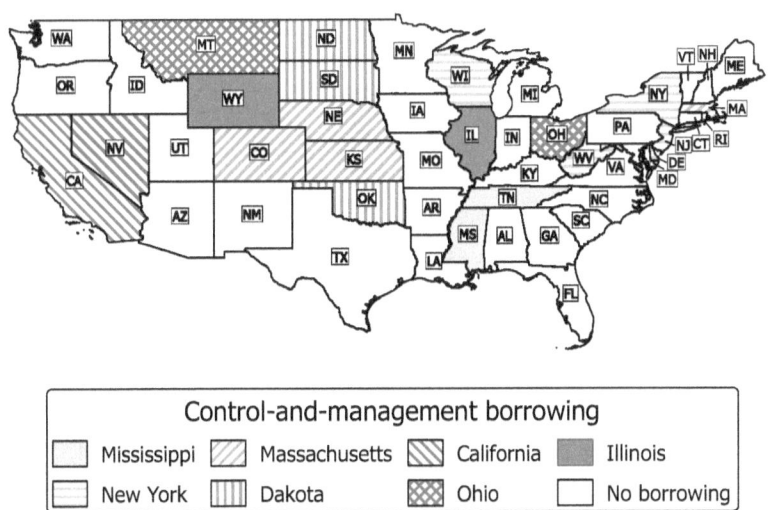

FIGURE 5.1. Borrowed language: control-and-management rights.

Decentralized Reform and Policy Diffusion 141

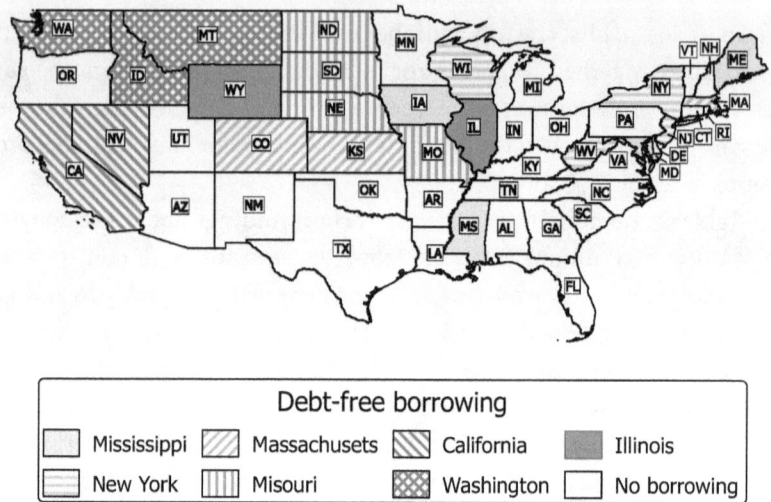

FIGURE 5.2. Borrowed language: debt-free separate estates.

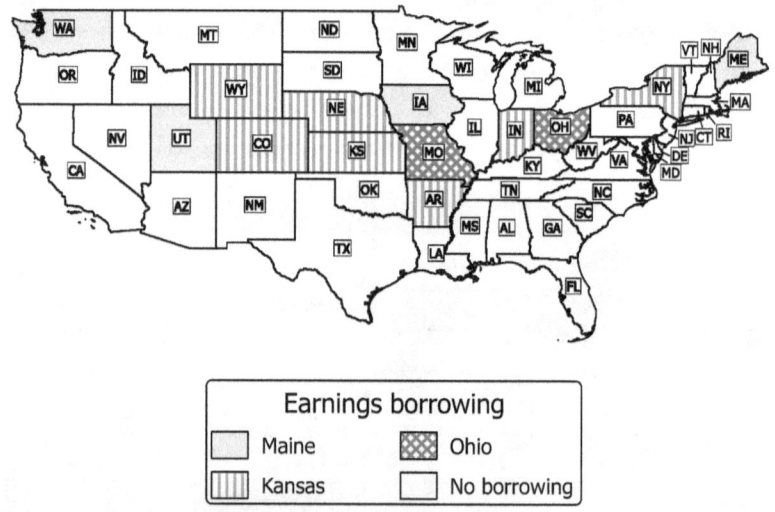

FIGURE 5.3. Borrowed language: earnings acts.

states in each cluster in chronological order. In comparison to the borrowing of statutory language, state constitutional conventions had a more limited number of clusters that contained several states, indicating a smaller number of more comprehensive networks of sharing. In the case of statutory language, there are more clusters, but they tend to include

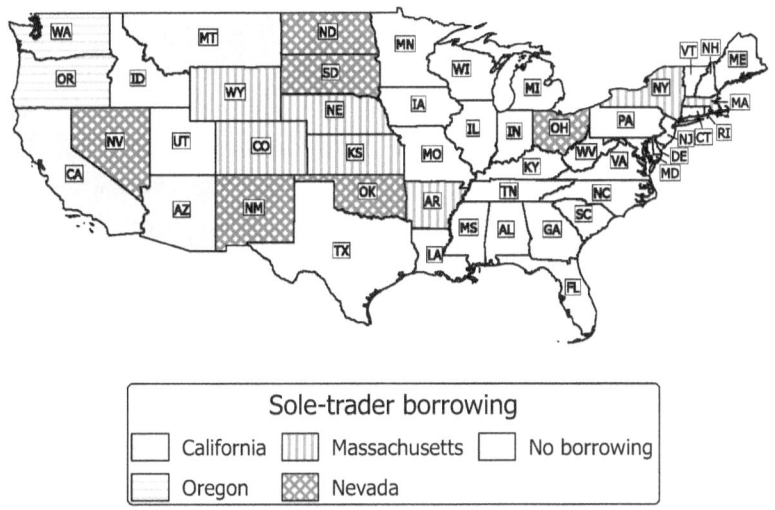

FIGURE 5.4. Borrowed language: sole-trader rights.

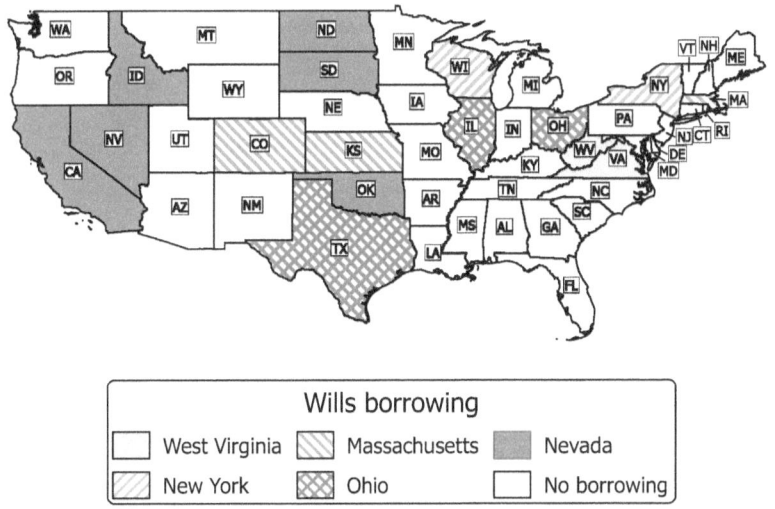

FIGURE 5.5. Borrowed language: testamentary rights.

fewer (sometimes only two) states. Thus, networks of sharing seem to have been smaller but more numerous in the case of statutory language.

Many of the statute-language clusters are regional, though this is not universally true. It is also clear that some states borrowed language across multiple reforms, often because they combined these reforms into a single statute. For example, Massachusetts, Colorado, and Kansas share significant language across multiple reform types. Each of these states passed comprehensive married women's property acts that addressed multiple issues: Massachusetts in 1855, Kansas in 1858, and Colorado in 1861. Although the three bills are not identical, each later bill was clearly modeled after an early one or earlier ones, with similar provisions listed in the same order and often with identical wording.

Other scholars have often identified New York as an early adopter that other states used as a model for their reforms.[18] The analysis here confirms that finding, with New York often being included in larger clusters of states with statutes that share similar language. But this analysis also points to other states and territories that adopted reforms early and whose language was subsequently used by other states: California, Kansas, Massachusetts, and Ohio were also early adopters that served as models and leaders on married women's property rights for the rest of the nation.

DECENTRALIZED REFORM

Decentralized reforms that don't have a major national "victory" can be challenging to study because different actors and dynamics are at play in each state. But studying these reforms illuminates lower-profile rights expansions in the states. There are not many accounts of such reforms in political science, but those that exist identify important alternate mechanisms for change. Alison Gash's study of strategic low-visibility activism in state and local governments, for example, finds that reformers and activists sometimes choose low-profile strategies that intentionally avoid publicity to avoid harsh political backlash and lengthy conflicts.[19] My study is different in that married women's property rights were not the sort of controversial policy that needed to fly "under the radar" like those examined in Gash's work. Here my focus is instead on incremental, patchwork, and interconnected change as it worked its way through state institutions. Each individual statute, constitutional provision, or court case did not dramatically change the national picture for married women, but together the reforms to married women's economic rights enacted across the states over the course of decades added up to a major shift in women's lived reality.

Without an organized, national campaign for or against the liberalization of married women's economic rights, these reforms were decentralized. States passed reforms at different times, and the comprehensiveness of these policies varied among states. There was significant unevenness in timing as well as in ultimate outcomes. Some states, such as Mississippi, adopted certain reforms early, in 1839, and ultimately ended up with one of the broadest and most expansive reforms in the nation, explicitly eliminating coverture's disabilities wholesale in the areas of contract and property law in 1880. Other nearby states, such as Alabama and Georgia, adopted only some of the more limited reforms and failed to adopt those that would have given married women more economic independence by 1920. This variability meant that married women living on opposite sides of a state border might have dramatically different economic opportunities available to them.

Because these laws were not federally mandated, states had the opportunity to experiment with different reforms and to borrow practices that seemed to be working well in other states. We can see this spread of reforms through a few mechanisms. Political actors actively discussed the successes and failures of married women's economic rights reforms in other states, making the case that successful policies should be replicated and that doing so would be necessary to attract women migrants. For example, California's first state constitution, written in 1849, was "scissored and pasted together" from copies of the Iowa and New York Constitutions—taking 85 of its 136 provisions from them.[20] The married women's provision specifically matched that of the Texas Constitution nearly verbatim. Delegates repeatedly referenced the successful reforms of married women's rights in the statute books and constitutions of other states and the need to compete with other states in terms of the rights afforded to women in order to attract them to their state; in 1850, the first year the U.S. census was taken in California, women made up less than 8 percent of the population.[21]

Parts of California's policies would later be adopted by other states. For example, Nevada's codebook of 1929 listed the California Civil Code as the origin for the state's limited earnings provision, which provided that earnings would be separate property only for wives living separately from their husbands.[22] In interpreting this and other sections of the state's married women's property law in 1916, the Nevada Supreme Court specifically referenced the idea that Nevada's statute had been copied from California's and in its ruling cited numerous California Supreme Court decisions on married women's property.[23]

Migration also mattered as westward settlement brought individuals with ideas from eastern states to territories and states on the frontier. One example is William Shannon, the California constitutional convention delegate from New York who introduced the married women's property provision to the California Constitution of 1849. This movement of information sometimes also took place through family relationships. The Hadley family, so influential in the passage of Mississippi's early debt-free separate-property law, may have also influenced the passage of Texas's first reform to marital-property rights at its constitutional convention in 1845. One of the delegates to this convention and a prominent committee chair, H. G. Runnels, was Mrs. Thomas Hadley's brother-in-law.[24] Although it is not entirely clear from convention debates who initially raised the idea of including a constitutional provision relating to married women's property rights, the presence of at least one delegate with close personal experience with this type of legislation is clearly relevant. Similarly, in 1872, California's statute covering control-and-management rights, earnings, and sole-trader powers was influenced by Stephen Field, who included ideas that his brother, David Dudley Field, had first developed in the prominent Field Code.[25] As families moved west, they brought with them the language of eastern and southern states' reforms.

Region influenced the context, goals, and outcomes of married women's economic rights reforms. As discussed in more detail in chapter 3, in the antebellum South states often included specific provisions for ownership and control of enslaved human property. Enslaved people were seen as highly valuable to white women slave owners both before and after marriage. In her book on slave ownership by white women, the historian Stephanie Jones-Rogers points out that slaveholding was a major form of property that white women brought to their marriages; white women would often receive enslaved people as gifts for special occasions or as property left to them in wills.[26] Jones-Rogers's work gives us a sense of how different the context of married women's economic experiences was—with white slaveholding women in the South experiencing an incredibly different economic environment and relationship to property ownership than women in the North. So, too, fathers' considerations about what types of property to give or bequeath to their daughters were very different in these different regional contexts.

In contrast, territories and states in the West faced dramatic gender imbalances because single men had moved west without families. As the historian Laurel Clark Shire argues in her account of married women's property acts in Florida, these reforms became important in frontier states to attract white women to these areas and to ensure the cooperation of white settler families in the colonial project.[27] Violence against Native populations alone could not accomplish U.S. leaders' goal of "permanent settlement" on the frontier; women and children would be needed to settle the land.[28] In states such as Texas, married white women both benefited from slaveholding and were a key component of settler colonialism because the nature of frontier life favored nuclear family structures.[29] The historian Mark Carroll writes: "Community property law and white supremacy policies that subjugated and dispossessed Tejanos, Native Americans, and free blacks thus placed Anglo-Texan husbands and wives securely in the upper echelon of the racial-caste structure."[30]

Despite these region- and time-bound contexts, married women's property acts could be molded to suit different ends and bolster state power. In part because political actors were focused on often-conflicting goals that might vary by region, period, legal context, and other factors, the reform process was piecemeal, and rights reform was patchwork and inconsistent. Married women's economic rights reforms were passed in different states at different times without top-down national coordination. Within each state, there were almost always multiple iterations of reforms spread out over the course of decades as political actors balanced varied goals and experimented with different formulations of married women's economic rights. On average, territories and states took about thirty-two years between passing their first reform and their last, although there was wide variation within this figure. Some passed all five reform policies as a bundle (Colorado, Kansas, and Wyoming), whereas others took substantially longer to pass all five reforms—for example, in Louisiana more than one hundred years passed between its first and last reform. Western states were especially likely to pass policies related to married women's property rights quickly once they started; on average, only eighteen years passed between their first and last reforms. Southern states were at the opposite end of the spectrum, with an average span of almost forty-eight years. Northern and midwestern states fell in the middle. Ultimately, because the passage of reforms spanned decades, it is clear that legislators, judges, and convention delegates used economic rights reforms for married women as a policy solution that could be molded to solve a huge number of economic and social "problems" facing states and territories over time.

CHAPTER SIX

Courts as Collaborators and Catalysts

State legislatures and constitutional conventions were not the only institutions to play a major role in shaping economic policy around married women's rights. In this chapter, I focus on the specific role of state courts as a particular type of institution with different behaviors and scope of action that played a catalytic role in the development of married women's rights. Through the examination of state court decisions and their timing vis-à-vis legislative and constitutional reform, I argue that state court judges' often cautious and narrow interpretations led to a cycle in which legislative actions were interpreted in ways that increased confusion and decreased predictability, thus creating popular pressure for further reforms. Legislators then modified laws, gradually expanding the rights of married women in a piecemeal fashion. This pattern points to an important role for courts in reform processes even when they are not engaged in direct conflict with elected bodies.

 The conventional wisdom around courts during this period—especially starting in the late 1800s—tends to focus on their conflictual relationships with elected bodies, largely over labor legislation. Although this story is complicated, court–legislature dynamics tended to be more cooperative when it came to married women's economic rights, with both venues tending to support incremental changes. Courts typically interpreted statutes relating to married women's rights narrowly, with an eye toward accepting the new legislation as valid but also leaving in place core components of the gender hierarchy, in particular a paternalistic attitude toward women that many legislators largely shared. Despite the deferential nature of their rulings, courts still played an important role in influencing how reform played out in each state. Legislators at the beginning of this period wrote general statutes with limited, modest expectations for how much the new laws would empower women. However, as specific cases worked their way through the court system, a piecemeal system of women's economic rights proved unworkable. Rulings that provided married women with partial rights and attempted to protect them from negative market outcomes often produced highly complex and confusing legal rules that left creditors on the hook for loans that they appeared to have made in good faith. Thus, a narrow approach to interpretation ultimately led elected bodies to gradually expand rights and enact more expansive reforms. In this chapter's analysis, I first discuss general patterns for understanding court–legislative interactions in the area of married women's property law and then trace legal developments in three case study states: New York, Mississippi, and South Carolina.

COURTS VERSUS LEGISLATURES? INSTITUTIONAL CONFLICT AND COOPERATION

One major narrative about the relationship between courts and legislatures in the late 1800s has been a story of conflict, with courts and legislatures clashing over issues of business and labor. Although this story is complicated in many ways, the Gilded Age is often characterized as a period in which courts were engaged in extensive conflict with majoritarian bodies. William Forbath writes, for example, that the judiciary played a uniquely combative role in blocking labor reforms and shaping labor activists' strategies: "Nowhere else among industrial nations . . . did trade unionists contend so constantly for so many decades with judge-made law."[1] In contrast, conflict between courts and legislatures was not as present in the area of married women's economic rights reforms, where these institutions tended to work more cooperatively. Two key differences between courts and legislatures/conventions are important in considering the path of reform through these institutions: differences in responsiveness to popular pressure and differences in the form of decision-making.

First, elected bodies can be expected to respond at least in part to the demands made by voters, whereas courts tend to be more, though not completely, insulated from popular pressure. Judges in this era, whether elected or appointed, tended to be selected from the elite and upper classes and to identify themselves with the business community and commercial interests.[2] In a study of judges in the Midwest from 1861 to 1899, Kermit Hall finds that party leaders, who often were lawyers themselves, tended to run candidates for judgeships who were at "the upper end of the social spectrum, with emphasis on the prosperous middle class," and typically had strong kinship connections to other judges and elected officials.[3] Further, Brian Balogh writes that after Reconstruction the judicial system was increasingly oriented toward the protection of corporate interests: "As the bar became professional and as prestigious positions were increasingly aligned with law firms that specialized in corporate work, there was no dearth of litigation to protect the interests of large employers and to create and stabilize a predictable national market."[4] Judges could also be expected to have an interest in preserving the common law as much as possible, both from self-interest (common law gave them more power over policy making as compared to legislatures) and because they were socialized in the legal profession and had family ties to other judges.

In the area of labor policy, each of these incentives tended to push judges in the direction of resisting the expansion of labor rights that was emerging through popular pressure and legislative action. In the case of liberalization of women's property rights, however, judges faced a more nuanced situation, with middle-class, business, and industrial interests often supporting reforms. Specifically, we can think of courts in this period as being both bastions of common-law conservatism and generally pro-business and aligned with commercial interests. In the areas of both labor rights and married women's rights, courts were inclined to follow common-law doctrines that enforced a social and legal hierarchy between master and servant or husband and wife, respectively. At the same time, judges also tended to be motivated in both areas by concerns for promoting business interests and commercial activity. In the case of labor, these two types of motivations pointed in the same outcome direction, whereas in the case of married women's property rights they were often at cross-purposes. As a result, court rulings on issues of married women's property rights were typically more mixed, often narrowing laws but not striking them down completely. Ultimately, all three state-level institutions—courts, legislatures, and conventions—could see some benefits to married women's economic rights, and all three institutions had some ambivalence about how far such rights should extend. Even in areas of the law where the judiciary tended to be more conflictual, as in labor law, gender dynamics colored court interpretations; courts were less likely to strike down labor legislation that singled out women.[5] In both property law and labor law, courts struggled to balance conceptions of women as independent economic actors and as vulnerable potential victims in need of state protection.[6]

Many court decisions on married women's rights in the 1800s and early 1900s did run counter to the more radical demands made by women's groups, but these rulings often fit well with the intentions of legislators, who typically had more modest and moderate goals. Similarly, although the new legislation did threaten to change courts' jurisdiction over family matters in some ways by altering the common law of coverture, it did not simultaneously present a major threat to a core constituency of the courts: business and commercial interests. Indeed, these interests often argued for more liberalization of property law, not less, in the interest of a better-functioning commercial economy. Married women's property acts were supported by a diverse and diffuse set of interests, many of which aligned with those of male legislators, delegates, and judges along multiple dimensions.

The second key difference between courts and elected bodies is the type of decisions they make. Statues and constitutional provisions are typically broad rules that cannot cover every contingency or special situation. Statutes and constitutional provisions defining married women's economic rights were typically short—sometimes a few paragraphs, but often just one or two sentences, especially in the case of constitutions. State courts were left to fill in the details. In contrast to legislative bodies, courts encounter law on a case-by-case basis, quite literally. In applying the general rules established in reforms to the particular cases brought before them in the nineteenth and early twentieth centuries, state courts often struggled to negotiate laws full of partial rights, which led to perverse outcomes that are explored in more detail in this chapter's case studies.

When courts did push the envelope and interpret reforms to grant broad rights, legislatures at least sometimes fought back and passed narrower laws to clarify their intentions. For instance, in 1881 the South Carolina Supreme Court expansively interpreted South Carolina's statute of 1870 to allow married women to mortgage their property for the benefit of a third party; in the case in question, a married woman had gone into debt to support her son's business, and the court ruled that this debt was legal and could be collected.[7] The South Carolina Legislature responded quickly, passing a new law in its very next session curtailing married women's general power to contract and limiting it to contracts specifically concerning their separate estates.[8] Thereafter, South Carolina courts fell in line with this more moderate interpretation of married women's economic rights.

By largely taking a middle path of narrow, cautious interpretations of married women's economic rights, courts mostly deferred to state legislatures in the gradual liberalization of married women's economic rights. The result was that courts could acquiesce to legislative action to liberalize feudal elements of marital-property law while also maintaining certain aspects of the ascriptive gender hierarchies that remained popular with male voters and legislators.

A cooperative, iterative process makes sense when considering that most male legislators advocated in favor of reforms not primarily for feminist reasons but rather to satisfy their own goals, which included protecting women from harm by both their husbands and the market—clearly a challenging balance to strike. We can view the liberalization of married women's economic rights as a dialogue between state courts and state legislative bodies in which courts weighed common-law precedents, gender hierarchies, and potentially transformative legislative enactments. Legislation granting married women partial rights to separate property created a complex legal situation, which often led to a cycle in which legislative actions were interpreted in courts in ways that increased confusion and decreased predictability, thus creating popular pressure for further reforms. Legislators then modified laws, gradually expanding the rights of married women in a piecemeal fashion. This pattern points to an important role for courts in reform processes even when they are not engaged in direct conflict with elected bodies.

"THE EXPERIENCE OF THE SAGES AND VENERABLE MEN": CONSTITUTIONAL INTERPRETATION IN NEW YORK'S LOWER COURTS

One possible option for courts—though rarely used—was to strike down married women's property laws in full or in part on various constitutional grounds, defending their turf as arbiters of the feudal common law and yielding no ground to legislators, especially with respect to reforms that contained a retroactive component. After the first married women's property act was passed in New York, two of the eight judicial districts in New York quickly responded by overturning the new statute, although these cases were not appealed to the Court of Appeals (the highest court in the state), and thus the law stood in the state as a whole. In *Holmes v. Holmes* (1848), the Second District Court dealt with a married couple who had separated, and the wife was suing to prevent an inheritance bequeathed to her from going to her estranged husband.[9] The court ruled that it had the power to assign the property to the woman under equity rules, independent of the existence of a statute to that effect, and, further, that the married women's property act was unconstitutional for a variety of reasons. Justice Barculo clearly saw the act as a sharp break from past traditions that could not be tolerated: "The experience of the sages and venerable men who have preceded us, is as nothing, compared to the intuition of the Solons of this 'progressive' age. Legal forms, authorities, precedents, maxims, adjudications, the knowledge of the past, the learning of the present, all fade away and disappear before the dazzling brightness of the new era."[10] He struck down the married women's property act on no less than three grounds: as beyond the state legislature's power to "destroy vested rights to property"; as a violation of the state constitution's due process clause; and as a violation of the U.S. Constitution's Contract Clause by impairing the marriage contract of couples who married before the law was passed (as was true for the couple in this case).[11]

The next year in *White v. White* (1849), the Sixth District also ruled the law void and on similar grounds that the New York Legislature had no power under the state constitution to interfere with vested property rights without due process.[12] The wife in this case had inherited real estate from her father, which had been willed to her under equity law.

She had been living on this real estate, managing it, and receiving profits from it until her husband violently evicted her from the land, causing her to bring a lawsuit against him. From the court's description, he was exactly the sort of husband that married women's property acts aimed to protect married women from: "The defendant was a man of idle habits and addicted to the use of spirituous liquors, to such a degree as to become frequently intoxicated[, and] he had been careless and improvident in the management and cultivation of the said farm and had greatly neglected the same."[13] Judge Mason, writing for the court, carefully considered whether the state legislature had exceeded its constitutional power under the Contract Clause[14] but ultimately concluded that the marriage contract is different enough from normal business contracts that the Contract Clause did not apply. However, he did strike down the law as violating state due process protections against the taking of vested property rights by the legislature. Mason wrote that "the people of the state of New-York [sic] have never delegated to their legislature the power to divest the vested rights of property legally acquired by any citizen of the state, and transfer them to another, against the will of the owner."[15] According to Mason, by taking property that belonged by right to Mr. White and giving it to Mrs. White without a trial, the legislature had exceeded its powers.

One interesting thing to note about both cases is that they represented less typical conflicts in which husband and wife were adverse parties. The dissolution of a well-functioning marital relationship was indeed one of the major issues raised by opponents of reforms to married women's economic rights, so it makes sense that these types of conflicts might lead to the most strident response from courts. However, this judicial holdout was very short-lived and ineffectual. The highest court in New York never took up these cases and never struck down a married women's property act. Rather, the New York Court of Appeals and most other New York courts took a middle path, avoiding either extreme resistance to reforms or broadly emancipatory interpretations.

For instance, in *Switzer v. Valentine* (1854),[16] the Superior Court of New York City interpreted the state's statute of 1849 to read that a married woman's separate property was narrowly defined and that the new statute did not confer any general right to contract, merely a specific one with regard to a married woman's separate estate. Caroline Switzer ran a boardinghouse with her husband's knowledge. She took out a mortgage on the boardinghouse, and when she failed to pay back the debt, the property was seized. Her husband sued the creditor, arguing that his wife had no legal right to mortgage the property. The court agreed, writing that although the boardinghouse was run by the wife and much of the business was done in her name, it was not Caroline Switzer's separate property, and thus the mortgage was void. The creditor, knowing that Switzer was a married woman, should not have agreed to the mortgage in her name without investigating whether the boardinghouse was in fact property completely separate from her husband's.

This interpretation is important in considering the relationship between the state legislature and state courts. The 1849 act could be read to give a married woman broad powers to mortgage property "as if she were a single female," but it could also be read more narrowly as giving married women rights specific to property held on a "sole and separate" account rather than general rights to engage in various types of economic activity. Although women organizing for property rights may have desired an expansive reading of the act, the male legislators who enacted it did not necessarily have this goal in mind. Rather, they hoped to restore some of the protection that had been provided by equity courts and shield a portion of family assets from creditors—goals that the Superior Court's interpretation of the act accomplished.

Switzer also illustrates how early reforms created legal difficulties for creditors, eventually leading to demands for expanding reforms. Even though Caroline Switzer was the boardinghouse's primary proprietor and did much of the business in her own name, this was still no guarantee that she could legally mortgage the property. In a case in 1874, Judge Church of the New York Court of Appeals urged the legislature to adopt more expansive rules regarding married women's economic rights, writing that partial rights had led to "a flood of expensive and vexatious litigation."[17]

"VALID DEBTS": THE LEGAL RESPONSE TO MARRIED WOMEN'S PROPERTY ACTS IN MISSISSIPPI

In line with the language of Mississippi's first married women's property statute of 1839, the Mississippi Supreme Court interpreted the law narrowly, with little sense that it would empower women economically. In a case in 1844, the Court concluded that a right to "separate property" included only ownership of enslaved people, not any profits or income from their labor. Sarah Spencer had purchased a carriage with the profits from hiring out enslaved people she had received from her father, and her husband's creditors attempted to seize the carriage as repayment for his debts. The court ruled that the carriage was not, in fact, Sarah's separate property and could legally be seized: "From the whole tenor of the act, it is plainly deducible that it was designed to guard the specific property from any liability for the debts and contracts of the husband. It reaches no further. . . . [U]nder [the law's] provisions, the productions of the slaves in question were the property, and liable for the debts and contracts of the husband."[18] This case indicates that the 1839 act functioned almost entirely as a debtor-protection law, exempting a very specific set of property for each family (i.e., a wife's real estate and enslaved human property, brought into the relationship through means outlined in the law) but without providing substantial economic empowerment for married women. In 1846, the Mississippi Supreme Court also found that the 1839 statute did not affect married women's broader economic rights, writing in *Davis v. Foy* that the law "has not the effect to extend [a married woman's] power of contracting, or of binding herself or her property."[19]

Later reforms expanded married women's property rights beyond the original law. In 1846 and 1857, the Mississippi Legislature passed reforms that kept in place the debtor protections of the 1839 act, while limiting husbands' control over their wives' separate property and giving married women limited rights to contract. For instance, the code of 1857 provided that husbands would no longer be able to "[sell], convey[], mortgage[], transfer[], or in any manner encumber[]" their wives' property without the wives' permission, and wives gained the right to purchase and sell property under their own name.[20] Further, married women would now receive the profits and income from their separate property rather than seeing this money go to their husbands, as under the 1839 act.[21] However, married women's right to mortgage separate property or otherwise take out loans remained limited. Married women could make these types of contracts only for specific purposes that were outlined in detail in the laws. The 1846 act, for example, allowed wives to mortgage their property for supplies for their enslaved human property and plantation, and the 1857 code enlarged these allowable purposes to include family supplies, clothing, children's education, household furniture, and improvements to the women's property.[22] Both reforms contained a mixture of protective and empowering elements for white wives and characterized enslaved women as property that was acted upon by the legislation.

As Mississippi's elected bodies gradually expanded the rights and powers available to married women under the law, the Mississippi Supreme Court heard a series of cases dealing with loans, contracts, and earnings that indicate a legal environment that would have been opaque and confusing for the average creditor or debtor. Many of the cases resulted in creditors being unable to collect even on debts that were seemingly made in good faith, without evidence that the creditors had attempted to fool or take advantage of the women who now appealed to coverture to escape their debts.

For instance, in a case in 1866 Sarah Pelan and her husband signed two promissory notes. Before the notes came due, her husband passed away, and Sarah claimed in court that she should not be liable to repay the debt because she had been under coverture when she signed the note. The court concluded that because the contract made no mention of Pelan's separate property, she was not liable despite the fact that she was a single woman at the time of the lawsuit. Justice Ellett wrote: "A married woman generally can make no valid contract, and her promises are prima facie void."[23] Though married women's property acts had enlarged married women's ability to make contracts in specific cases, those contracts had to abide by the specific rules and purposes laid out in the statutes.

Whitworth v. Carter (1870) spelled out exactly how those rules might be applied to a specific contract. In this case, Mary Whitworth purchased real estate on credit and failed to repay the loan. In ruling that Whitworth was not liable to repay the loan, the Mississippi Supreme Court wrote: "To hold that she can obligate herself to pay for property bought on credit . . . would overturn the beneficent policy of the law, and break down the barriers with which the corpus of her estate is hedged around. Whilst she can provide for the maintenance, comfort, and education of herself and family and for the improvement of her property, she is not permitted to embark in the hazards of trade or speculations."[24] The court reasoned that if Whitworth had taken out the loan for an allowable purpose under the statute—for example, the education of her children—she would indeed be liable. But a loan for land speculation was a different story; because the justices saw the purpose of the reform as protecting married women, they argued that it ought not allow them to take undue risks with their separate property.

Even where married women took out loans with the stated intent to use the funds for allowable purposes, it was incumbent upon the creditor to prove in court that she did, in fact, use the loan for these legal purposes. In a case in 1874, *Viser v. Scruggs*, the court was unsympathetic to a creditor who had a loan document that expressly laid out the way in which the borrower, a married woman, would use the funds:

> In making the loan Viser took the risk, that Mrs. Scruggs would use the money for the purposes recited in the note, "of purchasing family supplies and necessaries, and wearing apparel for herself and children." If the money was not appropriated to exonerate her estate from valid debts, or to improve her property, or to maintain the family, or for some other object for which she could incur liability, there is no obligation resting upon her, or her estate, which can be enforced. The appellant, Viser, has wholly failed to show such use of the money.[25]

This case lays out an almost impossible standard for creditors hoping to collect from married women who sought to escape their debts. Obtaining a signed contract that the lendee would use the loan in compliance with the purposes laid out in the law was not sufficient; the creditor was also required to show that the funds were actually used in that manner. Viser did have some recourse in this particular case: because Mrs. Scruggs had given the money in question to her husband, the court ruled that the debt legally became her husband's, and thus the income from her separate estate could be taken to repay the debt. But Viser was still unable to seize the property itself, as he would have been if Mrs. Scruggs were a man or single woman.

In cases throughout this period, the Mississippi Supreme Court issued similar rulings that limited the extent to which a married woman's separate property could be seized for her debts, writing that these limitations were "intended [by the legislature] to secure to the wife the enjoyment of her separate estate against any possible contingency of loss through the fraud, force or undue influence of her husband."[26] Although these rules limiting married women's liability may indeed have protected individual women who would otherwise have lost their property to bad business deals, it is also likely that many other women were unable to obtain credit at all because creditors were uncertain about whether these debts would ever be legally enforceable. Thus, there was a constant tension in court decisions between protecting women and empowering them economically, with the state's highest court tending to rule on the side of protection, even when this tendency created an unpredictable legal environment.

The other major legal issue surrounding married women's property during this period in Mississippi concerned their earnings. Industrial expansion during and after the Civil War led to more women working for wages, most commonly as domestic servants, seamstresses, and factory employees, though married women worked for wages less frequently than did unmarried women.[27] As was the case around the nation, earnings had traditionally been seen as fundamentally different from other types of property, such as real estate or a gift of funds, although this conception was beginning to change.[28] This distinction often benefited creditors to the detriment of women who believed that in their wages they held separate property that was exempt from their husbands' debts. As with the cases dealing with contracts made by married women, these rulings also sometimes led to outcomes that required extensive record keeping and high standards of evidence that would seemingly be difficult for many litigants to provide.

Apple v. Ganong (1872) demonstrates how different rules for earnings than for other sorts of property were becoming increasingly problematic.[29] As in many of these cases, this dispute concerned land that Louisa Ganong claimed as her separate property but that her husband's creditors claimed they should be able to seize for repayment of his debts. The court determined that Louisa had purchased the land using a combination of funds: money she had in her possession before being married, a gift of cotton from her mother, and income she earned after marriage from sewing. The first two categories of property could be claimed by married women as separate property, but the last could not, so the creditors could claim part but not all of Louisa's property.[30]

This type of case helps explain why Mississippi included an earnings act in its code of 1871. The new law placed earnings on the same footing as all other types of property, thus making unnecessary a thorough investigation into how married women purchased property.[31] The code also included an important new provision on married women's ability to make contracts, allowing them to make legally enforceable contracts in order to engage in trade or business.[32] The prominent lawyer Edward Mayes noted that this provision extended the right to contract in the course of business to "more than trade in a commercial sense. It meant any employment which required time, labor and skill."[33]

Throughout this transitional period, we see the Mississippi Legislature and Supreme Court gradually expanding married women's property rights over time, with continued concerns for protecting both indebted families and married women. There was an increasing tension between these protectionist concerns and a desire to prevent fraud and make legal principles clearer in ways that would empower women as economic actors. By 1876, the Mississippi Supreme Court had interpreted the "free-trader" provisions of the 1871 act broadly, ruling that married women could engage in trade and business just like men and unmarried women and could make legally enforceable contracts in the course of these business transactions. In a sharp shift from the protectionist stances of earlier cases, in *Netterville v. Barber* the Court wrote that "a married woman, like other persons, must take the chances and risks of her business transactions. The law will not intervene and relieve from all consequences of their mistakes, misfortunes, or follies."[34]

Clearly, this period saw a substantial expansion of women's property rights in Mississippi, both through legislative acts and through court rulings that cooperated with these expansionary statutes. But even the justices in *Netterville*, although announcing a ruling that broadly interpreted married women's right to contract, still insisted that "freedom from disability is not complete. She is not able to make every sort of contract."[35] Married women's property thus remained a confused area of law with serious consequences for both creditors and married women who hoped to obtain credit.

This complicated legal situation helps explain the expansive reforms found in Mississippi's statute of 1880 and constitution of 1890, which not only explicitly removed the disabilities of coverture with regard to property but also prevented the legislature from reversing these gains going forward. The context for the passage of these reforms had dramatically changed regarding concern for debtors and debt relief. Although the 1890 constitution did include a prohibition on imprisonment for debt (carried over from its 1868 constitution), there were no other provisions relating to debt relief, and the issue was not a major point of debate at the constitutional convention. By 1880, the debt-relief origins of Mississippi's 1839 law had essentially disappeared. The law made no reference to a married woman's husband's debts, and she now had the right to invest her separate property in his business ventures or to secure his loans as she pleased. Accordingly, many of the protective aspects of the early laws disappeared. For instance, in *Toof v. Brewer* (1888), the Mississippi Supreme Court ruled that a husband and wife could join together in a business partnership, and the wife would be personally liable for debts so incurred, as would her separate property.[36] In another example, the Court found in 1904 that married women were no longer protected against claims of adverse possession in court—with passage of the 1880 act, they were to be treated exactly like men and not have any special protections.[37] The law had now shifted, both in text and judicial interpretation, toward empowering women to make potentially risky economic decisions and away from carving out special protections for them.

However, despite the broad language of the 1880 and 1890 reforms, the Mississippi courts limited these statutes to property and economic rights only, with an emphasis on women's interactions with third parties outside the marital relationship. For example, in a case in 1924 the Mississippi Supreme Court ruled that a wife could not sue her husband for negligence, writing that "it was not the purpose of the makers of our Constitution nor of the legislature to entirely destroy the unity of man and wife with all the incidents flowing there from."[38] Similarly, work done in the home was clearly set outside the bounds of the statute and separate from wage labor done in the market when the 1880 code outlawed contracts between husband and wife that would compensate for household labor.[39] Thus, the transformation of married women's property law had its limits. Legislators and judges balanced liberalization in the market with a continued desire for gender hierarchy, especially in the home.

"A MUCH TANGLED ISSUE": LEGAL INTERPRETATION AND CONSTITUTIONAL RESPONSE IN SOUTH CAROLINA

The courts in South Carolina initially interpreted its married women's property act expansively and with more deference to creditors. In *Pelzer v. Campbell* (1881), the South Carolina Supreme Court held that a married woman was liable for a debt she contracted on behalf of her son's business. In discussing the history of married women's property rights reforms, the Court wrote:

> Most of the states of the Union originally adopted the old common law of the mother country, modified as it had been by the introduction of trusts and the peculiar doctrine of "the separate estate" of married women, created by act of the parties and administered exclusively in courts of equity. But later, as property increased and the relations of a highly civilized society become more complex, there was developed a tendency to escape what was regarded as the hard and unbending rules of the common law, and to bestow upon the wife a larger capacity to hold property in her own right, and to dispose of it without regard to the wishes of her husband.[40]

As this passage hints, the South Carolina Supreme Court extensively discussed married women's property law around the nation, describing the statutes of six states (Illinois, Maine, Massachusetts, New Jersey, New York, and Ohio) and explaining the legal reasoning of cases from six states (Kansas, Maine Massachusetts, New Jersey, New York, and Ohio). According to the Court, the expanding property rights of married women in South Carolina and elsewhere were largely in response to a growing commercial economy with more complex economic interactions among citizens. The Court wrote that the law clearly gave married women the right to contract with regard to their property as if they were single (and certainly a plain reading of the text would concur with this statement), and it quickly dismissed the impact this right might have on the protection of married women and/or its impact on possible debt-relief intentions behind the law: "It has been strongly urged upon us that to give a married woman the unrestricted right to bind herself by contract must result in the destruction of her separate estate . . . [and] that every good wife will contribute her last cent to promote the success or to maintain the credit and honor of her husband. . . . [But given] the right to contract, [married women] assume the liabilities of contractors."[41]

Thus, the Court took a stance that had implications for both married women and their creditors. On the one hand, the ruling took a less paternalistic stance toward married women: they had the right to contract with their property even to their own detriment or the detriment of their separate estate. On the other hand, this ruling also obviously benefited creditors, who would be able to collect on the debts of married women as if they were single; the ruling reduced uncertainty in a growing commercial economy that more frequently involved married women as economic actors by removing state protections.

Even as the South Carolina Supreme Court made a more expansive ruling in favor of married women's property rights, however, it seemed to signal to the legislature that the latter could be narrower in its legislation if it so chose. Referring to the intentions of the delegates at the recent constitutional convention, the judges wrote in 1881: "The main object of the provision in the constitution seems to have been, not so much to declare the rights of the wife, as to negative those of the husband in regard to her property—not to enable her, but to disable him and his creditors."[42] Thus, although the law passed by the legislature was broad both as written and as interpreted by the Court, the Court seemed to signal that a narrower law focused on debt relief would not be considered invalid under the state constitution if the legislature chose a different path.

The South Carolina Legislature responded quickly to *Pelzer* in its next session, including in the state's new code of 1882 a provision curtailing married women's general power to contract (limiting it to contracts specifically concerning their separate estates).[43] The legislature was also now overwhelmingly Democratic, a major shift since the statute had passed in 1870.[44] After 1882, the South Carolina courts reversed course and defined married women's separate estates very narrowly. The South Carolina Supreme Court would later write of the new policy:

"Its manifest purpose was to protect the wife by limiting her power to contract.... [I]f left to her own will, experience conclusively shows that a devoted and confiding wife could be very easily induced to sacrifice her all in, perhaps, what every one else would regard as a desperate attempt to shield a reckless or improvident husband from financial distress."[45]

Of course, at least in the cases that made it to court, the opposite was often true: women were trying to avoid repaying debts they had taken out, sometimes for their own business pursuits, by retroactively claiming they were not competent to have signed the contract. Specifically, the South Carolina Supreme Court ruled that contracts made by married woman must directly concern their separate property rather than merely making mention of it or using it to guarantee a debt unrelated to the separate estate.[46] That is, after the code was revised in 1882, married women were denied not only a general right to contract but also the right to contract with regard to their separate estates in all but the most limited circumstances. In *Aultman v. Rush* (1887), the Court extended this same principle to mortgages on separate estates.[47] The Court subsequently held that that a married woman had no right to her earnings and thus that those earnings could be claimed by a creditor for her husband's debts. In *Bridgers v. Howell* (1887), the Court argued that neither the South Carolina Constitution of 1868 nor the ensuing statute explicitly gave married women ownership of their earnings, so the common-law rule that earnings belonged to the husband still stood.[48]

The posture of the state legislature and courts toward debt relief is interesting here. After 1882, there was a clear concern for protecting women from their creditors even when the women acted to mortgage their separate property or otherwise to make contracts that would endanger that property. However, when it came to satisfying a husband's creditors, the justices were less willing to designate property as belonging solely to the wife and thus not accessible by creditors. Part of the story here relates to changing definitions of property in the broader society. According to William Scott, it was only in the decades just prior to the Civil War that Americans started viewing wages as property (and wage earners as property holders) at all.[49] The cases described here make it clear that the courts in the 1880s still viewed wages as being property of a different sort.

For instance, in *Bridgers* the South Carolina Supreme Court argued that the question in this case was not really about property but rather about the proper relationship between husband and wife under common law, referring to the doctrine of marital service and writing that the argument that married women have a property interest in their earnings "assumes... that a married woman's personal services belong to herself and not to her husband, whereas the reverse of this proposition was undoubtedly true at common law, and, as we have seen, neither the constitution nor any statute has made any change in the common law doctrine. Hence, as the services of the wife belong to her husband, all acquisitions made by such services belong to him also."[50]

Thus, wages were not seen as property in the same way that a tract of land was property; rather, they were payment for services rendered, and those services properly belonged to a woman's husband. The Court reiterated this point in *Gwynn v. Gwynn* (1887), this time siding with the debtors in the case.[51] In *Gwynn*, a husband and wife had signed a contract to enter into a business partnership together. When the business failed, creditors sued for both the husband's property and the wife's separate property. The Court ruled for the wife, first reiterating an argument from *Habenicht v. Rawls* (1886) that a married women had no general right to contract.[52] The Court distinguished between property and labor, writing that a business partnership is "an agreement that each of the parties named should combine their labor and skill in the proposed enterprise, [and] it is quite certain that no such partnership could be formed between husband and wife, for the simple reason that her labor and skill already belong to the husband." The Court described this labor arrangement as being central to "the very foundations of civilized society."[53] However foundational to civilization, this state of affairs was not to last long: at the end of 1887, the South Carolina Legislature decided that earnings were part of a wife's separate estate and would thereafter be treated according to the usual rules for separate estates.[54] However, this new statute did not seem to be about liberating women to use their earnings as they pleased because it did not remove any of the other liabilities of previous statutes and court rulings; as before, women still remained unable to make general contracts. Rather, the new statute simply clarified that a married woman's earnings would not be subject to her husband's debts. Indeed, the legislature continued along a protectionist path, specifying in 1891 that married women were not permitted to assume or guarantee the debts of any other person.[55]

By 1895, married women were clearly participating in the economy in various ways, but creditors could never be sure whether they would be able to collect on loans to women because lengthy legal battles could ensue when married women could not afford to pay their debts. As a result, married women's property rights were raised once again at the South Carolina constitutional convention of 1895. The new constitution affirmed the right of married women not only to hold separate property but also to make contracts and to have any other rights with regard to their property that "an unmarried woman or a man" would have.[56] In examining the motivations behind the constitutional change, it is important to recall that this constitution was not in general a rights-granting document. Like Mississippi's convention that ended Reconstruction, the South Carolina Constitution of 1895 disenfranchised large portions of the African American population in the state, mandated segregated schools, and failed to grant suffrage rights to women. Women's rights activists submitted petitions to the convention on the subject of woman suffrage, but these documents were not even forwarded to the suffrage committee, much less seriously considered by the convention as a whole.[57]

Rather, the delegates at the convention were more concerned with simplifying and rationalizing the legal status of married women's property ownership. In reporting on the convention, the *Charleston News and Courier* wrote that "everyone hopes [the married women's property clause] will settle the now much tangled issue." One delegate argued that "the Acts of the Legislature tinkering with the laws relating to the property of married women had caused more litigation and expense to the people of the State than any other one thing. He then pointed out in detail the dreadful botches the Legislature had made until now a Philadelphia lawyer could not tell what the law in this State on the subject was."[58] The delegates differed on the solution to this problem, which ranged from a return to coverture to various compromise positions that would limit the rights of married women in ways similar to previous statutes on the subject or to formal legal equality with regard to property rights. Ultimately, the delegates adopted the latter approach by a handy margin, including relatively expansive rights in the constitution.

This chapter emphasizes that it is important to look beyond highly conflictual battles between the U.S. Supreme Court and Congress in understanding the role of the judiciary in reform processes. State courts are important players, even when they largely defer to elected bodies. By making evident the contradictions inherent in vague and inconsistent legal reforms, nineteenth- and early twentieth-century state courts pushed forward the reforms of married women's economic rights. Legislative enactments—especially early legislative enactments—were the beginning of the story rather than the end. As courts began to interpret these laws in specific cases, legislatures had to confront the real-world implications of the sometimes-conflicting motivations for these laws—often a conflict between liberalizing the economic system and protecting women from the harsh realities of the free market.

State courts made it explicit in individual cases that the attempt to balance protectionist and free-market approaches to married women's property ownership could go only so far; at some point, the attempt would create a legal environment full of rules that were difficult—if not impossible—to understand and implement. This was especially the case when it came to lawsuits on the topic of married women's debts and contracts. Ultimately, through a gradual, iterative process with significant back-and-forth between different state-level government institutions, married women's economic rights were transformed. The process by which reforms were filtered through multiple institutions with different priorities and commitments shaped their trajectory in ways that enactment through a single institution would not have.

Conclusion

The story of married women's economic rights reform is not a straightforward or linear one. Reforms took place across states over the course of decades, with multiple state-level institutions working out the practicalities of rights expansions in an iterative process. The specifics of the reform process varied across the nation as married women's property acts proved to be a highly adaptable policy that could serve multiple goals in different state contexts. Liberalization of marital-property law was significant but far from complete by the end of the period discussed here, with many further reforms to married women's economic rights and divorce law enacted after 1920. The process as a whole has important lessons about the role of power dynamics and elite interests as well as about the role of marriage as an institution in American political development.

ITERATIVE, MULTIBRANCH REFORMS

Married women's property rights were enacted through a two-level process, with both intrastate and interstate dynamics playing important roles in their development. Within each state, elites established new policies across multiple years and multiple state-level institutions. States did not generally enact one statute reforming married women's property law and then cleanly implement it. Instead, reforms were interpreted and amended over the course of years—sometimes decades—and were passed around between multiple state-level institutions. States introduced new rights and affirmed statutory reforms in constitutional text, and then state courts interpreted both statutes and constitutional provisions. For the most part, state courts interpreted reforms narrowly in line with the preferences of many elected elites. But these narrow rulings often led to confusing and sometimes perverse outcomes, especially with respect to debt collection. Court rulings and legal complexity around married women's access to credit then led to further rounds of reform in elected bodies.

In drafting married women's property acts, male elites responded to a variety of interests and pressures, including but not limited to activism on the topic by women's organizations. Economic rights reforms for married women could serve a number of different policy goals, including social policy (temperance, reduction of women's dependency on the state); economic policy (responding to economic crises and industrialization); and the building of state power, especially in the areas of slavery and settler colonialism. Because of these dynamics, married women's economic rights reform was inherently limited both in terms of the extent to which it liberalized the marriage relationship as well as in terms of *which* women were granted new rights and which were left out or even lost rights as a result of the new reforms.

And reforms weren't just developing within individual states—they were also spreading across the nation. Because of the state-level status of both property law and marriage law, the national government did not coordinate reforms across states or require states to enact any reforms, but the policies still spread to every state in some form. Instead of a nationally led process, elites in multiple state venues learned about reforms elsewhere in the country and copied or adapted them to fit their needs. State legislators were aware of statutory developments in other states; they sought out policies that were working and tried to avoid the pitfalls of poorly drafted laws elsewhere in the nation. Constitutional convention delegates brought ideas about married women's rights with them as they moved west and carefully studied widely available compilations of constitutions. State courts at least sometimes cited and discussed out-of-state decisions. Then all this borrowing and learning fed back into the institutional cycle within each state.

POWER, ELITES, AND RIGHTS REFORMS

In his work on interest convergence, Derrick Bell argues that the interests of Black Americans have been successfully advanced in the courts only when those interests converged with the interests of white Americans, using the case study of racial equality in public schools. Bell argues that courts will require remedies not based on the level of discrimination or harm actually experienced by Black people but rather on the extent to which those remedies "secure, advance, or at least not harm societal interests deemed important by middle and upper class whites."[1] My study explores a dramatically different context from that of legal decisions on segregated schools in the twentieth century, but Bell's insights about power and social hierarchy are echoed in the case of married women's property rights reforms.

Male political actors in the 1800s and early 1900s benefited in many ways from extending economic rights to married women. This book illustrates that despite an appearance of men "giving up power," those with political power were able to use married women's property law to consolidate that power at least sometimes on dimensions other than gender. Stronger property rights for wives had important implications for policies such as slavery, settlement of the West, and the avoidance of women's dependency on the state. Therefore, although some women did benefit economically from these reforms, those benefits accrued to particular women in particular ways that also served the interests of male political elites and the state.

This understanding of rights reform does not discount the fact that reforms to the doctrine of coverture represented a major democratizing moment in U.S. history. Rather, this work contributes to broader understandings about the ways in which democratization and rights expansions not only accommodate the interests of politically, socially, and economically powerful actors but are often driven by those interests in various ways. We see this dynamic in a variety of contexts.

David Bateman describes the ways that extensions of the suffrage were paired with disenfranchising policies so that elite coalitions could both retain political power and define political communities in ways that were simultaneously inclusionary and exclusionary along different dimensions.[2] Relatedly, Paul Herron discusses the pairing of universal white male suffrage with constitutional protections for slavery in state constitutional development.[3] Ran Hirschl argues that the global trend toward the constitutionalization of rights and stronger judicial review is not—as some conventional wisdom has held—the result of movements seeking greater social justice and progressive values but rather the result of strategic actions of elites across multiple social and political sectors as they sought to maintain the status quo for their own self-interest.[4] Finally, Mary Dudziak presents compelling evidence that the movement for civil rights and desegregation after World War II was significantly bolstered not solely by a desire for justice but rather also by elites' calculation that such reforms would aid international diplomacy goals during the Cold War.[5] Although each of these studies discusses rights issues that are distinct from the development of married women's property rights in many ways, each shares key insights about the role of power in rights reforms and the ways that elites with political power can use reforms for their benefit. This dynamic often results in the pattern we see in the case of married women's economic rights, wherein democratizing reforms are fused with antidemocratic and illiberal policies.

EXPANDING ECONOMIC CITIZENSHIP

The path to full economic citizenship for women in the United States is a long and bumpy one that has continued far beyond the period studied in this book.[6] Economic citizenship encompasses two facets of rights: the right to participate in the economy and the right to be treated fairly and without discrimination once one is participating in the economy. This book addresses only the first of these aspects of economic rights, but this category of rights is clearly a prerequisite for full economic citizenship. Although reforms to married women's economic rights made meaningful changes to married women's legal status and ability to participate in the economy, they are certainly not the end to the story. After 1920 and the ratification of the Nineteenth Amendment, women's involvement in economic reform processes looked different, with more agency for both individual women and women organizing through groups. Two examples illustrate some of these differences.

The first comes from Florida, which was an outlier in the enactment of control-and-management rights for married women. Florida did not enact a control-and-management reform until 1943 and did so through a process that included women as more direct political actors, in contrast to the pre-1920 reforms discussed earlier in this book. Ethel Ernest Murrell, a Florida attorney, not only campaigned on behalf of changes to married women's property law over the course of almost a decade but was also the chair of the Florida Bar Association committee that rewrote the law and was credited by newspapers as the author of the bill.[7] After the law's passage, she also helped to successfully defend the reform before the Florida Supreme Court.[8] Murrell was not the only woman who played a crucial role in reform passage. Within the Florida Legislature, Representative Mary Lou Baker championed the reform as the only woman member of the legislature.[9] Fifty-three state-level women's organizations advocated for the passage of the law.[10] Overall, the passage of Florida's reform legislation in 1943 indicates that although women in that state might still not have enjoyed full economic citizenship, they were able to be much more active and effective advocates for their rights across multiple venues.

The fight against gender discrimination in the granting of credit—especially as relating to married women—in the 1970s provides another example of this dynamic in the slow extension of full economic citizenship to women.[11] Before the mid-1970s, lenders regularly discriminated against women in issuing mortgages and other forms of credit. Although policies varied by bank, practices affecting married women specifically included the refusal to count a married woman's full income in a credit application; an unwillingness to extend married women credit in their own name or without husbands acting as cosigner; and the requirement that women reapply for credit after marriage.[12] In order to obtain a loan, many married women also faced serious intrusion into their reproductive choices, such as encountering loan officials who asked married couples to agree not to have a child during the loan term, to show proof of birth control, or even to sign documents agreeing to an abortion if the wife became pregnant.[13] Single women, divorced women, and widows also faced policies that limited their access to credit on a basis equal to similarly situated men.[14]

In this area, feminist organizations played significant roles at all stages of the policy-reform process, including research; agenda setting; activism in legislative, judicial, and administrative arenas; and the activation of public opinion.[15] Lawrence Bowdish argues that women organizers did not see this activism as merely an effort to change lender's policies but also as a civil rights struggle that would grant women "full participation in the consumer's republic."[16] This work would ultimately culminate in the passage and implementation of the Housing and Community Development Act and the Equal Credit Opportunity Act of 1974.[17]

Although this struggle for new rights featured a more central role for women organizers, Chloe Thurston notes that the relatively quick success of the movement against credit discrimination was influenced by the fact that these reforms benefited elites in various ways. In contrast to legislation on more controversial issues championed by the women's movement, such as the Equal Rights Amendment and the right to abortion, legislation on credit discrimination allowed members of Congress to take an easier vote in favor of women's equality. Thurston writes: "This particular issue resonated with wide swaths of the public and did not overly challenge women's standing. Credit in particular was a politically advantageous issue, since it required no outlay of public funds."[18] But even this "easy" framing of the issue was shaped by feminist organizers, who eschewed coalitions based on race and class, avoided the issue of women's unpaid labor in the home in the context of creditworthiness, and generally aimed to "[keep] the scope of the issue narrow" and to avoid threatening "fundamental values."[19] Thus, both the interests of elites and the organizing efforts of women's groups were crucial factors in explaining the success of these credit reforms.

These examples illustrate the ways in which dynamics around economic rights reform changed after women gained greater political power, but they also highlight some areas of continuity. Before 1920, women did advocate for economic rights but were constrained along several dimensions. The interests of male elites with political power are central to explaining how and why reforms were enacted and ultimately took the shape that they did. Women had more direct agency and involvement across multiple institutional venues in later economic rights reforms. Yet elite interests still remained important in shaping those reforms, and race and class continued to be major areas of division in terms of who benefited from new policies.

MARRIAGE AND AMERICAN POLITICAL DEVELOPMENT

Throughout U.S. history, marriage has fundamentally shaped our politics. It is an institution that crosses both the public sphere and the private sphere, and it has proved central to the development of state power as well as to ongoing struggles for full inclusion and citizenship.[20] As Nancy Cott argues, through marriage policy the "state is actively involved in creating social and civic statuses for both men and women."[21] Married women's property rights reform significantly changed wives' civic and economic status. It is important to note, though, that when considered in conjunction with other state laws relating to marriage, property, and citizenship, these changes affected different women in dramatically different ways.

In addition to benefiting male elites in multiple ways, married women's property rights laws provided new protections as well as economic powers to women who had property to protect, to business owners, to women who owned enslaved people, and to women who played central roles in the settlement of the West. David Bateman writes that "democratization . . . is a political project through which the boundaries and character of the 'people' are redefined, with inclusions and exclusions not only compatible but also potentially reinforcing means to achieve this."[22] Even as some women were brought more fully into economic citizenship, others were treated as enslaved property in the South or were stripped of their property rights through the colonization of western territories.

As in other policy areas, marriage here proved to be an institution highly adaptable to accomplishing various state goals, including the definition of an ideal citizenry. Nancy Fraser and Linda Gordon argue that under the regimes of both coverture and slavery, white male civil citizenship was defined "by protecting, subsuming, and even owning [wives and enslaved people]" and by excluding them from the status of full citizenship.[23] When married women's property acts gave (some) women increased economic and legal power, in many places they did so by giving those women ownership and control over enslaved people and over land that had been seized from Native people. Ultimately, married women's economic rights were one piece of the broader structure in which states used marriage and marriage policy to exercise and consolidate power.

Methods Appendix

METHOD AND RESULTS FOR DATING OF STATUTES

Numerous previous studies have identified dates for married women's economic rights reforms. Some of this work is based on legal treatises, whereas other work has used statute books and state court cases. For my study, although I used these earlier works to identify some possible dates for the earliest statute within each state meeting the definitions laid out in chapter 1, I confirmed each date by locating the original statute in a state or territorial statute books. Table A.1 lists specific information on sources used for each reform type, and table A.2 identifies the date for each reform type in each state or territory.

TEXT ANALYSIS USING WCOPYFIND PLAGIARISM SOFTWARE

WCopyfind is software originally developed by the physicist Lou Bloomfield to detect plagiarism.[1] It compares two texts to identify shared words and phrases and then reports the percentage of the text that matches between the two documents. In comparing the texts of state constitutional provisions and statutes written during the period covered, I set the software to identify matching phrases of at least six words in length that

TABLE A.1

Sources of Statutes by Reform Type

Reform Type	Source Details
Debt-free separate estates	Initial list of dates compiled from: Chused, Richard H. "Married Women's Property Law: 1800–1850." *Georgetown Law Journal* 71 (1983): 1359–425. Kelly, John F. *A Treatise on the Law of Contracts of Married Women*. Legal Treatises, 1800–1926. Jersey City, NJ: F. D. Linn, 1882. Khan, B. Zorina. "Married Women's Property Laws and Female Commercial Activity: Evidence from United States Patent Records, 1790–1895." *Journal of Economic History* 56, no. 2 (1996): 356–88. Exceptions: Vermont date updated based on statute book—the date 1845 seems to have been a typo in Chused, "Married Women's Property Law." The date listed in Chused for New Hampshire addresses antenuptial and postnuptial contracts, not debts; updated to a later date that explicitly protects property from creditors. Nevada updated to an earlier date based on statute book. Maryland updated to one year later based on statute book (the statute passed during the 1842 legislative session, but the actual date of passage was 1843).
Control and management	Initial list of dates compiled from: Geddes, R. Richard, and Sharon Tennyson. "Passage of the Married Women's Property Acts and Earnings Acts in the United States: 1850 to 1920." *Research in Economic History* 29 (2013): 145–89. MacDonald, Daniel. "On the Question of Court Activism and Economic Interests in Nineteenth-Century Married Women's Property Law." In *Law and Social Economics: Essays in Ethical Values for Theory, Practice, and Policy*, edited by Mark D. White, 139–60. New York: Palgrave Macmillan, 2015.

Reform Type	Source Details
	Exceptions:
Oklahoma date was an error (off by ten years); confirmed with librarian at Oklahoma Department of Libraries. Macdonald and Geddes/Tennyson differ on the date for North Carolina, and MacDonald's date is correct (confirmed by date in statute book/constitutional provision). Maine updated to an earlier date based on statute book.
No passage date is listed for Georgia here. As late as 1914, statute language from 1866 only gave married women ownership of property, not control, and legal commentary related only to debt relief, not to control rights.[a] The case cited in MacDonald, "On the Question of Court Activism," references only debt relief as well. Later statute books were searched, but no statutory update was located through 1920.
Earnings	Initial list of dates compiled from:
Geddes, R. Richard, and Sharon Tennyson. "Passage of the Married Women's Property Acts and Earnings Acts in the United States: 1850 to 1920." *Research in Economic History* 29 (2013): 145–89.
Exceptions:
An earlier earnings act was found for Mississippi, referencing "fruits of her personal labor." An earlier date was also found for Minnesota, based on the state's statute books. Maryland was updated to one year later based on its statute book: the session date was 1842, but the statute was passed in 1843. There are no dates listed for either California or Nevada. In both of these community-property states, earnings were not considered separate property unless a woman was living separately from her husband or if he granted prior agreement that earnings could be considered separate property. Otherwise, earnings were considered community property and controlled by the husband.[b]

(continued)

TABLE A.1

Sources of Statutes by Reform Type (*continued*)

Reform Type	Source Details
Sole trader	Initial list of dates compiled from: Khan, B. Zorina. "Married Women's Property Laws and Female Commercial Activity: Evidence from United States Patent Records, 1790–1895." *Journal of Economic History* 56, no. 2 (1996): 356–88. Exceptions: Dates for Wyoming, Nebraska, Washington, Massachusetts, Arkansas, Minnesota, Maine, Maryland, Florida, Idaho, Kentucky, Colorado, Arizona, California, Louisiana, Vermont, and Kansas were updated after consulting statute books. Dates for Delaware, Indiana, North Carolina, Virginia, Rhode Island, Missouri, New Mexico, Ohio, Tennessee, Arizona, and Oklahoma were added after consulting statute books. The West Virginia date listed in Khan, "Married Women's Property Laws," applies only to women living separately from their husbands, and no later date was found, so a date is not listed for West Virginia. A sole-trader act also could not be located for Utah; Khan lists 1895, but the legislature did not meet in 1895, and the Utah Constitution of 1895 does not address sole-trader rights.
Wills	Initial list of dates compiled from: Hoff, Joan. *Law, Gender, and Injustice.* New York: New York University Press, 1991. Exceptions: Dates for South Carolina, Montana, Vermont, Iowa, Kentucky, Maine, North Carolina, Delaware, Oklahoma, Missouri, New Mexico, Virginia, Wisconsin, and Mississippi were added after consulting statute books or state constitutions.

Reform Type	Source Details
	Dates for Wyoming, Louisiana, West Virginia, Rhode Island, Colorado, Dakota Territory, Michigan, Nebraska, Maryland, and Indiana were updated after consulting statute books. Georgia is an interesting case where testamentary rights were first granted through a court ruling, citing the Georgia code and statutes despite there being no specific language in the code or statutes granting these rights. I used the first year the Georgia code confirmed this without choosing to reverse the ruling.[c]

[a] See Orville A. Park et al., *Park's Annotated Code of the State of Georgia 1914*, vol. 2 (Atlanta, GA: Harrison, 1915).
[b] For California, see James M. Kerr, *Codes of California as Amended and in Force at the Close of the Forty-Third [Forty-Fourth] Session of the Legislature, 1919–[1921]*, 2nd ed. (San Francisco: Bender-Moss, 1920–1922), 316. Nevada's statute is identical to California's, and a codebook from 1930 cites the California code on this issue. See Curtis Hillyer, *Nevada Compiled Laws 1929* (San Francisco: Bender-Moss, 1930), 1011.
[c] *Urquhart v. Oliver*, 56 Ga. 344 (1876).

overlap by at least 80 percent, allowing up to two imperfections per phrase. These settings are based on previous research in political science and account for slight differences in language between two provisions.[2] I also set the software to ignore punctuation and capitalization.

I used this software to compare the text of both state constitutional provisions and statutes. The comparison of constitutional provisions showed that there are 108 total matching pairs of documents in which at least some constitutional language is shared. In the main analysis presented in chapter 4, I include *only* unique state pair matches. For example, both Texas and California ratified multiple constitutional provisions on the topic of married women's economic rights during the nineteenth century, so there are multiple matches between various versions of their constitutions. To avoid double counting, I analyzed only the earliest match (the Texas Constitution of 1845 and the California Constitution of 1849) but not matches occurring later in time. This approach also avoids including states matching to themselves, as when a state might

TABLE A.2
Reform Dating (Date of First Passage, Through 1919)

State	Debt-Free Separate Estates	Control and Management	Earnings	Wills	Sole Trader
Alabama	1846		1887	1846	
Arizona	1864	1871		1901	1864
Arkansas	1835	1873	1873	1868	1873
California	1850	1872		1874	1852
Colorado	1861	1861	1861	1861	1861
Connecticut	1845	1877	1877	1809	1877
Delaware	1865	1873	1873	1875	1873
Florida	1845		1892	1823	
Georgia	1866		1861	1882	
Idaho	1863	1903	1915	1887	1903
Illinois	1861	1861	1869	1872	1874
Indiana	1847	1879	1879	1852	1879
Iowa	1846	1873	1873	1873	1873
Kansas	1858	1858	1858	1858	1858
Kentucky	1846	1894	1873	1894	1894
Louisiana		1916		1870	1807
Maine	1844	1852	1857	1848	1866
Maryland	1843	1860	1843	1860	1898
Massachusetts	1855	1855	1846	1855	1855
Michigan	1844	1855	1911	1855	
Minnesota	1866	1869	1863	1869	1869

State	Debt-Free Separate Estates	Control and Management	Earnings	Wills	Sole Trader
Mississippi	1839	1880	1871	1880	1871
Missouri	1849	1875	1875	1866	1889
Montana	1864	1887	1887	1887	1874
Nebraska	1855	1871	1871	1881	1871
Nevada	1865	1873		1873	1873
New Hampshire	1860	1860	1867	1854	1876
New Jersey	1852	1852	1874	1864	1874
New Mexico	1884	1884		1901	1907
New York	1848	1848	1860	1849	1860
North Carolina	1849	1911	1913	1872	1911
North Dakota	1862	1877		1877	1877
Ohio	1846	1861	1861	1808	1887
Oklahoma	1890	1890		1890	1890
Oregon	1857	1878	1872	1853	1880
Pennsylvania	1848	1848	1872	1848	
Rhode Island	1844	1872	1872	1844	1893
South Carolina	1868	1868	1887	1868	1870
South Dakota	1862	1877		1877	1877
Tennessee	1850	1919	1919	1852	1919
Texas	1840	1913	1913	1840	
Utah	1872	1872	1897	1895	
Vermont	1847	1884	1888	1847	1880

(continued)

TABLE A.2

Reform Dating (Date of First Passage, Through 1919) *(continued)*

State	Debt-Free Separate Estates	Control and Management	Earnings	Wills	Sole Trader
Virginia	1877	1877	1888	1899	1888
Washington	1860	1881	1881	1881	1881
West Virginia	1868	1868	1891	1868	
Wisconsin	1850	1850	1872	1850	
Wyoming	1869	1869	1869	1869	1869

use very similar language from one constitution to the next but without copying from anther state (i.e., Maryland's constitutions in 1851 and 1864 contain identical language on married women's property rights, but that language does not match the language of constitutions of any other state). This latter sort of match obviously does not reflect copying or borrowing between states. This distinction left forty-two unique state pair matches for the main analysis.

Statute text required more cleaning before analysis. I cleaned the data by isolating the portions of statutes that were specific to each reform type and then removed statute numbers, effective dates, statute titles, and phrases that did not contain policy content, such as "Be it enacted by the General Assembly of the Territory of Arkansas." I isolated the text referring to each specific reform from a statute as a whole as much as possible. For example, if the same law granted debt-free separate estates and control of earnings in separate sections, the text referring to the former would be compared to other debt-free statutes, while the text referring to the latter would be compared to other earnings acts. In some cases, multiple new rights might be granted in the same section or even the same sentence of a statute, in which case that text is included in the analysis of each reform. I then ran cleaned text through WCopyfind using the settings described earlier.

States within each cluster (table A.3) are listed from earliest adopter to latest adopter. In each case, a state in the cluster borrowed at least 40 percent of its language from one or more of the earlier adopting states.

EVENT HISTORY MODELS

The dependent variable in an event history model is the amount of time that an observation—in this case a state or territory—is at "risk" of experiencing some event. Here, that "risk" is the passing of a particular type of reform.[3] The process by which states and territories then experienced the event of reform enactment can be modeled as either continuous or discrete. In their book on event history analysis, the political scientists Janet Box-Steffensmeier and Bradford Jones note that policy adoption through legislative processes can often best be modeled as discrete-time processes "since legislation can only be adopted during a legislative session."[4] In my analyses, I recorded the year in which each type of reform was first enacted—during either a legislative session or a state constitutional convention—and thus treat the data as discrete. As a result, I used logit models to estimate the probability that states (or territories) would enact a particular reform, conditional on the amount of time that passed without enactment and a set of covariates that might be associated with earlier or later passage.[5] Thus, if the probability that a particular reform would be enacted is indicated by $\Pr(y_{it} = 1) = \lambda_i$, then the discrete-time logit model has the following functional form:[6]

$$\log(\lambda_i / 1 - \lambda_i) = \beta_0 + \beta_1 Suffrage_i + \beta_2 SuffrageOrganization_i + \beta_3 PercentFemale_i + \beta_4 HomesteadAct_i + \beta_5 CommunityProperty_i + \beta_6 Territory_i + \beta_7 NeighborAdopt_i + \beta_8 Duration_i + \beta_9 Duration^2_i + \beta_{10} Duration^3_i.$$

Each of the independent variables is summarized in table A.4. The final three terms are duration-dependence controls to allow for the risk of statute passage to vary over time.[7]

I examined a variety of independent variables, which are summarized in table A.4, where they are given the same names as those in the logit model. Two independent variables capture the role of suffrage and suffrage movements. First, I included a variable indicating whether women could

TABLE A.3
Clusters of States Borrowing Statutory and Constitutional Text

Debt-Free Separate Estates	Control and Management	Earnings	Sole Trader	Wills	Constitutional Text
Mississippi, Maryland, Maine, Iowa	Mississippi, Tennessee	Maine, Iowa, Washington, Utah	California, Arizona, Montana	West Virginia, Virginia	Texas, California, Oregon, Nevada, Florida
New York, Wisconsin, New Jersey, West Virginia	New York, Delaware, Wisconsin, New Jersey, West Virginia	Kansas, New York, Colorado, Wyoming, Nebraska, Arkansas, Indiana	Oregon, Washington	New York, Wisconsin	Michigan, Alabama, North Carolina, Arkansas, South Dakota, North Dakota, Utah
Massachusetts, Kansas, Colorado	Massachusetts, Kansas, Colorado, Nebraska	Ohio, Missouri	Massachusetts, Kansas, New York, Colorado, Wyoming, Nebraska, Arkansas	Massachusetts, Kansas, Colorado	
Missouri, Nebraska, Dakota Territory	Dakota Territory, Oklahoma		Nevada, Dakota Territory, Ohio, Oklahoma, New Mexico	Ohio, Texas, Illinois	
California, Nevada	California, Nevada			Nevada, California, Dakota Territory, Idaho, Oklahoma	
Washington, Idaho, Montana	Ohio, Montana				
Illinois, Wyoming	Illinois, Wyoming				

TABLE A.4
Logit Models: Independent Variables

Women's Political Organizing/Power	
Suffrage*	Dummy variable for whether white woman could vote in a particular year in a state or territory (1 for voting rights; 0 for no voting rights). This variable measures full suffrage rights (not school-vote suffrage or presidential-vote suffrage, which did come earlier to women in some jurisdictions). *Observed range: 0–1; date range: 1869–1920.*
Suffrage Organization	Dummy variable for whether a state woman suffrage organization was organized in a given year *or* woman suffrage had passed in that state or territory (1 for the presence of a suffrage organization or voting rights and 0 otherwise). *Observed range: 0–1; date range: 1869–1920.*
Political Context	
Percent Female	Percentage of the state or territorial population that was female in a given year, according to US census data. This figure is linearly interpolated between census years. *Observed range: 4.63–51.89 percent.*
Homestead Act	Dummy variable for whether a state or territory had passed a homestead-exemption act (1) or not (0). *Observed range: 0–1; date range: 1839–1920.*
Community Property	Dummy variable for whether a state or territory was a community-property regime (1) or not (0). *Observed range: 0–1.*
Territory	Dummy variable indicating territorial status (1) or statehood status (0). *Observed range: 0–1.*
Diffusion	
Neighbor Adopt	Dummy variable indicating whether any neighboring state had adopted a given reform in a given year (1) or not (0). *Observed range: 0–1.*

* The variable names in column 1 align with the variable names in the discrete-time logit model given in the "Methods Appendix."

vote at the state level because women in several states were granted the right to vote prior to the ratification of the Nineteenth Amendment in 1920. Although states were diverse in terms of how they granted suffrage rights to women (from allowing women to vote only in school-related elections to giving them full suffrage), I included this latter measure here because this broad electoral power would have been most relevant to whether women could place pressure on elected officials at the ballot box.[8] Second, I included a measure for the existence of a state-level woman suffrage organization, which provides a rough indication of suffrage-related women's organizing within each state.[9]

I also included a series of variables that capture the political context of states and territories. The "Percent Female" variable indicates the percentage of the population of each state that was female. As we saw earlier, gender imbalances could motivate reform. Western states and territories with few women sometimes passed economic rights laws to attract more women to move to the frontier, and southern states that had lost men of marriageable age to the Civil War wanted to protect propertied women from financial ruin if they married men lower in the class structure. This variable is based on U.S. census data.[10] Between census years, I used linear interpolation to estimate the percentage of women in a state's or territory's population. Some census data do exist for territories in the years prior to statehood, which is important given that some territories, such as Wyoming and Colorado, passed reforms before they became states.

Homestead-exemption acts are another important piece of context for the passage of married women's economic rights reforms. These laws provided debt relief to families and were often linked in political rhetoric to reforms regarding debt-free separate estates for married women in particular.[11] Another variable indicates community-property states because these states had a different baseline property rights system for married couples.[12] Some territories switched from a common-law to a community-property regime upon gaining statehood, in which case I coded them 0 before statehood and 1 thereafter. Finally, I included as a final measure of political context a dummy variable for whether a political unit was a territory or state in a given year. Although some scholars include separate equity courts in statistical analyses of married women's property laws, I do not do so here. Some states abolished equity courts during this period (such as New York), but, more importantly, the type of rights granted through equity jurisprudence were available not only through separate equity or chancery courts but also, depending on the state, sometimes through common-law courts or state legislatures.[13] Thus, the mere existence of separate equity courts did not necessarily indicate the presence of greater or different property rights for (wealthy) married women.

Finally, as a rough way to measure the geographic diffusion of married women's economic rights reforms among the states, I included a dummy variable indicating whether a neighboring state had passed a given reform in a given year.[14] For example, by the time Alabama passed its debt-free separate-estates law in 1846, two states neighboring Alabama had already passed a similar law (Mississippi and Florida), so this variable would take on a value of 1 in that year. Did Mississippi's early adoption of a debt-free provision encourage neighboring states to copy this sort of policy? Although the copying of reforms clearly could and did take place between states that were not neighbors, this neighboring-states variable allows for a rough measure of geographic closeness, with the idea that neighboring states might most likely observe the passage of married women's economic rights reforms, engage in communication among political elites, and experience similar conditions encouraging the passage of these laws. Because this diffusion variable already picks up on geographic variation, I did not include separate regional controls.

Acknowledgments

I am deeply grateful to the many people who have supported both my research and me as a scholar and a person throughout the process of writing this book. My interest in American political development began when I was an undergraduate. I read major works in the subfield and conducted research with Ron Kahn, my adviser at Oberlin College. This specific project began as a PhD dissertation, and I am thankful to my dissertation committee and others at the University of California at Berkeley who supported the project at that stage, especially Eric Schickler, Sean Gailmard, Devin Caughey, and Phil Rocco. Many thanks also to Adam Berinsky and Leanne Powner, who provided invaluable insight on the process of transforming the project from dissertation to book. My editor at Columbia University Press, Stephen Wesley, as well as the production team at the press were enormously helpful in walking me through the publishing process.

I am indebted to the many people who have offered thoughtful feedback on this project at conferences, workshops, and writing groups, including Michael Pisapia, Shamira Gelbman, Eileen McDonough, Julia Azari, Abby Matthews, Lia Merivaki, Anne Bloom, Liz Gerber, and the members of the junior faculty writing group and attendees of the Center on American Politics research workshop at the University of Denver. I was especially fortunate to receive a grant from the Center on American

Politics to hold a book conference in the winter of 2022, and the discussions from this day were very important in shaping the final manuscript. I thank Julie Novkov, Josh Wilson, Alena Wolflink, Nancy Wadsworth, Priscilla Yamin, Chloe Thurston, Emily Zackin, and Seth Masket for their careful reading and helpful comments at this conference. I also thank the publisher's peer reviewers, whose suggestions for revisions and encouragement about the value of the project were very beneficial.

Many people offered assistance with specific parts of this project, without whom this book would not be what it is. Holly McCammon and David Bateman generously shared data with me. Michael P. Fix, Nathan Kalmoe, and Tate Stiedley shared code and discussed methodological details. Chris Brown and Kate Crowe at the University of Denver, Brian Herder at the Kansas State Library, and Douglas Amos at the Oklahoma Department of Libraries helped me navigate sources. Arjen Bijl, Jesse Acevedo, and Cathy Durso helped me think through and create data visualizations, and Noelle Strom, Audra Sim, and Lexi Gillson provided invaluable research assistance. Andrea Wright and Jeanine Porck were accountability buddies par excellence with weekly calls throughout the COVID shutdown. Finally, I am indebted to Doug Booth, Darlene Squires, Samantha Register, and Katie Aker for their help with budgets, travel, and other practical aspects of this project.

I could never have written this book without the above-and-beyond support of my friends and family. I owe great thanks to my husband, Tim, and daughter, June; my parents, Laura and Jim; my sister, Anna; Pastor Chris and the rest of my church community at Sixth Avenue United Church of Christ; and the many friends who have cheered me on and lifted me up along the way (special shoutouts to Liz and Erin!). You all have been incredibly patient with me and have seen me through the ups and downs of writing this book. Your unconditional support and love are what made it possible for me to finish it.

Notes

INTRODUCTION

1. "Radical Legal Changes—Married Woman's Rights in Mississippi," *Chicago Daily Tribune*, September 13, 1880.
2. Elizabeth Gaspar Brown, "Husband and Wife: Memorandum on the Mississippi Woman's Law of 1839," *Michigan Law Review* 42, no. 6 (1944): 1110–21; Sandra Moncrief, "The Mississippi Married Women's Property Act of 1839," *Journal of Mississippi History* 47, no. 2 (1985): 110–25; Joseph A. Ranney, *In the Wake of Slavery: Civil War, Civil Rights, and the Reconstruction of Southern Law* (Westport, CT: Praeger, 2006); "Removal of the Disabilities of Married Women in Mississippi," *American Law Review* 26 (1892): 115–16.
3. J. Ross Browne, ed., *Report of the Debates in the Convention of California on the Formation of the State Constitution* (Washington, DC: J. T. Towers, 1850), 257–69.
4. For an excellent discussion of married women's property laws and property ownership by Black women in South Carolina, see Damita L. Green, "'Occupation: Land Owner': African American Female Property Ownership in Clarendon County, South Carolina, 1870–1910," MA thesis, Morgan State University, 2019.
5. See, for example, Emily Zackin, *Looking for Rights in All the Wrong Places: Why State Constitutions Contain America's Positive Rights* (Princeton, NJ: Princeton University Press, 2013); Robinson Woodward-Burns, *Hidden Laws: How State Constitutions Stabilize American Politics* (New Haven, CT: Yale University Press, 2021).

6. Gretchen Ritter, "Gender as a Category of Analysis in American Political Development," in *Political Women and American Democracy*, ed. Christina Wolbrecht, Lisa Baldez, and Karen Beckwith (New York: Cambridge University Press, 2008), 26.
7. Louis Hartz, *The Liberal Tradition in America* (New York: Harcourt, Brace & World, 1955); Theodore J. Lowi, *The End of Liberalism: Ideology, Policy, and the Crisis of Public Authority* (New York: Norton, 1969).
8. Duncan Bell, "What Is Liberalism?," *Political Theory* 42, no. 6 (2014): 682.
9. James A. Morone, "Political Culture: Consensus, Conflict, and Culture War," in *The Oxford Handbook of American Political Development*, ed. Richard Valelly, Suzanne Mettler, and Robert Lieberman (Oxford: Oxford University Press, 2016), 132–47.
10. See, for example, Karen Orren on the liberalization of labor politics, Rogers Smith on liberalization and citizenship, as well as Eileen McDonough on the persistence of feudalism in the family: Karen Orren, *Belated Feudalism: Labor, the Law, and Liberal Development in the United States* (Cambridge: Cambridge University Press, 1991); Rogers M. Smith, *Civic Ideals: Conflicting Visions of Citizenship in U.S. History* (New Haven, CT: Yale University Press, 1997); Eileen McDonagh, "The Feudal Family Versus American Political Development: From Separate Spheres to Woman Suffrage," in *Stating the Family: New Directions in the Study of American Politics*, ed. Julie Novkov and Carol Nackenoff (Lawrence: University Press of Kansas, 2020), 164–96.
11. An important exception here is Kathleen Sullivan's work on married women's property acts, which traces the development of legal rights discourse around women's rights through this period. See Kathleen Sullivan, *Constitutional Context: Women and Rights Discourse in Nineteenth-Century America* (Baltimore, MD: Johns Hopkins University Press, 2007).

1. LIFE UNDER COVERTURE AND HOW IT CHANGED

1. These categories were derived based on my reading of multiple statutes and/or constitutional provisions for each state or territory as well as a careful review of the secondary literature.
2. See Marlene Stein Wortman, *Women in American Law: From Colonial Times to the New Deal* (New York: Holmes & Meier, 1985), 14. As discussed later in the chapter, there were some exceptions to and variations on the strict rules of coverture, each exception dependent on state law.
3. Linda Kerber, *Women of the Republic: Intellect and Ideology in Revolutionary America* (Chapel Hill: University of North Carolina Press, 1980), 152.

4. Sandra F. VanBurkleo, *"Belonging to the World": Women's Rights and American Constitutional Culture* (New York: Oxford University Press, 2001), 10.
5. In return, husbands were required to support their wives financially. See Hendrik Hartog, *Man and Wife in America: A History* (Cambridge, MA: Harvard University Press, 2000), 115.
6. Marylynn Salmon, *Women and the Law of Property in Early America* (Chapel Hill: University of North Carolina Press, 1986), 15.
7. Salmon, *Women and the Law of Property*, 53–54.
8. B. Zorina Khan, "Married Women's Property Laws and Female Commercial Activity: Evidence from United States Patent Records, 1790–1895," *Journal of Economic History* 56, no. 2 (1996): 360.
9. Hartog, *Man and Wife in America*, 115–16.
10. Norma Basch, *In the Eyes of the Law: Women, Marriage, and Property in Nineteenth-Century New York* (Ithaca, NY: Cornell University Press, 1982), 65; Joan Hoff, *Law, Gender, and Injustice* (New York: New York University Press, 1991), 132.
11. Nancy Isenberg, *Sex and Citizenship in Antebellum America* (Chapel Hill: University of North Carolina Press, 1998), 162–63; Jill Elaine Hasday, "Contest and Consent: A Legal History of Marital Rape," *California Law Review* 88, no. 5 (2000): 1373–506.
12. A few women had voting rights prior to the early 1800s, and women began to be enfranchised at the state level starting in 1869, but the vast majority of women were disenfranchised under coverture. The timing of voting rights and economic rights reform passage is discussed further in later chapters.
13. Rebecca M. Ryan, "The Sex Right: A Legal History of the Marital Rape Exemption," *Law & Social Inquiry* 20, no. 4 (1995): 941–1001; Equal Credit Opportunity Act, 15 U.S.C. 1691 (1974).
14. Salmon, *Women and the Law of Property*, 44–56.
15. Salmon, *Women and the Law of Property*, 57.
16. Basch, *In the Eyes of the Law*, 20.
17. Basch, *In the Eyes of the Law*.
18. Basch, *In the Eyes of the Law*, 75–79.
19. Salmon, *Women and the Law of Property*, 11.
20. Peter Winthrop Bardaglio, *Reconstructing the Household: Families, Sex, and the Law in the Nineteenth-Century South*, Studies in Legal History (Chapel Hill: University of North Carolina Press, 1995), 31–32. See also Norma Basch, "Invisible Women: The Legal Fiction of Marital Unity in Nineteenth-Century America," in *Women and the American Legal Order*, ed. Karen J. Maschke (New York: Garland, 1997), 44–45.

21. Joseph A. Ranney, "Anglicans, Merchants, and Feminists: A Comparative Study of the Evolution of Married Women's Rights in Virginia, New York, and Wisconsin," *William & Mary Journal of Race, Gender, and Social Justice* 6, no. 3 (2000): 496.
22. VanBurkleo, *"Belonging to the World,"* 11.
23. See Basch, *In the Eyes of the Law*, and Kerber, *Women of the Republic*. Kathleen Sullivan argues that reformers could have pushed for an expansion of equity protections, which could theoretically have set the law and jurisprudence around gender discrimination on a different path, one more conscious of the social context and lived experiences of married women. But, ultimately, reformers, male or female, did not pursue this strategy. Starting in the late 1830s, states instead began to codify married women's economic rights in ways that both extended some of the equitable exceptions to coverture, moving them out of equity courts and making them more widely available to married women from a broader cross-section of society, and liberalized married women's economic rights more broadly by granting entirely new rights. See Kathleen Sullivan, *Constitutional Context: Women and Rights Discourse in Nineteenth-Century America* (Baltimore, MD: Johns Hopkins University Press, 2007), 4–15.
24. Sara Brooks Sundberg, "Women and Property in Early Louisiana: Legal Systems at Odds," *Journal of the Early Republic* 32, no. 4 (2012): 633–65; Daniel MacDonald, "On the Question of Court Activism and Economic Interests in Nineteenth-Century Married Women's Property Law," in *Law and Social Economics: Essays in Ethical Values for Theory, Practice, and Policy*, ed. Mark D. White (New York: Palgrave Macmillan, 2015), 139–60; Raquel Fernández, "Women's Rights and Development," *Journal of Economic Growth* 19, no. 1 (2014): 37–80.
25. Clarence J. Morrow, "Matrimonial Property Law in Louisiana," in *Matrimonial Property Law*, ed. W. Friedmann (Toronto: Carswell, 1955), 29–88.
26. Alice Kessler-Harris, *Out to Work: A History of Wage-Earning Women in the United States* (New York: Oxford University Press, 1982), 184.
27. South Carolina is an important exception here, discussed further in the case studies in chapter 6.
28. William B. Scott, *In Pursuit of Happiness: American Conceptions of Property from the Seventeenth to the Twentieth Century* (Bloomington: Indiana University Press, 1977), 92–93.
29. Many thanks to my research assistant Arjen Bijl for creating these maps.
30. Megan Benson, "*Fisher v. Allen*: The Southern Origins of Married Women's Property Acts," *Journal of Southern Legal History* 6 (1998): 97–122; Sandra Moncrief, "The Mississippi Married Women's Property Act of 1839," *Journal of Mississippi History* 47, no. 2 (1985): 110–25.

31. During the earliest years of married women's property rights reforms, southern territories and states such as Florida and Arkansas were considered part of the frontier, so scholarly analyses of the frontier do not consider the West exclusively.
32. Michael B. Dougan, "The Arkansas Married Woman's Property Law," *Arkansas Historical Quarterly* 46, no. 1 (1987): 3–26.
33. Laurel Clark Shire, *The Threshold of Manifest Destiny: Gender and National Expansion in Florida* (Philadelphia: University of Pennsylvania Press, 2016); Laurel A. Clark, "The Rights of a Florida Wife: Slavery, U.S. Expansion, and Married Women's Property Law," *Journal of Women's History* 22, no. 4 (2010): 39–63; Mark M. Carroll, *Homesteads Ungovernable: Families, Sex, Race, and the Law in Frontier Texas, 1823–1860* (Austin: University of Texas Press, 2001). Note that parts of the South were still considered to be "the frontier" in the early 1800s.
34. Joyce L. Broussard, "Naked Before the Law: Married Women and the Servant Ideal in Antebellum Natchez," in *Mississippi Women: Their Histories, Their Lives*, ed. Martha H. Swain, Elizabeth Anne Payne, and Marjorie Julian Spruill (Athens: University of Georgia Press, 2010), 61.
35. See Jessica M. Lepler, *The Many Panics of 1837: People, Politics, and the Creation of a Transatlantic Financial Crisis* (New York: Cambridge University Press, 2013); Elmus Wicker, *Banking Panics of the Gilded Age* (Cambridge: Cambridge University Press, 2000); Hannah Catherine Davies, *Transatlantic Speculations: Globalization and the Panics of 1873* (New York : Columbia University Press, 2018); Brigitte Koenig, "Panic of 1907," in *Encyclopedia of American Recessions and Depressions*, ed. Daniel J. Leab (Santa Barbara, CA: ABC-CLIO, 2014), 329–46; Hugh Rockoff, "Crisis of 1857," in *Business Cycles and Depressions: An Encyclopedia*, ed. David Glasner (New York: Garland, 1997), 128–31.
36. Brian Bixby, "Panic of 1837," in *Encyclopedia of American Recessions and Depressions*, ed. Leab, 133–51; Wicker, *Banking Panics*.
37. See Bixby, "Panic of 1837," 144–45; and Michael Shapiro, "Panic of 1857," in *Encyclopedia of American Recessions and Depressions*, ed. Leab, 191.
38. Edward J. Balleisen, *Navigating Failure: Bankruptcy and Commercial Society in Antebellum America* (Chapel Hill: University of North Carolina Press, 2001); Basch, *In the Eyes of the Law*.
39. Suzanne D. Lebsock, "Radical Reconstruction and the Property Rights of Southern Women," *Journal of Southern History* 43, no. 2 (1977): 195–216; Linda E. Speth, "The Married Women's Property Acts, 1839–1965: Reform, Reaction, or Revolution?," in *Women and the Law: A Social Historical Perspective*, ed. D. Kelly Weisberg (Cambridge, MA: Schenkman, 1982), 69–91; Richard H. Chused, "Married Women's Property Law: 1800–1850," *Georgetown Law Journal* 71

(1983): 1359–425; Moncrief, "Mississippi Married Women's Property Act"; Dougan, "Arkansas Married Woman's Property Law"; Hoff, *Law, Gender, and Injustice*; Broussard, "Naked Before the Law."

40. Peggy A. Rabkin, *Fathers to Daughters: The Legal Foundations of Female Emancipation* (Westport, CT: Greenwood Press, 1980); Basch, *In the Eyes of the Law*.
41. Gregory Alexander, *Commodity & Propriety: Competing Visions of Property in American Legal Thought, 1776–1970* (Chicago: University of Chicago Press, 1997), 1.
42. See especially Rabkin, *Fathers to Daughters*.
43. Kathleen Elizabeth Lazarou, *Concealed Under Petticoats: Married Women's Property and the Law of Texas, 1840–1913*, American Legal and Constitutional History: A Garland Series of Outstanding Dissertations (New York: Garland, 1986); Elizabeth Bowles Warbasse, *The Changing Legal Rights of Married Women: 1800–1861*, American Legal and Constitutional History: A Garland Series of Outstanding Dissertations (New York: Garland, 1987); Nancy F. Cott, *Public Vows: A History of Marriage and the Nation* (Cambridge, MA: Harvard University Press, 2000); Holly J. McCammon, Sandra C. Arch, and Erin M. Bergner, "A Radical Demand Effect: Early US Feminists and the Married Women's Property Acts," *Social Science History* 38, nos. 1–2 (2014): 221–50.
44. Basch, *In the Eyes of the Law*; Hoff, *Law, Gender, and Injustice*; Peggy A. Rabkin, "The Origins of Law Reform: The Social Significance of the Nineteenth-Century Codification Movement and Its Contribution to the Passage of the Early Married Women's Property Acts," *Buffalo Law Review* 24 (1975): 683–760.
45. Rabkin, "Origins of Law Reform"; Rabkin, *Fathers to Daughters*; Lebsock, "Radical Reconstruction"; Chused, "Married Women's Property Law"; Dougan, "Arkansas Married Woman's Property Law."
46. Reva B. Siegel, "Home as Work: The First Woman's Rights Claims Concerning Wives' Household Labor, 1850–1880," *Yale Law Journal* 103, no. 5 (1994): 1073–217. For a study that addresses women's failed efforts to convince legislators to recognize joint property claims in a different geographic context, see Donna C. Schuele, "Community Property Law and the Politics of Married Women's Rights in Nineteenth-Century California," in *The American West: Interactions, Intersections, and Injunctions*, ed. Gordon Morris Bakken and Brenda Farrington (New York: Garland, 2001), 413–49.
47. Richard A. Rapaport, "Relationship of the Women's Movement to the Passage of Married Women's Property Acts in the Mid–Nineteenth Century," Stanford Law School, Stanford University, 1973; Warbasse, *Changing Legal Rights of Married Women*; McCammon, Arch, and Bergner, "A Radical Demand Effect."
48. Rapaport, "Relationship of the Women's Movement"; Daniel Carpenter, *Democracy by Petition: Popular Politics in Transformation, 1790–1870* (Cambridge, MA: Harvard University Press, 2021).

49. Carpenter, *Democracy by Petition*, 383.
50. McCammon, Arch, and Bergner, "A Radical Demand Effect."
51. MacDonald, "On the Question of Court Activism"; Sara L. Zeigler, "Uniformity and Conformity: Regionalism and the Adjudication of the Married Women's Property Acts," *Polity* 28, no. 4 (1996): 467–95; Reva B. Siegel, "The Modernization of Marital Status Law: Adjudicating Wives' Rights to Earning, 1860–1930," *Georgetown Law Journal* 82 (1995): 2127–211.
52. See, for example, Khan, "Married Women's Property Laws."
53. See R. Richard Geddes and Sharon Tennyson, "Passage of the Married Women's Property Acts and Earnings Acts in the United States: 1850 to 1920," *Research in Economic History* 29 (2013): 145–89.
54. Rick Geddes and Dean Lueck, "The Gains from Self-Ownership and the Expansion of Women's Rights," *American Economic Review* 92, no. 4 (2002): 1079–92; Fernández, "Women's Rights and Development."
55. Jayme S. Lemke, "Interjurisdictional Competition and the Married Women's Property Acts," *Public Choice* 166, no. 3 (2016): 291–313.
56. Carole Shammas, "Re-assessing the Married Women's Property Acts," *Journal of Women's History* 6, no. 1 (1994): 9–30; Khan, "Married Women's Property Laws."
57. Catherine L. McDevitt and James R. Irwin, "The Narrowing of the Gender Wealth Gap Across the Nineteenth-Century United States," *Social Science History* 41, no. 2 (2017): 255–81.
58. Evan Roberts, *Women's Rights and Women's Labor: Married Women's Property Laws and Labor Force Participation*, working paper (Minneapolis: Minnesota Population Center, University of Minnesota, 2014).
59. Rick Geddes, Dean Lueck, and Sharon Tennyson, "Human Capital Accumulation and the Expansion of Women's Economic Rights," *Journal of Law and Economics* 55, no. 4 (2012): 839–67; Roberts, *Women's Rights and Women's Labor*.
60. Roberts, *Women's Rights and Women's Labor*.
61. Daniel MacDonald and Yasemin Dildar, "Married Women's Economic Independence and Divorce in the Nineteenth- and Early-Twentieth-Century United States," *Social Science History* 42, no. 3 (2018): 601–29.
62. Hazem Alshaikhmubarak, R. Richard Geddes, and Shoshana A. Grossbard, "Single Motherhood and the Abolition of Coverture in the United States," *Journal of Empirical Legal Studies* 16, no. 1 (2019): 94–118.
63. Moshe Hazan, David Weiss, and Hosny Zoabi, "Women's Liberation as a Financial Innovation," *Journal of Finance* 74, no. 6 (2019): 2915–56; Peter Koudijs and Laura Salisbury, "Limited Liability and Investment: Evidence from Changes in Marital Property Laws in the US South, 1840–1850," *Journal of Financial Economics* 138, no. 1 (2020): 1–26.

2. MARRIED WOMEN'S RIGHTS REFORMS IN AMERICAN POLITICAL DEVELOPMENT

1. John W. Kingdon, *Agendas, Alternatives, and Public Policies*, 2nd ed. (New York: Longman, 1995). Kingdon's analysis focuses on the federal government, where policy windows are fleeting because of limited agendas, multiple veto points, and constraints on action. Married women's property acts were passed in the states, so sometimes there were fewer veto points—as in constitutional conventions, where delegates merely needed a simple majority vote to include a married women's provision in the new document. And, of course, there were forty-seven territories and states, so even if reforms stalled in one state, they progressed in many other venues. Despite the different context, married women's property acts did operate in many ways as a solution in search of a problem in the nineteenth century.
2. On women's vulnerability to exploitation, see Suzanne D. Lebsock, "Radical Reconstruction and the Property Rights of Southern Women," *Journal of Southern History* 43, no. 2 (1977): 195–216.
3. Priscilla Yamin, *American Marriage: A Political Institution* (Philadelphia: University of Pennsylvania Press, 2012), 11.
4. Maryland Const. of 1867, art. 3, §2; Mississippi Const. of 1890, art. 3, §94.
5. Given the involvement of multiple courts in many states, this statement is not absolute. Courts occasionally interpreted reforms very broadly or even struck down the laws as unconstitutional. However, these exceptions were far from the norm in state courts. See, for example, *Holmes v. Holmes*, 4 Barbour 295 (1848), and *White v. White*, 5 Barbour 474 (1849), both in New York, as well as *Pelzer v. Campbell*, 15 SC 581 (1881), in South Carolina.
6. Norma Basch, *In the Eyes of the Law: Women, Marriage, and Property in Nineteenth-Century New York* (Ithaca, NY: Cornell University Press, 1982); Reva B. Siegel, "The Modernization of Marital Status Law: Adjudicating Wives' Rights to Earning, 1860–1930," *Georgetown Law Journal* 82 (1995): 2127–211; Sara L. Zeigler, "Uniformity and Conformity: Regionalism and the Adjudication of the Married Women's Property Acts," *Polity* 28, no. 4 (1996): 467–95.
7. From a transcript of the convention given in the *Charleston News and Courier*, October 1, 1895.
8. An important exception was a married women's property act concerning women in Washington, DC, whose property rights were governed by Congress. This law was passed in 1869, but efforts to pass a national reform never gained traction. See Jean H. Baker, *Women and the U.S. Constitution, 1776–1920*, New Essays on American Constitutional History (Washington, DC: American Historical Association, 2009), 22. See also Richard H.

Chused, "The Oregon Donation Act of 1850 and Nineteenth Century Federal Married Women's Property Law," *Law and History Review* 2, no. 1 (1984): 44–78.
9. David D. Meyer, "The Constitutionalization of Family Law," *Family Law Quarterly* 42, no. 3 (2008): 529–72.
10. *Frontiero v. Richardson*, 411 U.S. 677 (1973), 685.

3. SOCIAL MOVEMENTS AND STATE POWER: REFORM IN STATE LEGISLATURES

1. Chapter 1 outlines this evidence in greater detail.
2. Elizabeth Bowles Warbasse, *The Changing Legal Rights of Married Women: 1800–1861*, American Legal and Constitutional History: A Garland Series of Outstanding Dissertations (New York: Garland, 1987), 57.
3. Kathleen Sullivan, *Constitutional Context: Women and Rights Discourse in Nineteenth-Century America* (Baltimore, MD: Johns Hopkins University Press, 2007).
4. See, for example, Holly J. McCammon, Sandra C. Arch, and Erin M. Bergner, "A Radical Demand Effect: Early US Feminists and the Married Women's Property Acts," *Social Science History* 38, nos. 1–2 (2014): 221–50; Richard A. Rapaport, "Relationship of the Women's Movement to the Passage of Married Women's Property Acts in the Mid–Nineteenth Century," Stanford Law School, Stanford University, 1973; Peggy A. Rabkin, "The Origins of Law Reform: The Social Significance of the Nineteenth-Century Codification Movement and Its Contribution to the Passage of the Early Married Women's Property Acts," *Buffalo Law Review* 24 (1975): 683–760; Linda E. Speth, "The Married Women's Property Acts, 1839–1965: Reform, Reaction, or Revolution?," in *Women and the Law: A Social Historical Perspective*, ed. D. Kelly Weisberg (Cambridge, MA: Schenkman, 1982), 69–91; Sullivan, *Constitutional Context*.
5. *Council Journal of the Legislative Assembly of the Territory of Colorado. First Session [1861]* (Denver: Thos. Gibson, Colorado Republican and Herald Office, 1862), 6.
6. Keith Eugene Melder, *Beginnings of Sisterhood: The American Woman's Rights Movement, 1800–1850*, Studies in the Life of Women (New York: Schocken, 1977), 144.
7. Reva B. Siegel, "Home as Work: The First Woman's Rights Claims Concerning Wives' Household Labor, 1850–1880," *Yale Law Journal* 103, no. 5 (1994): 1073–217.
8. Karen O'Connor, *Women's Organizations' Use of the Courts* (Lexington, MA: Lexington Books, 1980).

9. Karen Sánchez-Eppler, "Bodily Bonds: The Intersecting Rhetorics of Feminism and Abolition," *Representations*, no. 24 (1988): 29.
10. Blanche Glassman Hersh, *The Slavery of Sex: Feminist-Abolitionists in America* (Urbana: University of Illinois Press, 1978), 48.
11. Warbasse, *Changing Legal Rights of Married Women*, 248; Siegel, "Home as Work," 1098.
12. Joseph A. Ranney, *A Legal History of Mississippi: Race, Class, and the Struggle for Opportunity* (Jackson: University Press of Mississippi, 2019), 67.
13. Stanton's speech was printed in the *Una*, April 1, 1854.
14. Mary Livermore, quoted in Amy Dru Stanley, *From Bondage to Contract: Wage Labor, Marriage, and the Market in the Age of Slave Emancipation* (Cambridge: Cambridge University Press, 1998), 485.
15. DC Court of Claims case quoted in *Woman's Journal*, May 23, 1874.
16. Amy Dru Stanley, "Conjugal Bonds and Wage Labor: Rights of Contract in the Age of Emancipation," *Journal of American History* 75, no. 2 (1988): 484–85; Siegel, "Home as Work," 1176.
17. Peter Winthrop Bardaglio, *Reconstructing the Household: Families, Sex, and the Law in the Nineteenth-Century South*, Studies in Legal History (Chapel Hill: University of North Carolina Press, 1995), 9; Gregory Alexander, *Commodity & Propriety: Competing Visions of Property in American Legal Thought, 1776–1970* (Chicago: University of Chicago Press, 1997), 169.
18. Rabkin, "Origins of Law Reform," 686.
19. Norma Basch, *In the Eyes of the Law: Women, Marriage, and Property in Nineteenth-Century New York* (Ithaca, NY: Cornell University Press, 1982), 37–38.
20. "Radical Legal Changes—Married Woman's Rights in Mississippi," *Chicago Daily Tribune*, September 13, 1880.
21. Revised Code of the Statute Laws of the State of Mississippi (1880), chap. 42, §1167.
22. "Removal of the Disabilities of Married Women in Mississippi," *American Law Review* 26 (1892): 115.
23. Dunbar Rowland, *Courts, Judges, and Lawyers of Mississippi, 1798–1935* (Jackson, MS: Hederman Bros., 1935), 107.
24. *Journal of the Senate of the State of Mississippi* (Jackson, MS: J. L. Power, 1880), 40–42.
25. This issue of legal complexity created by piecemeal reforms is discussed in more detail in chapter 6.
26. Rosamond Parma, "The History of the Adoption of the Codes of California," *Law Library Journal* 22 (1929): 14–15; Henry M. Field, *The Life of David Dudley Field* (New York: Scribner's, 1898), 74–75, 78.

27. Rabkin, "Origins of Law Reform," 715.
28. *New York Field Codes 1850–1865*, vol. 3: *The Civil Code of the State of New York* (1865; reprint, Union, NJ: Lawbook Exchange, 1998), §§75–85, 320–21, and 337.
29. *Civil Code of the State of New York*, §§76–77 and 320.
30. Field, *The Life of David Dudley Field*, 86–88. See also Daun van Ee, *David Dudley Field and the Reconstruction of the Law*, American Legal and Constitutional History: A Garland Series of Outstanding Dissertations (New York: Garland, 1986), 332–35, on Field's failure to have his codes adopted in New York; and Alison Reppy, "The Field Codification Concept," in *David Dudley Field: Centenary Essays*, ed. Alison Reppy (New York: New York University School of Law, 1949), 17–54.
31. Field wrote multiple codes (five in total). The civil code is one of them. It is also the most widely adopted and tends to be referred to as the "Field Code." California, Montana, Idaho, South Dakota, and North Dakota adopted large portions of Field's civil code, which included his provisions on married women's property and economic rights. See Maurice E. Harrison, "The First Half-Century of the California Civil Code," *California Law Review* 10, no. 3 (1922): 187. In "The Field Codification Concept," Alison Reppy also adds Georgia to this list.
32. William Wirt Blume, "Adoption in California of the Field Code of Civil Procedure: A Chapter in American Legal History," *Hastings Law Journal* 17 (1966): 701–2.
33. Blume, "Adoption in California of the Field Code of Civil Procedure," 707.
34. Albert Hart, *The Civil Code of the State of California* (San Francisco: Sumner Whitney, 1880), §§155–81.
35. Donna Clare Schuele, "'A Robbery to the Wife': Culture, Gender and Marital Property in California Law and Politics, 1850–1890," PhD diss., University of California, Berkeley, 1999, 201–2.
36. Schuele, "'Robbery to the Wife,'" 203.
37. McCammon, Arch, and Bergner, "A Radical Demand Effect," 235.
38. Rabkin, "Origins of Law Reform."
39. Rabkin, "Origins of Law Reform," 716–20; Marlene Stein Wortman, *Women in American Law: From Colonial Times to the New Deal* (New York: Holmes & Meier, 1985), 119.
40. Rabkin, "Origins of Law Reform," 715.
41. Alison D. Morantz, "There's No Place Like Home: Homestead Exemption and Judicial Constructions of Family in Nineteenth-Century America," *Law and History Review* 24, no. 2 (2006): 254; Paul Goodman, "The Emergence of Homestead Exemption in the United States: Accommodation and Resistance to the Market Revolution, 1840–1880," *Journal of American History* 80, no. 2 (1993): 483, 488.

42. Goodman, "Emergence of Homestead Exemption," 470.
43. Goodman, "Emergence of Homestead Exemption," 472.
44. Claire Priest, "Creating an American Property Law: Alienability and Its Limits in American History," *Harvard Law Review* 120, no. 2 (2006): 455–56.
45. Chapters 4 and 5 explore these processes in more detail.
46. *Laws of the State of Missouri [Fifteenth General Assembly]* (Jefferson, MO: Hampton L. Boon, 1849), 67–68.
47. Goodman, "Emergence of Homestead Exemption," 488.
48. Morantz, "There's No Place Like Home," 258.
49. Morantz, "There's No Place Like Home," 266.
50. For example, Amanda Ray argues that Republican Party politics was especially important to the passage of married women's property acts in Reconstruction-era West Virginia. See Amanda J. Ray, "The Impact of Statehood and Republican Politics on Women's Legal Rights in West Virginia, 1863–1872," MA thesis, West Virginia University, 2001.
51. For my examination, I used "National Political Party Platforms," in *The American Presidency Project*, ed. John T. Woolley and Gerhard Peters (Santa Barbara: University of California, 1999–2020), http://www.presidency.ucsb.edu/platforms.php.
52. Republican Party platform, 1872, in "National Political Party Platforms."
53. Republican Party platform, 1876, in "National Political Party Platforms."
54. Republican Party platform, 1896, 1908, 1912, 1920, in "National Political Party Platforms."
55. Democratic Party platform, 1908, 1916, 1920, in "National Political Party Platforms."
56. See chapter 4 for more details on partisanship and constitutional conventions.
57. Elmus Wicker, *Banking Panics of the Gilded Age* (Cambridge: Cambridge University Press, 2000).
58. Edward J. Balleisen, *Navigating Failure: Bankruptcy and Commercial Society in Antebellum America* (Chapel Hill: University of North Carolina Press, 2001), 2.
59. Nancy F. Cott, *Public Vows: A History of Marriage and the Nation* (Cambridge, MA: Harvard University Press, 2000), 52.
60. On the diffusion of indebtedness throughout American society, see Balleisen, *Navigating Failure*.
61. Suzanne D. Lebsock, "Radical Reconstruction and the Property Rights of Southern Women," *Journal of Southern History* 43, no. 2 (1977): 202.
62. Sandra Moncrief, "The Mississippi Married Women's Property Act of 1839," *Journal of Mississippi History* 47, no. 2 (1985): 111–12; Act of June 28, 1834, chap. 95 (Coinage Act); Act of June 23, 1836, chap. 115 (Distribution Act).

63. Reginald Charles McGrane, *The Panic of 1837: Some Financial Problems of the Jacksonian Era* (New York: Russel & Russel, 1965), 117.
64. "State Homestead Exemption Laws," *Yale Law Journal* 46, no. 6 (1937): 1026.
65. Megan Benson, "*Fisher v. Allen*: The Southern Origins of Married Women's Property Acts," *Journal of Southern Legal History* 6 (1998): 113; Elizabeth Gaspar Brown, "Husband and Wife: Memorandum on the Mississippi Woman's Law of 1839," *Michigan Law Review* 42, no. 6 (1944): 1113–14.
66. Gaspar Brown, "Husband and Wife"; Moncrief, "Mississippi Married Women's Property Act of 1839"; Joseph A. Ranney, *In the Wake of Slavery: Civil War, Civil Rights, and the Reconstruction of Southern Law* (Westport, CT: Praeger, 2006); "Removal of Disabilities."
67. Gaspar Brown, "Husband and Wife," 1114.
68. Gaspar Brown, "Husband and Wife," 1116.
69. Benson, "*Fisher v. Allen*," 112.
70. June Cabone and Naomi Cahn, "Democracy and Family," in *Stating the Family: New Directions in the Study of American Politics*, ed. Julie Novkov and Carol Nackenoff (Lawrence: University Press of Kansas, 2020), 28.
71. Rick Geddes and Dean Lueck, "The Gains from Self-Ownership and the Expansion of Women's Rights," *American Economic Review* 92, no. 4 (2002): 1079–92.
72. Peter Koudijs and Laura Salisbury, "Limited Liability and Investment: Evidence from Changes in Marital Property Laws in the US South, 1840–1850," *Journal of Financial Economics* 138, no. 1 (2020): 8.
73. Gavin Wright, *Slavery and American Economic Development* (Baton Rouge: Louisiana State University Press, 2006), 60–61.
74. Bonnie Martin, "Neighbor-to-Neighbor Capitalism: Local Credit Networks and the Mortgaging of Slaves," in *Slavery's Capitalism: A New History of American Economic Development*, ed. Sven Beckert and Seth Rockman (Philadelphia: University of Philadelphia Press, 2016), 107.
75. These statutes were passed in 1839 (Mississippi), 1840 (Texas), 1843 (Maryland), and 1846 (Arkansas and Kentucky).
76. *Laws of the State of Mississippi* (Jackson, MS: B. D. Howard, 1839), 72.
77. Stephanie E. Jones-Rogers, *They Were Her Property: White Women as Slave Owners in the American South* (New Haven, CT: Yale University Press, 2019), xiii.
78. Jones-Rogers, *They Were Her Property*, 2, 19, 29.
79. Jones-Rogers, *They Were Her Property*, 2–3.
80. Michael B. Dougan, "The Arkansas Married Woman's Property Law," *Arkansas Historical Quarterly* 46, no. 1 (1987): 25.

81. Laurel A. Clark, "The Rights of a Florida Wife: Slavery, U.S. Expansion, and Married Women's Property Law," *Journal of Women's History* 22, no. 4 (2010): 49.
82. Martin, "Neighbor-to-Neighbor Capitalism," 107; Sarah L. Quinn, *American Bonds: How Credit Markets Shaped a Nation* (Princeton, NJ: Princeton University Press, 2019), 37.
83. Quinn, *American Bonds*, 39.
84. Edward Baptist, *The Half Has Never Been Told: Slavery and the Making of American Capitalism* (New York: Basic, 2014), 274.
85. Warbasse, *Changing Legal Rights of Married Women*, 143–44.
86. Alexander Tsesis, *The Thirteenth Amendment and American Freedom: A Legal History* (New York: New York University Press, 2004), 51.
87. Mehrsa Baradaran, *The Color of Money: Black Banks and the Racial Wealth Gap* (Cambridge, MA: Harvard University Press, 2018), 18; Emily Zackin and Chloe Thurston, *The Political Economy of American Debt Relief* (Chicago: University of Chicago Press, forthcoming).
88. Kate Masur, *Until Justice Be Done: America's First Civil Rights Movement, from the Revolution to Reconstruction* (New York: Norton, 2021), 2–3; Richard Wormser, *The Rise and Fall of Jim Crow* (New York: St. Martin's Press, 2003), 8.
89. Baradaran, *Color of Money*, 18, 293 n. 53; Act of May 20, 1862, chap. 75 (Homestead Act). Meanwhile, although the Southern Homestead Act (Act of June 21, 1866, chap. 127) was intended to create homesteads for formerly enslaved people after the Civil War, it failed to transfer meaningful property to Black Americans. See Christie Farnham Pope, "Southern Homesteads for Negroes," *Agricultural History* 44, no. 2 (1970): 201–12.
90. Delilah L. Beasley, *The Negro Trail Blazers of California* (Los Angeles: R and E Research Associates, 1919), 60.
91. Beasley, *Negro Trail Blazers*, 60–61; Masur, *Until Justice Be Done*, 18.
92. Zackin and Thurston, *American Debt Relief*.
93. Tonia M. Compton, "Proper Women/Propertied Women: Federal Land Laws and Gender Order(s) in the Nineteenth-Century Imperial American West," PhD diss., University of Nebraska, 2009, 4.
94. Mari J. Matsuda, "The West and the Legal State of Women: Explanations of Frontier Feminism," *Journal of the West* 24, no. 1 (1985): 52.
95. Compton, "Proper Women," 6.
96. Sebastian Braun and Michael Kvasnicka, "Men, Women, and the Ballot: Gender Imbalances and Suffrage Extensions in the United States," *Explorations in Economic History* 50, no. 3 (2013): 405–26; Julie Roy Jeffrey, *Frontier Women: The Trans-Mississippi West 1840–1880* (New York: Hill and Wang, 1979), 191.

97. *General Laws, Memorials, and Resolutions of the Territory of Wyoming, Passed at the First Session of the Legislative Assembly (1869)* (Cheyenne, WY: S. Allan Bristol, 1870).
98. Mark M. Carroll, *Homesteads Ungovernable: Families, Sex, Race, and the Law in Frontier Texas, 1823–1860* (Austin: University of Texas Press, 2001), 68.
99. Peggy Pascoe, *What Comes Naturally: Miscegenation Law and the Making of Race in America* (Oxford: Oxford University Press, 2009), 98.
100. Julie Novkov, "*Pace v. Alabama*: Interracial Love, the Marriage Contract, and Post-bellum Foundations of the Family," in *The Supreme Court and American Political Development*, ed. Ronald Kahn and Kenneth Kersch (Lawrence: University Press of Kansas, 2006), 342.
101. Pascoe, *What Comes Naturally*, 103–08.
102. Bardaglio, *Reconstructing the Household*, xiv, 236 n. 15.
103. Bardaglio, *Reconstructing the Household*, 35.
104. Ranney, *In the Wake of Slavery*, 114–15.
105. *Southern Sun* (Jackson, MS), February 5, 1839, quoted in Moncrief, "Mississippi Married Women's Property Act of 1839," 122.
106. "New York," in *History of Woman Suffrage*, vol. 1, ed. Elizabeth Cady Stanton, Susan B. Anthony, and Matilda Joslyn Gage (New York: Fowler & Wells, 1881), 63–64.
107. Geoffrey Geddes, quoted in "New York," in *History of Woman Suffrage*, ed. Stanton, Anthony, and Gage, 64.
108. *Report of the Debates and Proceedings of the Convention for the Revision of the Constitution of the State of Indiana* (Indianapolis, IN: A. H. Brown, 1850), 467.
109. Sullivan, *Constitutional Context*, 9.
110. Siegel, "Home as Work."
111. *Proceedings of the Woman's Rights Convention, Held at Worcester, October 23d and 24th, 1850*, quoted in Siegel, "Home as Work," 1113.
112. Reva B. Siegel, "The Modernization of Marital Status Law: Adjudicating Wives' Rights to Earning, 1860–1930," *Georgetown Law Journal* 82 (1995): 2127–211.
113. "An Act in Relation to the Rights of Married Women," chap. 59, 36th Legislature, Regular Session, Maine, 1857.

4. CONSTITUTIONAL CONVENTIONS AS KEY REFORM MOMENTS

1. The delegates' motivation was not necessarily benevolent here: many pro-debtor reforms were at least partially driven by the need to reduce state support of individuals and families who fell on hard times.

2. Noelle Strom, my research assistant, and I compiled these constitutional provisions largely through John Joseph Wallis, National Bureau of Economic Research (NBER)/University of Maryland State Constitution Project, n.d., http://www.stateconstitutions.umd.edu. Strom conducted searches by state for the following terms: *married, woman, women, female, wife, wives,* and *femme covert.* The findings from the searches were supplemented with information on and copies of the constitutions of Georgia and Oregon from the digital platform State Constitutions Illustrated, available through HeinOnline, https://heinonline-org.du.idm.oclc.org/HOL/Index?collection=statecon.

3. Georgia Const. of 1983, art. 1, §1, para. 27.

4. Florida Const. of 1861, art. 4, §21.

5. All ten of these amendments were ratified after 1920. Thus, all the provisions considered in detail in this chapter and included in tables 4.2–4.4 were the result of constitutional conventions.

6. Bruce E. Cain and Roger G. Noll, "Malleable Constitutions: Reflections on State Constitutional Reform Symposium. What, If Anything, Do We Know About Constitutional Design: Constitutional Change," *Texas Law Review* 87, no. 7 (2009): 1517–44.

7. Christian G. Fritz, "The American Constitutional Tradition Revisited: Preliminary Observations on State Constitution-Making in the Nineteenth-Century West," *Rutgers Law Journal* 25, no. 4 (1994): 963–71.

8. Emily Zackin, *Looking for Rights in All the Wrong Places: Why State Constitutions Contain America's Positive Rights* (Princeton, NJ: Princeton University Press, 2013), 11.

9. Zackin, *Looking for Rights*, 34.

10. Zackin, *Looking for Rights*, 37–42.

11. Richard A. Posner, "The Cost of Rights: Implications for Central and Eastern Europe—and for the United States," *Tulsa Law Journal* 32, no. 1 (1996): 1–20; Henry Shue, *Basic Rights: Subsistence, Affluence, and U.S. Foreign Policy* (Princeton, NJ: Princeton University Press, 1996); Stephen Holmes and Cass R. Sunstein, *The Cost of Rights: Why Liberty Depends on Taxes* (New York: Norton, 2000).

12. Posner, "Cost of Rights."

13. Holmes and Sunstein, *Cost of Rights*, 60.

14. Frank B. Cross, "The Error of Positive Rights," *UCLA Law Review* 48, no. 4 (2001): 867.

15. Arkansas Const. of 1874, art. 9, §8.

16. Laurel Clark Shire, *The Threshold of Manifest Destiny: Gender and National Expansion in Florida* (Philadelphia: University of Pennsylvania Press, 2016), 10.

17. Here, "the South" is defined as the states that seceded from the Union. For an excellent analysis of southern constitutions from the antebellum period through the early 1900s, see Paul E. Herron, *Framing the Solid South: The State Constitutional Conventions of Secession, Reconstruction, and Redemption, 1860–1902* (Lawrence: University Press of Kansas, 2017).
18. Richard L. Hume and Jerry B. Gough, *Blacks, Carpetbaggers, and Scalawags: The Constitutional Conventions of Radical Reconstruction* (Baton Rouge: Louisiana State University Press, 2008), 250.
19. Louisiana included married women's property rights in its Constitution of 1868 but not in its Constitution of 1879. North Carolina included these reforms in its Constitution of 1868 and did not ratify a new constitution until 1971, although Democrats did add several amendments in 1873 and 1875 that rolled back Reconstruction reforms.
20. Joseph A. Ranney, *In the Wake of Slavery: Civil War, Civil Rights, and the Reconstruction of Southern Law* (Westport, CT: Praeger, 2006), 119.
21. Peter Wallenstein, *Tell the Court I Love My Wife: Race, Marriage, and Law—an American History* (New York: Palgrave Macmillan, 2002), 162.
22. Peggy Pascoe, *What Comes Naturally: Miscegenation Law and the Making of Race in America* (Oxford: Oxford University Press, 2009), 46.
23. John G. Price, ed., *Debates and Proceedings of the Convention Which Assembled at Little Rock, January 7th, 1868* (Little Rock, AR: J. G. Price, 1868), 206–7.
24. Price, *Debates*, 701–2.
25. Price, *Debates*, 704–7.
26. Price, *Debates*, 708.
27. Price, *Debates*, 724.
28. *Journal of the Proceedings of the Constitutional Convention of the State of Mississippi, 1868* (Jackson, MS: E. Stafford, 1871), 345.
29. Suzanne D. Lebsock, "Radical Reconstruction and the Property Rights of Southern Women," *Journal of Southern History* 43, no. 2 (1977): 197–201.
30. *Journal of the Proceedings of the Constitutional Convention of the State of Mississippi, 1868*, 80–81. At another point, a different delegate proposed a similar provision that would have allowed exemptions only for clothing and property owned by a married woman before marriage; this proposal also failed (*Journal of the Proceedings of the Constitutional Convention of the State of Mississippi, 1868*, 584).
31. *Journal of the Proceedings of the Constitutional Convention of the State of Mississippi, 1868*, 80.
32. Alexander F. Roehrkasse, "Failure, Fraud, and Force: The Rise and Fall of the Debtor's Prison in New York, 1760–1840," MA thesis, University of California, Berkeley, 2014, 49.

33. *Journal of the Proceedings of the Constitutional Convention of the State of Mississippi, 1868*, 43–44.
34. Mississippi Const. of 1868, art. 1, §11 (ban on imprisonment for debt); art. 12, §24 (legislative power to pass homestead-exemption and debt-relief laws); art. 1, §16 (married women's property rights).
35. Mississippi Const. of 1890, art. 3, §94.
36. *Journal of the Proceedings of the Constitutional Convention of the State of Mississippi, 1890* (Jackson, MS: E. L. Martin, 1890), 168.
37. *Journal of the Proceedings of the Constitutional Convention of the State of Mississippi, 1890*, 220.
38. See also *Journal of the Proceedings of the Constitutional Convention of the State of Mississippi, 1890*.
39. Paul Goodman, "The Emergence of Homestead Exemption in the United States: Accommodation and Resistance to the Market Revolution, 1840–1880," *Journal of American History* 80, no. 2 (1993): 496.
40. *Journal of the Proceedings of the Constitutional Convention of the State of Mississippi, 1890*, 122. Thompson later was one of the drafters of the Mississippi Code.
41. Walter Edgar, *South Carolina: A History* (Columbia: University of South Carolina Press, 1998), 386.
42. *Proceedings of the Constitutional Convention of South Carolina* (Charleston, SC: Denny & Perry, 1868), 62–63.
43. *Proceedings of the Constitutional Convention of South Carolina*, 64–65.
44. *Proceedings of the Constitutional Convention of South Carolina*, 785–86.
45. *Proceedings of the Constitutional Convention of South Carolina*, 786.
46. *Proceedings of the Constitutional Convention of South Carolina*, 787.
47. South Carolina Const. of 1868, art. 16, §8.
48. *Proceedings of the Constitutional Convention of South Carolina*, 786.
49. J. David Hacker, Libra Hilde, and James Holland Jones, "The Effect of the Civil War on Southern Marriage Patterns," *Journal of Southern History* 76, no. 1 (2010): 39–70.
50. Hacker, Hilde, and Jones, "Effect of the Civil War on Southern Marriage Patterns," 46.
51. South Carolina Const. of 1868, art. 16, §8.
52. *Proceedings of the Constitutional Convention of South Carolina*, 785.
53. *Proceedings of the Constitutional Convention of South Carolina*, 783–84.
54. The roll-call vote comes from *Journal of the Proceedings of the Constitutional Convention of the State of Mississippi, 1868*, 345. Data on delegates' race and Conservative/Radical voting patterns come from Hume and Gough, *Blacks, Carpetbaggers, and Scalawags*, 282–405.

55. *Journal of the Proceedings of the Constitutional Convention of the State of Mississippi, 1890*, 704–8.
56. Hume and Gough, *Blacks, Carpetbaggers, and Scalawags*, 170.
57. The roll-call vote comes from *Proceedings of the Constitutional Convention of South Carolina*, 787–88. Data on delegates' race come from Hume and Gough, *Blacks, Carpetbaggers, and Scalawags*, 282–405.
58. D. D. Wallace, "The South Carolina Constitutional Convention of 1895," *Sewanee Review* 4, no. 3 (1896): 351.
59. Amy Bridges, *Democratic Beginnings: Founding the Western States* (Lawrence: University Press of Kansas, 2015), 9–10.
60. Fritz, "American Constitutional Tradition Revisited," 978; Bridges, *Democratic Beginnings*, 142–43.
61. Leonard L. Richards, *The California Gold Rush and the Coming of the Civil War* (New York: Knopf, 2007), 72.
62. Richards, *California Gold Rush*, 70.
63. Richards, *California Gold Rush*, 77–78.
64. J. Ross Browne, ed., *Report of the Debates in the Convention of California on the Formation of the State Constitution* (Washington, DC: J. T. Towers, 1850), 375, 377.
65. Orrin K. McMurray, "The Beginnings of the Community Property System in California and the Adoption of the Common Law," *California Law Review* 3, no. 5 (1915): 369.
66. Browne, *Report of the Debates in the Convention of California*, 258.
67. Browne, *Report of the Debates in the Convention of California*, 264.
68. Browne, *Report of the Debates in the Convention of California*, 262.
69. Browne, *Report of the Debates in the Convention of California*, 268–69.
70. Browne, *Report of the Debates in the Convention of California*, 257–60.
71. Browne, *Report of the Debates in the Convention of California*, 259, 265–67.
72. Browne, *Report of the Debates in the Convention of California*, 263.
73. Browne, *Report of the Debates in the Convention of California*, 258.
74. Browne, *Report of the Debates in the Convention of California*, 259.
75. Browne, *Report of the Debates in the Convention of California*, 258.
76. Andrew J. Marsh, *Official Report of the Debates and Proceedings in the Constitutional Convention of the State of Nevada, Assembled at Carson City, July 4th, 1864, to Form a Constitution and State Government* (San Francisco: Frank Eastman, 1866), 154.
77. Marsh, *Official Report of the Debates and Proceedings in the Constitutional Convention of the State of Nevada*, 154.
78. Marsh, *Official Report of the Debates and Proceedings in the Constitutional Convention of the State of Nevada*, 154.

79. Marsh, *Official Report of the Debates and Proceedings in the Constitutional Convention of the State of Nevada*, 154.
80. Marsh, *Official Report of the Debates and Proceedings in the Constitutional Convention of the State of Nevada*, 154, 277.
81. Marsh, *Official Report of the Debates and Proceedings in the Constitutional Convention of the State of Nevada*, 276.
82. Marsh, *Official Report of the Debates and Proceedings in the Constitutional Convention of the State of Nevada*, 275, 277.
83. Marsh, *Official Report of the Debates and Proceedings in the Constitutional Convention of the State of Nevada*, 278.
84. Marsh, *Official Report of the Debates and Proceedings in the Constitutional Convention of the State of Nevada*, xvi.
85. Marsh, *Official Report of the Debates and Proceedings in the Constitutional Convention of the State of Nevada*, xvi.
86. Oregon Const. of 1859, art. 1, §31.
87. Texas Const. of 1845, art. 3, §§1–2; California Const. of 1850, art. 2, §1; Kansas Const. of 1861, art. 5, §1; Nevada Const. of 1864, art. 2, §1; North Dakota Const. of 1889, art. 5, §121.
88. Goodman, "Emergence of Homestead Exemption," 496.
89. "State Homestead Exemption Laws," *Yale Law Journal* 46, no. 6 (1937): 1027.
90. Lebsock, "Radical Reconstruction," 202.
91. Goodman, "Emergence of Homestead Exemption," 493.
92. Goodman, "Emergence of Homestead Exemption."
93. "State Homestead Exemption Laws," 1030 n. 62.
94. Alison D. Morantz, "There's No Place Like Home: Homestead Exemption and Judicial Constructions of Family in Nineteenth-Century America," *Law and History Review* 24, no. 2 (2006): 245–95. See also Lebsock, "Radical Reconstruction," 202. Not all of these proposals made it into the state's final constitutional text: some were debated and rejected or were initially packaged together and later separated. Wisconsin, for example, considered a homestead exemption and married women's property protections together but ultimately rejected both and instead included a more general debtor-protection measure in its constitution. See *Journal of the Convention to Form a Constitution for the State of Wisconsin, with a Sketch of the Debates* (Madison, WI: Tenney, Smith & Holt, 1848), 556–58.
95. Marsh, *Official Report of the Debates and Proceedings in the Constitutional Convention of the State of Nevada*, 282.
96. Marsh, *Official Report of the Debates and Proceedings in the Constitutional Convention of the State of Nevada*, 286.
97. Marsh, *Official Report of the Debates and Proceedings in the Constitutional Convention of the State of Nevada*, 287.

98. *Debates and Proceedings of the Constitutional Convention of the State of Illinois*, vol. 1 (Springfield, IL: Merritt, 1870), 895, https://heinonline-org.du.idm.oclc.org/HOL/P?h=hein.cow/dpccil0001&i=1.
99. *Debates and Proceedings of the Constitutional Convention of the State of Illinois*, 1:900.
100. Browne, *Report of the Debates in the Convention of California*, 271.
101. Alabama, Florida, and Texas included such protections in their constitutions. See Lebsock, "Radical Reconstruction," 204; and Goodman, "Emergence of Homestead Exemption."
102. Jack H. Garrett, "The Wife's Illusory Homestead Rights," *Baylor Law Review*, no. 2 (1970): 178–90.
103. Zackin, *Looking for Rights*, 20.
104. Fritz, "American Constitutional Tradition Revisited," 980–81.
105. Fritz, "American Constitutional Tradition Revisited," 975–76. One typical example is *The American's Guide: Comprising the Declaration of Independence; the Articles of Confederation; the Constitution of the United States; and the Constitutions of the Several States Composing the Union* (Philadelphia: Hogan and Thompson, 1849).
106. Bridges, *Democratic Beginnings*, 15.
107. Herron, *Framing the Solid South*, 176.
108. For more on text as data more generally, see Matthew Gentzkow, Bryan Kelly, and Matt Taddy, "Text as Data," *Journal of Economic Literature* 57, no. 3 (2019): 535–74.
109. Lou Bloomfield, WCopyfind, version 4.1.5, https://plagiarism.bloomfieldmedia.com/software/wcopyfind/.
110. See, for example, Pamela C. Corley, "The Supreme Court and Opinion Content: The Influence of Parties' Briefs," *Political Research Quarterly* 61, no. 3 (2008): 468–78; Justin Grimmer, "A Bayesian Hierarchical Topic Model for Political Texts: Measuring Expressed Agendas in Senate Press Releases," *Political Analysis* 18, no. 1 (2010): 1–35; Pamela C. Corley, Paul M. Collins Jr., and Bryan Calvin, "Lower Court Influence on U.S. Supreme Court Opinion Content," *Journal of Politics* 73, no. 1 (2011): 31–44; Matthew Eshbaugh-Soha, "Presidential Influence of the News Media: The Case of the Press Conference," *Political Communication* 30, no. 4 (2013): 548–64; Michael F. Salamone, "Community and Persuasion: The Influence of the Federalist Society on the Supreme Court," paper presented at the American Political Science Association Annual Meeting, Washington, DC, 2014; Rachael K. Hinkle, "Into the Words: Using Statutory Text to Explore the Impact of Federal Courts on State Policy Diffusion," *American Journal of Political Science* 59, no. 4 (2015): 1002–21; Adam Feldman, "All Copying Is Not Created Equal: Borrowed Language in Supreme Court

Opinions," *Journal of Appellate Practice and Process* 17, no. 1 (2016): 21–112; Shane A. Gleason, Jennifer J. Jones, and Jessica Rae McBean, "The Role of Gender Norms in Judicial Decision-Making at the U.S. Supreme Court: The Case of Male and Female Justices," *American Politics Research* 47, no. 3 (2019): 494–529.

111. Texas Const. of 1845, art. 7, §19.
112. California Const. of 1850, art. 11, §14.
113. Michigan Const. of 1850, art. 16, §5.
114. North Carolina Const. of 1868, art. 10, §6.

5. DECENTRALIZED REFORM AND POLICY DIFFUSION

1. *Proceedings of the Constitutional Convention of South Carolina* (Charleston, SC: Denny & Perry, 1868), 785.
2. The number of states and territories analyzed is forty-seven because Alaska and Hawaii were not yet territories, and Dakota Territory passed every major category of married women's property rights reform in its territorial legislature prior to splitting into North Dakota and South Dakota.
3. Virginia Gray, "Innovation in the States: A Diffusion Study," *American Political Science Review* 67, no. 4 (1973): 1175–76.
4. See, for example, Craig Volden, Michael M. Ting, and Daniel P. Carpenter, "A Formal Model of Learning and Policy Diffusion," *American Political Science Review* 102, no. 3 (2008): 319–32; Andrew Karch, "Emerging Issues and Future Directions in State Policy Diffusion Research," *State Politics & Policy Quarterly* 7, no. 1 (2007): 55; and Brady Baybeck, William D. Berry, and David A. Siegel, "A Strategic Theory of Policy Diffusion Via Intergovernmental Competition," *Journal of Politics* 73, no. 1 (2011): 232–47.
5. Baybeck, Berry, and Siegel, "A Strategic Theory of Policy Diffusion."
6. Jayme S. Lemke, "Interjurisdictional Competition and the Married Women's Property Acts," *Public Choice* 166, no. 3 (2016): 291–313.
7. Volden, Ting, and Carpenter, "A Formal Model of Learning," 319.
8. See, for example, Frances Stokes Berry and William D. Berry, "State Lottery Adoptions as Policy Innovations: An Event History Analysis," *American Political Science Review* 84, no. 2 (1990): 395–415.
9. Craig Volden, "States as Policy Laboratories: Emulating Success in the Children's Health Insurance Program," *American Journal of Political Science* 50, no. 2 (2006): 294–312.
10. Bruce A. Desmarais, Jeffrey J. Harden, and Frederick J. Boehmke, "Persistent Policy Pathways: Inferring Diffusion Networks in the American States," *American Political Science Review* 109, no. 2 (2015): 392–406.

11. To be more precise, the odds ratio for control-and-management acts is 2.68, and the odds ratio for earnings acts is 2.41.
12. Specifically, a one percentage point increase in the female population of a state or territory is associated with a 0.92–0.93 increase in the odds ratio. Community-property states are associated with a 0.04–0.27 increase in the odds ratio as compared to common-law states.
13. Idaho Civil Practice Act (1863), §221.
14. Laws of Montana Territory (1864), chap. 5, §193.
15. An Act to Exempt the Property of Married Women from Execution in Certain Cases, Nebraska (1855), §§1–2.
16. An Act to Exempt the Property of Married Women from Execution in Certain Cases, Dakota Territory (1862), §1.
17. The 40 percent cutoff was chosen by examining the pairs of documents. Those with 40 and greater match percentages do seem to share substantial similar or identical language and ideas, while those with match percentages less than 40 tend to share more limited "stock" phrases, such as "the separate property of the wife" and "the debts of the husband."
18. See, for example, R. Richard Geddes and Sharon Tennyson, "Passage of the Married Women's Property Acts and Earnings Acts in the United States: 1850 to 1920," *Research in Economic History* 29 (2013): 154.
19. Alison L. Gash, *Below the Radar: How Silence Can Save Civil Rights* (Oxford: Oxford University Press, 2015).
20. Leonard L. Richards, *The California Gold Rush and the Coming of the Civil War* (New York: Knopf, 2007), 72.
21. Census Office, *1850 Census: Compendium of the Seventh Census* (Washington, DC: Census Office, 1854), https://www.census.gov/library/publications/1854/dec/1850c.html.
22. Curtis Hillyer, *Nevada Compiled Laws 1929* (San Francisco: Bender-Moss, 1930), 1011.
23. *In re Estate of Williams*, 40 Nev. 241 (1916), 246.
24. Sandra Moncrief, "The Mississippi Married Women's Property Act of 1839," *Journal of Mississippi History* 47, no. 2 (1985): 123–24.
25. Rosamond Parma, "The History of the Adoption of the Codes of California," *Law Library Journal* 22 (1929): 14–15. See also Henry M. Field, *The Life of David Dudley Field* (New York: Scribner's, 1898), 74–75, 78.
26. Stephanie E. Jones-Rogers, *They Were Her Property: White Women as Slave Owners in the American South* (New Haven, CT: Yale University Press, 2019), 2.
27. Laurel Clark Shire, *The Threshold of Manifest Destiny: Gender and National Expansion in Florida* (Philadelphia: University of Pennsylvania Press, 2016).
28. Shire, *Threshold of Manifest Destiny*, 10.

29. Mark M. Carroll, *Homesteads Ungovernable: Families, Sex, Race, and the Law in Frontier Texas, 1823–1860* (Austin: University of Texas Press, 2001), 81.
30. Carroll, *Homesteads Ungovernable*, 105.

6. COURTS AS COLLABORATORS AND CATALYSTS

1. William E. Forbath, "The Shaping of the American Labor Movement," *Harvard Law Review* 102, no. 6 (1989): 1114. See also Brian Balogh, *A Government out of Sight: The Mystery of National Authority in Nineteenth-Century America* (Cambridge: Cambridge University Press, 2009), 312–43.
2. Forbath, "Shaping of the American Labor Movement," 1130–31.
3. Kermit L. Hall, "Constitutional Machinery and Judicial Professionalism: The Careers of Midwestern State Appellate Court Judges, 1861–1899," in *The New High Priests: Lawyers in Post–Civil War America*, ed. Gerard Gawalt (Westport, CT: Greenwood Press, 1984), 42.
4. Balogh, *A Government out of Sight*, 318–19.
5. Julie Novkov, *Constituting Workers, Protecting Women: Gender, Law, and Labor in the Progressive Era and New Deal Years* (Ann Arbor: University of Michigan Press, 2001).
6. Sara Chatfield, "Competing Social Constructions of Women Workers in Lochner-Era Judicial Decision-Making," *Constitutional Studies* 4 (2019): 105–30.
7. *Pelzer v. Campbell*, 15 SC 581 (1881).
8. Code of Civil Procedure of the State of South Carolina (1882), 93.
9. *Holmes v. Holmes*, 4 Barbour 295 (1848).
10. *Holmes v. Holmes*, 4 Barbour 295 (1848), 299.
11. *Holmes v. Holmes*, 4 Barbour 295 (1848), 300–301.
12. *White v. White*, 5 Barbour 474 (1849).
13. *White v. White*, 5 Barbour 474 (1849), 475.
14. "No State shall enter into any Treaty, Alliance, or Confederation; grant Letters of Marque and Reprisal; coin Money; emit Bills of Credit; make any Thing but gold and silver Coin a Tender in Payment of Debts; *pass any* Bill of Attainder, ex post facto Law, *or Law impairing the Obligation of Contracts*, or grant any Title of Nobility" (U.S. Const., art. 1, §10 , cl. 1, emphasis added).
15. *White v. White*, 5 Barbour 474 (1849), 485.
16. *Switzer v. Valentine*, 10 HOW 109 (NY) (1854).
17. *Manhattan Brass & Mfg. Co. v. Thompson*, 58 NY 80 (1874), 85.
18. *Grand Gulf Bank v. Barnes*, 10 Miss. 165 (1844), 186.
19. *Davis v. Foy*, 15 Miss. 64 (1846), 67.
20. Revised Code of the Statute Laws of the State of Mississippi (1857), chap. 40, §5, art. 23–24.

21. Revised Code of the Statute Laws of the State of Mississippi (1857), chap. 40, §5, art. 24.
22. Revised Code of the Statute Laws of the State of Mississippi (1857), chap. 40, §5, art. 25.
23. *Hardin v. Pelan*, 41 Miss. 112 (1866), 114.
24. *Whitworth v. Carter*, 43 Miss. 61 (1870), 72–73.
25. *Viser v. Scruggs*, 49 Miss. 705 (1874), 711.
26. *Dibrell v. Carlisle*, 48 Miss. 691 (1873), 706. See also *Foxworth v. Magee*, 44 Miss. 430 (1870).
27. Alice Kessler-Harris, *Out to Work: A History of Wage-Earning Women in the United States* (New York: Oxford University Press, 1982), 75–77.
28. For a discussion of popular conceptions of wages versus other types of property that is relevant to both genders, see William B. Scott, *In Pursuit of Happiness: American Conceptions of Property from the Seventeenth to the Twentieth Century* (Bloomington: Indiana University Press, 1977).
29. *Apple v. Ganong*, 47 Miss. 189 (1872). Note that although this case reached the Mississippi Supreme Court after the Mississippi Legislature had passed an earnings act (in 1871), the purchases and debts in question occurred prior to the passage of the act, so the earnings act was not controlling.
30. *Apple v. Ganong*, 47 Miss. 189 (1872), 199.
31. Revised Code of the Statute Laws of the State of Mississippi (1871), chap. 23, art. 5: "Property of the Wife," §1778.
32. Revised Code of the Statute Laws of the State of Mississippi (1871), chap. 23, art. 5: "Property of the Wife," §1780.
33. Edward Mayes, "The Legal and Judicial History," in *Biographical and Historical Memoirs of Mississippi: Embracing an Authentic and Comprehensive Account of the Chief Events of the History of the State and a Record of the Lives of Many of the Most Worthy and Illustrious Families and Individuals*, ed. Goodspeed Brothers (Chicago: Goodspeed, 1891), 124.
34. *Netterville v. Barber*, 52 Miss. 168 (1876), 173–74.
35. *Netterville v. Barber*, 52 Miss. 168 (1876), 170.
36. *Toof v. Brewer*, 96 Miss. 19 (1888).
37. *Southworth v. Brownlow*, 84 Miss. 405 (1904).
38. *Austin v. Austin*, 136 Miss. 61 (1924), 71.
39. Revised Code of the Statute Laws of the State of Mississippi (1880), chap. 42, §1177.
40. *Pelzer v. Campbell*, 15 SC 581 (1881), 588–89.
41. *Pelzer v. Campbell*, 15 SC 581 (1881), 601.
42. *Pelzer v. Campbell*, 15 SC 581 (1881), 596.
43. Code of Civil Procedure of the State of South Carolina (1882), 93; *Habenicht v. Rawls*, 24 SC 461 (1886), 464–65.

44. Michael J. Dubin, *Party Affiliations in the State Legislatures: A Year by Year Summary, 1796–2006* (Jefferson, NC: McFarland, 2007), 171.
45. *Gwynn v. Gwynn*, 27 SC 525 (1887), 538.
46. *Habenicht v. Rawls*, 24 SC 461 (1886), 466–67.
47. *Aultman v. Rush*, 26 SC 517 (1887).
48. *Bridgers v. Howell*, 27 SC 425 (1887), 429–30.
49. Scott, *In Pursuit of Happiness*.
50. *Bridgers v. Howell*, 27 SC 425 (1887), 430–31.
51. *Gwynn v. Gwynn*, 27 SC 525 (1887).
52. *Habenicht v. Rawls*, 24 SC 461 (1886).
53. *Gwynn v. Gwynn*, 27 SC 525 (1887), 540, 541.
54. South Carolina Acts (1887), 819; *Mitchell v. Mitchell*, 42 SC 475 (1894).
55. Acts and Joint Resolutions of the General Assembly of the State of South Carolina (1891), 1121.
56. South Carolina Const. of 1895, art. 17, §9.
57. Walter Edgar, *South Carolina: A History* (Columbia: University of South Carolina Press, 1998), 445.
58. *Charleston News and Courier*, October 1, 1895.

CONCLUSION

1. Derrick A. Bell, "*Brown v. Board of Education* and the Interest-Convergence Dilemma," *Harvard Law Review* 93, no. 3 (1980): 523.
2. David A. Bateman, *Disenfranchising Democracy: Constructing the Electorate in the United States, the United Kingdom, and France* (Cambridge: Cambridge University Press, 2018).
3. Paul E. Herron, "Slavery and Freedom in American State Constitutional Development," *Journal of Policy History* 27, no. 2 (2015): 301–36.
4. Ran Hirschl, *Towards Juristocracy: The Origins and Consequences of the New Constitutionalism* (Cambridge, MA: Harvard University Press, 2004).
5. Mary L. Dudziak, *Cold War Civil Rights: Race and the Image of American Democracy*, Politics and Society in Twentieth-Century America (Princeton, NJ: Princeton University Press, 2000).
6. To follow this story later in time, see Alice Kessler-Harris, *In Pursuit of Equity: Women, Men, and the Quest for Economic Citizenship in 20th-Century America* (Oxford: Oxford University Press, 2001).
7. Genevieve Reynolds, "Ethel Ernest Murrell Arrives in Capital to Pursue Equal Rights for Women in U.S.," *Washington Post*, August 14, 1943.
8. *Taylor v. Dorsey*, 155 Fla. 305 (1944).
9. "Florida Votes Equal Rights Bill," *New York Times*, May 27, 1943.

10. Mary Hornaday, "Women's Rights Advanced in Florida," *Christian Science Monitor*, September 7, 1943.
11. Lawrence Bowdish, "American Women's Struggle to End Credit Discrimination in the Twentieth Century," in *The Development of Consumer Credit in Global Perspective: Business, Regulation, and Culture*, ed. Jan Logemann (New York: Palgrave Macmillan, 2012), 110.
12. Chloe Thurston, *At the Boundaries of Homeownership: Credit, Discrimination, and the American State* (Cambridge: Cambridge University Press, 2018), 154; Bowdish, "American Women's Struggle " 110.
13. Thurston, *At the Boundaries of Homeownership*, 157–58; Bowdish, "American Women's Struggle " 110.
14. Thurston, *At the Boundaries of Homeownership*, 154.
15. Thurston, *At the Boundaries of Homeownership*, 143.
16. Bowdish, "American Women's Struggle," 113.
17. Thurston, *At the Boundaries of Homeownership*, 143; Housing and Community Development Act, 42 U.S.C. 69 (1974); Equal Credit Opportunity Act, 15 U.S.C. 1691 (1974).
18. Thurston, *At the Boundaries of Homeownership*, 172.
19. Thurston, *At the Boundaries of Homeownership*, 181–82.
20. Priscilla Yamin, *American Marriage: A Political Institution* (Philadelphia: University of Pennsylvania Press, 2012); Nancy F. Cott, *Public Vows: A History of Marriage and the Nation* (Cambridge, MA: Harvard University Press, 2000).
21. Nancy F. Cott, "Giving Character to Our Whole Civil Polity: Marriage and the Public Order in the Late Nineteenth Century," in *U.S. History as Women's History: New Feminist Essays*, ed. Linda K. Kerber, Alice Kessler-Harris, and Kathryn Kish Sklar (Chapel Hill: University of North Carolina Press, 1995), 108.
22. Bateman, *Disenfranchising Democracy*, 6.
23. Nancy Fraser and Linda Gordon, "Contract Versus Charity: Why Is There No Social Citizenship in the United States?," *Socialist Review* 22, no. 3 (1993): 56.

METHODS APPENDIX

1. Lou Bloomfield, WCopyfind, version 4.1.5, https://plagiarism.bloomfieldmedia.com/software/wcopyfind/.
2. Pamela C. Corley, "The Supreme Court and Opinion Content: The Influence of Parties' Briefs," *Political Research Quarterly* 61, no. 3 (2008): 468–78.
3. Janet M. Box-Steffensmeier and Bradford S. Jones, *Event History Modeling: A Guide for Social Scientists* (Cambridge: Cambridge University Press, 2004), 1.
4. Box-Steffensmeier and Jones, *Event History Modeling*, 69. For further discussion of the choice to model legislative enactments using discrete-time models,

see Holly McCammon, "Using Event History Analysis in Historical Research: With Illustrations from a Study of the Passage of Women's Protective Legislation," *International Review of Social History* 43 (1998): 33–55.

5. Box-Steffensmeier and Jones, *Event History Modeling*, 73.
6. For more details on this approach, see Box-Steffensmeier and Jones, *Event History Modeling*, 73.
7. Box-Steffensmeier and Jones, *Event History Modeling*.
8. Data on state-level woman suffrage come from Holly J. McCammon, Karen E. Campbell, Ellen M. Granberg, and Christine Mowery, "How Movements Win: Gendered Opportunity Structures and U.S. Women's Suffrage Movements, 1866 to 1919," *American Sociological Review* 66, no. 1 (2001): 49–70.
9. I thank Holly McCammon for generously sharing her data on state-level suffrage organizations. Also see her analysis of these data in McCammon et al., "How Movements Win."
10. I thank David Bateman for his help with wrangling census data. Historical population data come from Michael R. Haines, "Historical, Demographic, Economic, and Social Data: The United States, 1790–2002," Inter-university Consortium for Political and Social Research, 2010.
11. Dates of homestead-exemption acts come from Paul Goodman, "The Emergence of Homestead Exemption in the United States: Accommodation and Resistance to the Market Revolution, 1840–1880," *Journal of American History* 80, no. 2 (1993): 470–98.
12. Data on community property come from Raquel Fernández, *Women's Rights and Development*, National Bureau of Economic Research (NBER) Working Paper (Cambridge, MA: NBER, 2009).
13. Elizabeth Bowles Warbasse, *The Changing Legal Rights of Married Women: 1800–1861*, American Legal and Constitutional History: A Garland Series of Outstanding Dissertations (New York: Garland, 1987), 39.
14. I thank Michael Fix for generously sharing Stata code to create the neighboring-states variable. See Michael P. Fix and Joshua L. Mitchell, "Examining the Policy Learning Dynamics of Atypical Policies with an Application to State Preemption of Local Dog Laws," *Statistics, Politics, and Policy* 8, no. 2 (2017): 223–47.

Bibliography

Alexander, Gregory. *Commodity & Propriety: Competing Visions of Property in American Legal Thought, 1776–1970*. Chicago: University of Chicago Press, 1997.
Alshaikhmubarak, Hazem, R. Richard Geddes, and Shoshana A. Grossbard. "Single Motherhood and the Abolition of Coverture in the United States." *Journal of Empirical Legal Studies* 16, no. 1 (2019): 94–118.
The American's Guide: Comprising the Declaration of Independence; the Articles of Confederation; the Constitution of the United States; and the Constitutions of the Several States Composing the Union. Philadelphia: Hogan and Thompson, 1849.
Baker, Jean H. *Women and the U.S. Constitution, 1776–1920*. New Essays on American Constitutional History. Washington, DC: American Historical Association, 2009.
Balleisen, Edward J. *Navigating Failure: Bankruptcy and Commercial Society in Antebellum America*. Chapel Hill: University of North Carolina Press, 2001.
Balogh, Brian. *A Government out of Sight: The Mystery of National Authority in Nineteenth-Century America*. Cambridge: Cambridge University Press, 2009.
Baptist, Edward. *The Half Has Never Been Told: Slavery and the Making of American Capitalism*. New York: Basic, 2014.
Baradaran, Mehrsa. *The Color of Money: Black Banks and the Racial Wealth Gap*. Cambridge, MA: Harvard University Press, 2018.
Bardaglio, Peter Winthrop. *Reconstructing the Household: Families, Sex, and the Law in the Nineteenth-Century South*. Studies in Legal History. Chapel Hill: University of North Carolina Press, 1995.

Basch, Norma. *In the Eyes of the Law: Women, Marriage, and Property in Nineteenth-Century New York*. Ithaca, NY: Cornell University Press, 1982.

———. "Invisible Women: The Legal Fiction of Marital Unity in Nineteenth-Century America." In *Women and the American Legal Order*, edited by Karen J. Maschke, 42–62. New York: Garland, 1997.

Bateman, David A. *Disenfranchising Democracy: Constructing the Electorate in the United States, the United Kingdom, and France*. Cambridge: Cambridge University Press, 2018.

Baybeck, Brady, William D. Berry, and David A. Siegel. "A Strategic Theory of Policy Diffusion Via Intergovernmental Competition." *Journal of Politics* 73, no. 1 (2011): 232–47.

Beasley, Delilah L. *The Negro Trail Blazers of California*. Los Angeles: R and E Research Associates, 1919.

Bell, Derrick A. "*Brown v. Board of Education* and the Interest-Convergence Dilemma." *Harvard Law Review* 93, no. 3 (1980): 518–33.

Bell, Duncan. "What Is Liberalism?" *Political Theory* 42, no. 6 (2014): 682–715.

Benson, Megan. "*Fisher v. Allen*: The Southern Origins of Married Women's Property Acts." *Journal of Southern Legal History* 6 (1998): 97–122.

Berry, Frances Stokes, and William D. Berry. "State Lottery Adoptions as Policy Innovations: An Event History Analysis." *American Political Science Review* 84, no. 2 (1990): 395–415.

Bixby, Brian. "Panic of 1837." In *Encyclopedia of American Recessions and Depressions*, edited by Daniel J. Leab, 133–51. Santa Barbara, CA: ABC-CLIO, 2014.

Blume, William Wirt. "Adoption in California of the Field Code of Civil Procedure: A Chapter in American Legal History." *Hastings Law Journal* 17 (1966): 701–25.

Bowdish, Lawrence. "American Women's Struggle to End Credit Discrimination in the Twentieth Century." In *The Development of Consumer Credit in Global Perspective: Business, Regulation, and Culture*, edited by Jan Logemann, 109–28. New York: Palgrave Macmillan, 2012.

Box-Steffensmeier, Janet M., and Bradford S. Jones. *Event History Modeling: A Guide for Social Scientists*. Cambridge: Cambridge University Press, 2004.

Braun, Sebastian, and Michael Kvasnicka. "Men, Women, and the Ballot: Gender Imbalances and Suffrage Extensions in the United States." *Explorations in Economic History* 50, no. 3 (2013): 405–26.

Bridges, Amy. *Democratic Beginnings: Founding the Western States*. Lawrence: University Press of Kansas, 2015.

Broussard, Joyce L. "Naked Before the Law: Married Women and the Servant Ideal in Antebellum Natchez." In *Mississippi Women: Their Histories, Their Lives*, edited by Martha H. Swain, Elizabeth Anne Payne, and Marjorie Julian Spruill, 57–76. Athens: University of Georgia Press, 2010.

Browne, J. Ross, ed. *Report of the Debates in the Convention of California on the Formation of the State Constitution.* Washington, DC: J. T. Towers, 1850.

Cabone, June, and Naomi Cahn. "Democracy and Family." In *Stating the Family: New Directions in the Study of American Politics,* edited by Julie Novkov and Carol Nackenoff, 21–44. Lawrence: University Press of Kansas, 2020.

Cain, Bruce E., and Roger G. Noll. "Malleable Constitutions: Reflections on State Constitutional Reform Symposium. What, If Anything, Do We Know About Constitutional Design: Constitutional Change." *Texas Law Review* 87, no. 7 (2009): 1517–44.

Carpenter, Daniel. *Democracy by Petition: Popular Politics in Transformation, 1790–1870.* Cambridge, MA: Harvard University Press, 2021.

Carroll, Mark M. *Homesteads Ungovernable: Families, Sex, Race, and the Law in Frontier Texas, 1823–1860.* Austin: University of Texas Press, 2001.

Census Office. *1850 Census: Compendium of the Seventh Census.* Washington, DC: Census Office, 1854. https://www.census.gov/library/publications/1854/dec/1850c.html.

Chatfield, Sara. "Competing Social Constructions of Women Workers in Lochner-Era Judicial Decision-Making." *Constitutional Studies* 4 (2019): 105–30.

Chused, Richard H. "Married Women's Property Law: 1800–1850." *Georgetown Law Journal* 71 (1983): 1359–425.

——. "The Oregon Donation Act of 1850 and Nineteenth Century Federal Married Women's Property Law." *Law and History Review* 2, no. 1 (1984): 44–78.

Clark, Laurel A. "The Rights of a Florida Wife: Slavery, U.S. Expansion, and Married Women's Property Law." *Journal of Women's History* 22, no. 4 (2010): 39–63.

Compton, Tonia M. "Proper Women/Propertied Women: Federal Land Laws and Gender Order(s) in the Nineteenth-Century Imperial American West." PhD diss., University of Nebraska, 2009.

Corley, Pamela C. "The Supreme Court and Opinion Content: The Influence of Parties' Briefs." *Political Research Quarterly* 61, no. 3 (2008): 468–78.

Corley, Pamela C., Paul M. Collins Jr., and Bryan Calvin. "Lower Court Influence on U.S. Supreme Court Opinion Content." *Journal of Politics* 73, no. 1 (2011): 31–44.

Cott, Nancy F. "Giving Character to Our Whole Civil Polity: Marriage and the Public Order in the Late Nineteenth Century." In *U.S. History as Women's History: New Feminist Essays,* edited by Linda K. Kerber, Alice Kessler-Harris, and Kathryn Kish Sklar, 107–21. Chapel Hill: University of North Carolina Press, 1995.

——. *Public Vows: A History of Marriage and the Nation.* Cambridge, MA: Harvard University Press, 2000.

Council Journal of the Legislative Assembly of the Territory of Colorado. First Session [1861]. Denver: Thos. Gibson, Colorado Republican and Herald Office, 1862.

Cross, Frank B. "The Error of Positive Rights." *UCLA Law Review* 48, no. 4 (2001): 857–924.

Davies, Hannah Catherine. *Transatlantic Speculations: Globalization and the Panics of 1873*. New York: Columbia University Press, 2018.

Debates and Proceedings of the Constitutional Convention of the State of Illinois. Vol. 1. Springfield, IL: Merritt, 1870. https://heinonline-org.du.idm.oclc.org/HOL/P?h=hein.cow/dpccil0001&i=1.

Desmarais, Bruce A., Jeffrey J. Harden, and Frederick J. Boehmke. "Persistent Policy Pathways: Inferring Diffusion Networks in the American States." *American Political Science Review* 109, no. 2 (2015): 392–406.

Dougan, Michael B. "The Arkansas Married Woman's Property Law." *Arkansas Historical Quarterly* 46, no. 1 (1987): 3–26.

Dubin, Michael J. *Party Affiliations in the State Legislatures: A Year by Year Summary, 1796–2006*. Jefferson, NC: McFarland, 2007.

Dudziak, Mary L. *Cold War Civil Rights: Race and the Image of American Democracy*. Politics and Society in Twentieth-Century America. Princeton, NJ: Princeton University Press, 2000.

Edgar, Walter. *South Carolina: A History*. Columbia: University of South Carolina Press, 1998.

Eshbaugh-Soha, Matthew. "Presidential Influence of the News Media: The Case of the Press Conference." *Political Communication* 30, no. 4 (2013): 548–64.

Feldman, Adam. "All Copying Is Not Created Equal: Borrowed Language in Supreme Court Opinions." *Journal of Appellate Practice and Process* 17, no. 1 (2016): 21–112.

Fernández, Raquel. "Women's Rights and Development." *Journal of Economic Growth* 19, no. 1 (2014): 37–80.

———. *Women's Rights and Development*. National Bureau of Economic Research (NBER) Working Paper. Cambridge, MA: NBER, 2009.

Field, Henry M. *The Life of David Dudley Field*. New York: Scribner's, 1898.

Fix, Michael P., and Joshua L. Mitchell. "Examining the Policy Learning Dynamics of Atypical Policies with an Application to State Preemption of Local Dog Laws." *Statistics, Politics, and Policy* 8, no. 2 (2017): 223–47.

Forbath, William E. "The Shaping of the American Labor Movement." *Harvard Law Review* 102, no. 6 (1989): 1109–256.

Fraser, Nancy, and Linda Gordon. "Contract Versus Charity: Why Is There No Social Citizenship in the United States?" *Socialist Review* 22, no. 3 (1993): 45–67.

Fritz, Christian G. "The American Constitutional Tradition Revisited: Preliminary Observations on State Constitution-Making in the Nineteenth-Century West." *Rutgers Law Journal* 25, no. 4 (1994): 945–98.

Garrett, Jack H. "The Wife's Illusory Homestead Rights." *Baylor Law Review*, no. 2 (1970): 178–90.

Gash, Alison L. *Below the Radar: How Silence Can Save Civil Rights.* Oxford: Oxford University Press, 2015.

Gaspar Brown, Elizabeth. "Husband and Wife: Memorandum on the Mississippi Woman's Law of 1839." *Michigan Law Review* 42, no. 6 (1944): 1110–21.

Geddes, Rick, and Dean Lueck. "The Gains from Self-Ownership and the Expansion of Women's Rights." *American Economic Review* 92, no. 4 (2002): 1079–92.

Geddes, Rick, Dean Lueck, and Sharon Tennyson. "Human Capital Accumulation and the Expansion of Women's Economic Rights." *Journal of Law and Economics* 55, no. 4 (2012): 839–67.

Geddes, R. Richard, and Sharon Tennyson. "Passage of the Married Women's Property Acts and Earnings Acts in the United States: 1850 to 1920." *Research in Economic History* 29 (2013): 145–89.

General Laws, Memorials, and Resolutions of the Territory of Wyoming, Passed at the First Session of the Legislative Assembly (1869). Cheyenne, WY: S. Allan Bristol, 1870.

Gentzkow, Matthew, Bryan Kelly, and Matt Taddy. "Text as Data." *Journal of Economic Literature* 57, no. 3 (2019): 535–74.

Gleason, Shane A., Jennifer J. Jones, and Jessica Rae McBean. "The Role of Gender Norms in Judicial Decision-Making at the U.S. Supreme Court: The Case of Male and Female Justices." *American Politics Research* 47, no. 3 (2019): 494–529.

Goodman, Paul. "The Emergence of Homestead Exemption in the United States: Accommodation and Resistance to the Market Revolution, 1840–1880." *Journal of American History* 80, no. 2 (1993): 470–98.

Gray, Virginia. "Innovation in the States: A Diffusion Study." *American Political Science Review* 67, no. 4 (1973): 1174–85.

Green, Damita L. "'Occupation: Land Owner': African American Female Property Ownership in Clarendon County, South Carolina, 1870–1910." MA thesis, Morgan State University, 2019.

Grimmer, Justin. "A Bayesian Hierarchical Topic Model for Political Texts: Measuring Expressed Agendas in Senate Press Releases." *Political Analysis* 18, no. 1 (2010): 1–35.

Gubernatorial Elections: 1787–1997. Washington, DC: Congressional Quarterly, 1998.

Hacker, J. David, Libra Hilde, and James Holland Jones. "The Effect of the Civil War on Southern Marriage Patterns." *Journal of Southern History* 76, no. 1 (2010): 39–70.

Haines, Michael R. "Historical, Demographic, Economic, and Social Data: The United States, 1790–2002." Inter-university Consortium for Political and Social Research, 2010.

Hall, Kermit L. "Constitutional Machinery and Judicial Professionalism: The Careers of Midwestern State Appellate Court Judges, 1861–1899." In *The New High Priests:*

Lawyers in Post–Civil War America, edited by Gerard Gawalt, 29–49. Westport, CT: Greenwood Press, 1984.

Harrison, Maurice E. "The First Half-Century of the California Civil Code." *California Law Review* 10, no. 3 (1922): 185–201.

Hart, Albert. *The Civil Code of the State of California*. San Francisco: Sumner Whitney, 1880.

Hartog, Hendrik. *Man and Wife in America: A History*. Cambridge, MA: Harvard University Press, 2000.

Hartz, Louis. *The Liberal Tradition in America*. New York: Harcourt, Brace & World, 1955.

Hasday, Jill Elaine. "Contest and Consent: A Legal History of Marital Rape." *California Law Review* 88, no. 5 (2000): 1373–506.

Hazan, Moshe, David Weiss, and Hosny Zoabi. "Women's Liberation as a Financial Innovation." *Journal of Finance* 74, no. 6 (2019): 2915–56.

Herron, Paul E. *Framing the Solid South: The State Constitutional Conventions of Secession, Reconstruction, and Redemption, 1860–1902*. Lawrence: University Press of Kansas, 2017.

———. "Slavery and Freedom in American State Constitutional Development." *Journal of Policy History* 27, no. 2 (2015): 301–36.

Hersh, Blanche Glassman. *The Slavery of Sex: Feminist-Abolitionists in America*. Urbana: University of Illinois Press, 1978.

Hillyer, Curtis. *Nevada Compiled Laws 1929*. San Francisco: Bender-Moss, 1930.

Hinkle, Rachael K. "Into the Words: Using Statutory Text to Explore the Impact of Federal Courts on State Policy Diffusion." *American Journal of Political Science* 59, no. 4 (2015): 1002–21.

Hirschl, Ran. *Towards Juristocracy: The Origins and Consequences of the New Constitutionalism*. Cambridge, MA: Harvard University Press, 2004.

Hoff, Joan. *Law, Gender, and Injustice*. New York: New York University Press, 1991.

Holmes, Stephen, and Cass R. Sunstein. *The Cost of Rights: Why Liberty Depends on Taxes*. New York: Norton, 2000.

Hume, Richard L., and Jerry B. Gough. *Blacks, Carpetbaggers, and Scalawags: The Constitutional Conventions of Radical Reconstruction*. Baton Rouge: Louisiana State University Press, 2008.

Isenberg, Nancy. *Sex and Citizenship in Antebellum America*. Chapel Hill: University of North Carolina Press, 1998.

Jeffrey, Julie Roy. *Frontier Women: The Trans-Mississippi West 1840–1880*. New York: Hill and Wang, 1979.

Jones-Rogers, Stephanie E. *They Were Her Property: White Women as Slave Owners in the American South*. New Haven, CT: Yale University Press, 2019.

Journal of the Convention to Form a Constitution for the State of Wisconsin, with a Sketch of the Debates. Madison, WI: Tenney, Smith & Holt, 1848.

Journal of the Proceedings of the Constitutional Convention of the State of Mississippi, 1868. Jackson, MS: E. Stafford, 1871.

Journal of the Proceedings of the Constitutional Convention of the State of Mississippi, 1890. Jackson, MS: E. L. Martin, 1890.

Journal of the Senate of the State of Mississippi. Jackson, MS: J. L. Power, 1880.

Karch, Andrew. "Emerging Issues and Future Directions in State Policy Diffusion Research." *State Politics & Policy Quarterly* 7, no. 1 (2007): 54–80.

Kelly, John F. *A Treatise on the Law of Contracts of Married Women.* Legal Treatises, 1800–1926. Jersey City, NJ: F. D. Linn, 1882.

Kerber, Linda. *Women of the Republic: Intellect and Ideology in Revolutionary America.* Chapel Hill: University of North Carolina Press, 1980.

Kerr, James M. *Codes of California as Amended and in Force at the Close of the Forty-Third [Forty-Fourth] Session of the Legislature, 1919–[1921].* 2nd ed. San Francisco: Bender-Moss, 1920–1922.

Kessler-Harris, Alice. *In Pursuit of Equity: Women, Men, and the Quest for Economic Citizenship in 20th-Century America.* Oxford: Oxford University Press, 2001.

———. *Out to Work: A History of Wage-Earning Women in the United States.* New York: Oxford University Press, 1982.

Khan, B. Zorina. "Married Women's Property Laws and Female Commercial Activity: Evidence from United States Patent Records, 1790–1895." *Journal of Economic History* 56, no. 2 (1996): 356–88.

Kingdon, John W. *Agendas, Alternatives, and Public Policies.* 2nd ed. New York: Longman, 1995.

Koenig, Brigitte. "Panic of 1907." In *Encyclopedia of American Recessions and Depressions*, edited by Daniel J. Leab, 329–46. Santa Barbara, CA: ABC-CLIO, 2014.

Koudijs, Peter, and Laura Salisbury. "Limited Liability and Investment: Evidence from Changes in Marital Property Laws in the US South, 1840–1850." *Journal of Financial Economics* 138, no. 1 (2020): 1–26.

Laws of the State of Mississippi. Jackson, MS: B. D. Howard, 1839.

Laws of the State of Missouri [Fifteenth General Assembly]. Jefferson, MO: Hampton L. Boon, 1849.

Lazarou, Kathleen Elizabeth. *Concealed Under Petticoats: Married Women's Property and the Law of Texas, 1840–1913.* American Legal and Constitutional History: A Garland Series of Outstanding Dissertations. New York: Garland, 1986.

Lebsock, Suzanne D. "Radical Reconstruction and the Property Rights of Southern Women." *Journal of Southern History* 43, no. 2 (1977): 195–216.

Lemke, Jayme S. "Interjurisdictional Competition and the Married Women's Property Acts." *Public Choice* 166, no. 3 (2016): 291–313.

Lepler, Jessica M. *The Many Panics of 1837: People, Politics, and the Creation of a Transatlantic Financial Crisis*. New York: Cambridge University Press, 2013.

Lowi, Theodore J. *The End of Liberalism: Ideology, Policy, and the Crisis of Public Authority*. New York: Norton, 1969.

MacDonald, Daniel. "On the Question of Court Activism and Economic Interests in Nineteenth-Century Married Women's Property Law." In *Law and Social Economics: Essays in Ethical Values for Theory, Practice, and Policy*, edited by Mark D. White, 139–60. New York: Palgrave Macmillan, 2015.

MacDonald, Daniel, and Yasemin Dildar. "Married Women's Economic Independence and Divorce in the Nineteenth- and Early-Twentieth-Century United States." *Social Science History* 42, no. 3 (2018): 601–29.

Marsh, Andrew J. *Official Report of the Debates and Proceedings in the Constitutional Convention of the State of Nevada, Assembled at Carson City, July 4th, 1864, to Form a Constitution and State Government*. San Francisco: Frank Eastman, 1866.

Martin, Bonnie. "Neighbor-to-Neighbor Capitalism: Local Credit Networks and the Mortgaging of Slaves." In *Slavery's Capitalism: A New History of American Economic Development*, edited by Sven Beckert and Seth Rockman, 107–21. Philadelphia: University of Philadelphia Press, 2016.

Masur, Kate. *Until Justice Be Done: America's First Civil Rights Movement, from the Revolution to Reconstruction*. New York: Norton, 2021.

Matsuda, Mari J. "The West and the Legal State of Women: Explanations of Frontier Feminism." *Journal of the West* 24, no. 1 (1985): 47–56.

Mayes, Edward. "The Legal and Judicial History." In *Biographical and Historical Memoirs of Mississippi: Embracing an Authentic and Comprehensive Account of the Chief Events of the History of the State and a Record of the Lives of Many of the Most Worthy and Illustrious Families and Individuals*, edited by Goodspeed Brothers, 100–131. Chicago: Goodspeed, 1891.

McCammon, Holly. "Using Event History Analysis in Historical Research: With Illustrations from a Study of the Passage of Women's Protective Legislation." *International Review of Social History* 43 (1998): 33–55.

McCammon, Holly J., Sandra C. Arch, and Erin M. Bergner. "A Radical Demand Effect: Early US Feminists and the Married Women's Property Acts." *Social Science History* 38, nos. 1–2 (2014): 221–50.

McCammon, Holly J., Karen E. Campbell, Ellen M. Granberg, and Christine Mowery. "How Movements Win: Gendered Opportunity Structures and U.S. Women's Suffrage Movements, 1866 to 1919." *American Sociological Review* 66, no. 1 (2001): 49–70.

McDevitt, Catherine L., and James R. Irwin. "The Narrowing of the Gender Wealth Gap Across the Nineteenth-Century United States." *Social Science History* 41, no. 2 (2017): 255–81.

McDonagh, Eileen. "The Feudal Family Versus American Political Development: From Separate Spheres to Woman Suffrage." In *Stating the Family: New Directions in the Study of American Politics*, edited by Julie Novkov and Carol Nackenoff, 164–96. Lawrence: University Press of Kansas, 2020.

McGrane, Reginald Charles. *The Panic of 1837: Some Financial Problems of the Jacksonian Era*. New York: Russel & Russel, 1965.

McMurray, Orrin K. "The Beginnings of the Community Property System in California and the Adoption of the Common Law." *California Law Review* 3, no. 5 (1915): 359–80.

Melder, Keith Eugene. *Beginnings of Sisterhood: The American Woman's Rights Movement, 1800–1850*. Studies in the Life of Women. New York: Schocken, 1977.

Meyer, David D. "The Constitutionalization of Family Law." *Family Law Quarterly* 42, no. 3 (2008): 529–72.

Moncrief, Sandra. "The Mississippi Married Women's Property Act of 1839." *Journal of Mississippi History* 47, no. 2 (1985): 110–25.

Morantz, Alison D. "There's No Place Like Home: Homestead Exemption and Judicial Constructions of Family in Nineteenth-Century America." *Law and History Review* 24, no. 2 (2006): 245–95.

Morone, James A. "Political Culture: Consensus, Conflict, and Culture War." In *The Oxford Handbook of American Political Development*, edited by Richard Valelly, Suzanne Mettler, and Robert Lieberman, 132–47. Oxford: Oxford University Press, 2016.

Morrow, Clarence J. "Matrimonial Property Law in Louisiana." In *Matrimonial Property Law*, edited by W. Friedmann, 29–88. Toronto: Carswell, 1955.

"National Political Party Platforms." In *The American Presidency Project*, ed. John T. Woolley and Gerhard Peters. Santa Barbara: University of California, 1999–2020. http://www.presidency.ucsb.edu/platforms.php.

New York Field Codes 1850–1865. Vol. 3: *The Civil Code of the State of New York*. 1865. Reprint. Union, NJ: Lawbook Exchange, 1998.

Novkov, Julie. *Constituting Workers, Protecting Women: Gender, Law, and Labor in the Progressive Era and New Deal Years*. Ann Arbor: University of Michigan Press, 2001.

———. "*Pace v. Alabama*: Interracial Love, the Marriage Contract, and Post-bellum Foundations of the Family." In *The Supreme Court and American Political Development*, edited by Ronald Kahn and Kenneth Kersch, 329–65. Lawrence: University Press of Kansas, 2006.

O'Connor, Karen. *Women's Organizations' Use of the Courts*. Lexington, MA: Lexington Books, 1980.

Orren, Karen. *Belated Feudalism: Labor, the Law, and Liberal Development in the United States*. Cambridge: Cambridge University Press, 1991.

Park, Orville A., et al. *Park's Annotated Code of the State of Georgia 1914*. Vol. 2. Atlanta, GA: Harrison, 1915.

Parma, Rosamond. "The History of the Adoption of the Codes of California." *Law Library Journal* 22 (1929): 8–21.

Pascoe, Peggy. *What Comes Naturally: Miscegenation Law and the Making of Race in America*. Oxford: Oxford University Press, 2009.

Pope, Christie Farnham. "Southern Homesteads for Negroes." *Agricultural History* 44, no. 2 (1970): 201–12.

Posner, Richard A. "The Cost of Rights: Implications for Central and Eastern Europe—and for the United States." *Tulsa Law Journal* 32, no. 1 (1996): 1–20.

Price, John G., ed. *Debates and Proceedings of the Convention Which Assembled at Little Rock, January 7th, 1868*. Little Rock, AR: J. G. Price, 1868.

Priest, Claire. "Creating an American Property Law: Alienability and Its Limits in American History." *Harvard Law Review* 120, no. 2 (2006): 385–459.

Proceedings of the Constitutional Convention of South Carolina. Charleston, SC: Denny & Perry, 1868.

Quinn, Sarah L. *American Bonds: How Credit Markets Shaped a Nation*. Princeton, NJ: Princeton University Press, 2019.

Rabkin, Peggy A. *Fathers to Daughters: The Legal Foundations of Female Emancipation*. Westport, CT: Greenwood Press, 1980.

———. "The Origins of Law Reform: The Social Significance of the Nineteenth-Century Codification Movement and Its Contribution to the Passage of the Early Married Women's Property Acts." *Buffalo Law Review* 24 (1975): 683–760.

Ranney, Joseph A. "Anglicans, Merchants, and Feminists: A Comparative Study of the Evolution of Married Women's Rights in Virginia, New York, and Wisconsin." *William & Mary Journal of Race, Gender, and Social Justice* 6, no. 3 (2000): 493–559.

———. *In the Wake of Slavery: Civil War, Civil Rights, and the Reconstruction of Southern Law*. Westport, CT: Praeger, 2006.

———. *A Legal History of Mississippi: Race, Class, and the Struggle for Opportunity*. Jackson: University Press of Mississippi, 2019.

Rapaport, Richard A. "Relationship of the Women's Movement to the Passage of Married Women's Property Acts in the Mid–Nineteenth Century." Stanford Law School, Stanford University, 1973.

Ray, Amanda J. "The Impact of Statehood and Republican Politics on Women's Legal Rights in West Virginia, 1863–1872." MA thesis, West Virginia University, 2001.

"Removal of the Disabilities of Married Women in Mississippi." *American Law Review* 26 (1892): 115–16.

Report of the Debates and Proceedings of the Convention for the Revision of the Constitution of the State of Indiana. Indianapolis, IN: A. H. Brown, 1850.

Reppy, Alison. "The Field Codification Concept." In *David Dudley Field: Centenary Essays*, edited by Alison Reppy, 17–54. New York: New York University School of Law, 1949.
Richards, Leonard L. *The California Gold Rush and the Coming of the Civil War.* New York: Knopf, 2007.
Ritter, Gretchen. "Gender as a Category of Analysis in American Political Development." In *Political Women and American Democracy*, edited by Christina Wolbrecht, Lisa Baldez, and Karen Beckwith, 12–30. New York: Cambridge University Press, 2008.
Roberts, Evan. *Women's Rights and Women's Labor: Married Women's Property Laws and Labor Force Participation.* Working paper. Minneapolis: Minnesota Population Center, University of Minnesota, 2014.
Rockoff, Hugh. "Crisis of 1857." In *Business Cycles and Depressions: An Encyclopedia*, edited by David Glasner, 128–31. New York: Garland, 1997.
Roehrkasse, Alexander F. "Failure, Fraud, and Force: The Rise and Fall of the Debtor's Prison in New York, 1760–1840." MA thesis, University of California, Berkeley, 2014.
Rowland, Dunbar. *Courts, Judges, and Lawyers of Mississippi, 1798–1935.* Jackson, MS: Hederman Bros., 1935.
Rusk, Jerrold G. *A Statistical History of the American Electorate.* Washington, DC: CQ Press, 2001.
Ryan, Rebecca M. "The Sex Right: A Legal History of the Marital Rape Exemption." *Law & Social Inquiry* 20, no. 4 (1995): 941–1001.
Salamone, Michael F. "Community and Persuasion: The Influence of the Federalist Society on the Supreme Court." Paper presented at the American Political Science Association Annual Meeting, Washington, DC, 2014.
Salmon, Marylynn. *Women and the Law of Property in Early America.* Chapel Hill: University of North Carolina Press, 1986.
Sánchez-Eppler, Karen. "Bodily Bonds: The Intersecting Rhetorics of Feminism and Abolition." *Representations*, no. 24 (1988): 28–59.
Schuele, Donna C. "Community Property Law and the Politics of Married Women's Rights in Nineteenth-Century California." In *The American West: Interactions, Intersections, and Injunctions*, edited by Gordon Morris Bakken and Brenda Farrington, 413–49. New York: Garland, 2001.
———. "'A Robbery to the Wife': Culture, Gender, and Marital Property in California Law and Politics, 1850–1890." PhD diss., University of California, Berkeley, 1999.
Scott, William B. *In Pursuit of Happiness: American Conceptions of Property from the Seventeenth to the Twentieth Century.* Bloomington: Indiana University Press, 1977.

Shammas, Carole. "Re-assessing the Married Women's Property Acts." *Journal of Women's History* 6, no. 1 (1994): 9–30.

Shapiro, Michael. "Panic of 1857." In *Encyclopedia of American Recessions and Depressions*, edited by Daniel J. Leab, 181–99. Santa Barbara, CA: ABC-CLIO, 2014.

Shire, Laurel Clark. *The Threshold of Manifest Destiny: Gender and National Expansion in Florida*. Philadelphia: University of Pennsylvania Press, 2016.

Shue, Henry. *Basic Rights: Subsistence, Affluence, and U.S. Foreign Policy*. Princeton, NJ: Princeton University Press, 1996.

Siegel, Reva B. "Home as Work: The First Woman's Rights Claims Concerning Wives' Household Labor, 1850–1880." *Yale Law Journal* 103, no. 5 (1994): 1073–217.

———. "The Modernization of Marital Status Law: Adjudicating Wives' Rights to Earning, 1860–1930." *Georgetown Law Journal* 82 (1995): 2127–211.

Smith, Rogers M. *Civic Ideals: Conflicting Visions of Citizenship in U.S. History*. New Haven, CT: Yale University Press, 1997.

Speth, Linda E. "The Married Women's Property Acts, 1839–1965: Reform, Reaction, or Revolution?" In *Women and the Law: A Social Historical Perspective*, edited by D. Kelly Weisberg, 69–91. Cambridge, MA: Schenkman, 1982.

Stanley, Amy Dru. "Conjugal Bonds and Wage Labor: Rights of Contract in the Age of Emancipation." *Journal of American History* 75, no. 2 (1988): 471–500.

———. *From Bondage to Contract: Wage Labor, Marriage, and the Market in the Age of Slave Emancipation*. Cambridge: Cambridge University Press, 1998.

Stanton, Elizabeth Cady, Susan B. Anthony, and Matilda Joslyn Gage, eds. *History of Woman Suffrage*. Vol. 1. New York: Fowler & Wells, 1881.

"State Homestead Exemption Laws." *Yale Law Journal* 46, no. 6 (1937): 1023–41.

Sullivan, Kathleen. *Constitutional Context: Women and Rights Discourse in Nineteenth-Century America*. Baltimore, MD: Johns Hopkins University Press, 2007.

Sundberg, Sara Brooks. "Women and Property in Early Louisiana: Legal Systems at Odds." *Journal of the Early Republic* 32, no. 4 (2012): 633–65.

Thurston, Chloe. *At the Boundaries of Homeownership: Credit, Discrimination, and the American State*. Cambridge: Cambridge University Press, 2018.

Tsesis, Alexander. *The Thirteenth Amendment and American Freedom: A Legal History*. New York: New York University Press, 2004.

VanBurkleo, Sandra F. *"Belonging to the World": Women's Rights and American Constitutional Culture*. New York: Oxford University Press, 2001.

Van Ee, Daun. *David Dudley Field and the Reconstruction of the Law*. American Legal and Constitutional History: A Garland Series of Outstanding Dissertations. New York: Garland, 1986.

Volden, Craig. "States as Policy Laboratories: Emulating Success in the Children's Health Insurance Program." *American Journal of Political Science* 50, no. 2 (2006): 294–312.

Volden, Craig, Michael M. Ting, and Daniel P. Carpenter. "A Formal Model of Learning and Policy Diffusion." *American Political Science Review* 102, no. 3 (2008): 319–32.

Wallace, D. D. "The South Carolina Constitutional Convention of 1895." *Sewanee Review* 4, no. 3 (1896): 348–60.

Wallenstein, Peter. *Tell the Court I Love My Wife: Race, Marriage, and Law—an American History*. New York: Palgrave Macmillan, 2002.

Wallis, John Joseph. National Bureau of Economic Research (NBER)/University of Maryland State Constitution Project. N.d. http://www.stateconstitutions.umd.edu.

Warbasse, Elizabeth Bowles. *The Changing Legal Rights of Married Women: 1800–1861*. American Legal and Constitutional History: A Garland Series of Outstanding Dissertations. New York: Garland, 1987.

Wicker, Elmus. *Banking Panics of the Gilded Age*. Cambridge: Cambridge University Press, 2000.

Woodward-Burns, Robinson. *Hidden Laws: How State Constitutions Stabilize American Politics*. New Haven, CT: Yale University Press, 2021.

Wormser, Richard. *The Rise and Fall of Jim Crow*. New York: St. Martin's Press, 2003.

Wortman, Marlene Stein. *Women in American Law: From Colonial Times to the New Deal*. New York: Holmes & Meier, 1985.

Wright, Gavin. *Slavery and American Economic Development*. Baton Rouge: Louisiana State University Press, 2006.

Yamin, Priscilla. *American Marriage: A Political Institution*. Philadelphia: University of Pennsylvania Press, 2012.

Zackin, Emily. *Looking for Rights in All the Wrong Places: Why State Constitutions Contain America's Positive Rights*. Princeton, NJ: Princeton University Press, 2013.

Zackin, Emily, and Chloe Thurston. *The Political Economy of American Debt Relief*. Chicago: University of Chicago Press, forthcoming.

Zeigler, Sara L. "Uniformity and Conformity: Regionalism and the Adjudication of the Married Women's Property Acts." *Polity* 28, no. 4 (1996): 467–95.

Index

abolitionist movement, 63
abortion rights, 174
Alabama reforms, *94*, 128, 145, 231n101
Alexander, Gregory, 27
Allen, James, 130
American political development (APD) perspective, 4–7, 32
antimiscegenation laws, 82–83, 107–108
Apple v. Ganong, 160–161
Arch, Sandra C., 29
Arkansas, enslaved human property, 78
Arkansas reforms, *97*, *105*, 108, 197n31
Aultman v. Rush, 165

Baker, Mary Lou, 173
Balleisen, Edward, 74
Balogh, Brian, 151
Baptist, Edward, 79
Bardaglio, Peter, 83
Bateman, David, 171, 175
Bell, Derrick, 171
Bell, Duncan, 6
Benson, Megan, 76

Bergner, Erin M., 29
Black codes, 79–80
Boehmke, Frederick, 134
Bowdish, Lawrence, 174
Box-Steffensmeier, Janet, 185
Brennan, William J., 42
Bridgers v. Howell, 165–166
Bridges, Amy, 116, 124
Broussard, Joyce, 26
business interests, 40, 76, 151, 152
business ownership, 12–13, *18*, 20, 24

California reforms: civil law and, 14; codification movement and, 67–68, 203n31; constitutional provisions, 68, *99*, *103*, 116–119, 120, 121, 125; frontier settlement projects and, 1; interstate reform diffusion and, 144, 145–146; migration and, 146; overview, *47*; racial hierarchies and, 80; timing of, *54–56*; wills law, *18*
Campbell, Josiah A. P., 66
Carpenter, Daniel, 133
Carroll, Mark, 83, 147

case studies, 44–45, 46–48
chancery courts. *See* equity courts
chattel slavery. *See* enslaved human property
Chickasaw tribal law, 25
child custody, 11–12
civil law, 14, 51, 117
Civil War: constitutional provisions and, 38, 90, 92; economic crisis and, 75, 111, 112; gender imbalances and, 113, 188; industrialization and, 160
Clark, Laurel, 78–79
codification movement, 28, 36, 64–69, 65, 67–68, 146, 203n31
Coinage Act (1834), 75
Colorado reforms, 48, 54–56, 59, 144, 147
commercialization: codification movement and, 64; credit markets and, 164; female labor-force participation and, 76; indebtedness and, 27, 74, 110; male beneficiaries and, 6, 27; state court interpretations and, 163
common law, 117, 119, 151. *See also* coverture
community property, 14, 117, 119, 137, 147, 188
Compton, Tonia, 80, 81
Congress, 42, 200n8
constitutional conventions: frequency of, 102; general interstate diffusion and, 128; ideal citizen and, 89; occasions for, 38, 88, 90; woman suffrage and, 108, 111, 114, 167. *See also* constitutional provisions
constitutional provisions, 38–39, 103–104, 128–129, 208n5; codification movement and, 68; homestead exemptions, 39, 104, 109–110, 111, 112, 121–124, 122, 212n94, 213n101; importance of, 88–89; interstate reform diffusion and, 89, 109, 116–118, 119–120, 121, 124–128, 127, 129, 181, 184; iterative process and, 4, 38–39, 40, 41; liminal nature of, 89, 104–105, 128; partial rights and, 114; partisan politics and, 71, 74, 107, 114–115, 120–121; paternalism and, 84–85, 109, 112–114, 115, 118, 120, 121; racial hierarchies and, 88, 89, 105–106, 107, 111, 115, 121, 167; as social safety net, 89, 102, 104, 124, 207n1; southern states, 39, 91–98, 106–115, 209nn17,30, 210n34; statehood constitutions, 99–102, 115–121. *See also* positive rights
control-and-management provisions: interstate reform diffusion and, 135, 141; overview, 16–17, 19–20; post-suffrage reforms and, 172–173; reform timing, 23, 141, 172–173; statute dating methods, 178–179
Cott, Nancy, 74–75, 175
coverture, 2; broad relevance of, 14–15; constitutional provisions on, 112; constraints under, 11–12, 14–15; exceptions to, 12–13, 14, 64, 196n23; feudal elements of, 6; financial support for women under, 195n5; state court interpretations and, 152, 158; Supreme Court on, 42; woman suffrage and, 195n12
credit markets: debtor protection and, 79, 110, 111, 160, 161; enslaved human property and, 77, 79; modern reforms, 12, 173–174; state court interpretations and, 156; trends in, 36
Cross, Frank, 105

Dakota Territory reforms, *16*, 139, 214n2
Davis v. Foy, 157
debt-free separate estates exemptions: constitutional provisions, 112, 116; enslaved human property and, 19; event history analysis and, 137; homestead exemptions and, 69, 188; interstate reform diffusion and, 138–139, 141, *142*; overview, 15, *16*, 19; reform timing, 23; statute dating methods, *178*
debtor-creditor disputes: codification movement and, 64; constitutional provisions and, 110; debtor protection and, 38, 76; earnings acts and, 160; partial rights and, 40; reform legislation and, 38; state court interpretations and, 40, 155–156, 157, 158, 159–161, 163–164, 167
debtor protection: constitutional provisions and, 104, 109–110, 115, 118; credit markets and, 79, 110, 111, 160, 161; earnings acts and, 166; enslaved human property and, 76, 77–78, 79, 205n75; family property and, 13, 14, 27, 28, 83–84, 113; fraud concerns and, 76, 114, 118; historical studies of, 27; increase in indebtedness and, 27, 36, 74–75, 109–111, 112; personal motivations for, 1, 3, 75–76; racial hierarchies and, 80; as social safety net, 75, 89, 104, 124, 207n1; state court interpretations and, 157, 158–159, 161. *See also* debt-free separate estates exemptions; homestead exemptions
debt relief, 1, 75–76, 112. *See also* debtor protection
Democratic Party, 71

democratization, 6
Desmarais, Bruce, 134
Distribution Act (1836), 75
domestic violence, 12
Dougan, Michael, 78
Dudziak, Mary, 172

earnings acts: event history analysis and, 135, 137; household labor and, 86; interstate reform diffusion and, *142*; overview, *17*, 20; societal views of property and, 165–166; state court interpretations and, 160, 165, 217n29; statute dating methods, *179*; timing of, *24*
economic crises, 26–27, 36, 74, 110–111
economic forces. *See* credit markets; economic crises; indebtedness, increase in
elite power, 56, 171–172, 174. *See also* male beneficiaries; state power
enslaved human property: credit markets and, 77, 79; debt-free separate estates exemptions and, 19; debtor protection and, 76, 77–78, 79, 205n75; historical studies of, 26; inheritance and, 78–79; reform pathways and, 45; regional differences and, 146–147; state court interpretations and, 157, 158; state power and, 5; state projects and, 37
Equal Credit Opportunity Act (1974), 12, 174
Equal Rights Amendment, 174
equity courts, 13, 19, 83, 154–155, 188–189
event history analysis, 132, 134–135, *136*, 137; discrete-time processes and, 185; outcome table, *136*; variables for, 134, *135*, 185, *187*, 188–189, 215n12

Index 237

family law, 42
family property protection, 13, 14, 27, 28, 83–84, 113
federalism, 5
female labor-force participation, 76, 160. *See also* earnings acts
feminist groups. *See* women's rights activism
feme-sole provisions: codification movement and, 67, 68; constitutional provisions, 109, 113–114, 116, 119–120, 167; control-and-management provisions and, 19; as coverture exceptions, 12–13; event history analysis and, 137; fraud concerns and, 120; interstate reform diffusion and, *143*; overview, *18*, 20; reform timing, *24*; state court interpretations and, 156, 161, 163–164; statute dating methods, *180*
fertility rates, 36
Field, David Dudley, 67, 146
Field, Stephen J., 67–68, 146
Field Code, 67, 68, 146, 203n31
First National Woman's Rights Convention (1850), 86
Florida: enslaved human property, 78–79; frontier status of, 197n31; post-suffrage reforms, 172–173. *See also* Florida reforms
Florida reforms: constitutional provisions, 90, 92–93, 231n101; gender imbalances and, 106, 147; overview, *46*; timing of, *43*, *45*, *49–51*
Forbath, William, 150
Fraser, Nancy, 175
fraud concerns: codification movement and, 68; debtor protection and, 76, 114, 118; sole-trader provisions and, 120
French civil law, 14
Fritz, Christian, 102, 124
Frontiero v. Richardson, 42
frontier settlement projects: competition among states and, 31, 116, 145; constitutional provisions and, 1, 106, 116, 119; event history analysis and, 137, 188; Native American displacement and, 5, 26, 37, 106, 147; reform pathways and, 51; woman suffrage and, 81. *See also* settler colonialism
frontier territories/states: land speculation in, 75, 118–119; southern states as part of, 197nn31,33. *See also* frontier territories/states, reforms in
frontier territories/states, reforms in, 197n31; constitutional provisions and, 38; historical studies of, 26; overview, 51; racial hierarchies and, 147; timing of, 81–82, *82*. *See also* frontier settlement projects; statehood constitutions; *specific states*

Gash, Alison, 144
Geddes, Geoffrey, 84
Geddes, R. Richard, 30
gender imbalances: Civil War and, 113, 188; event history analysis and, 135, 137, 188, 215n12; interstate reform diffusion and, 145. *See also* frontier settlement projects
Georgia reforms, *94*, 145
Gilded Age, 150
Goodman, Paul, 69
Gordon, Linda, 175
Gray, Virginia, 132
Gwynn v. Gwynn, 166

238 *Index*

Habenicht v. Rawls, 166
Hacker, J. David, 113
Hadley, Thomas, 1, 75–76
Hall, Kermit, 151
Harden, Jeffrey, 134
Herron, Paul, 124–125, 171–172
Hersh, Blanche Glassman, 63
Hilde, Libra, 113
Hirschl, Ran, 172
History of Woman Suffrage (Stanton, Anthony, and Gage), 84
Holmes, Stephen, 105
Holmes v. Holmes, 154
Homestead Act (1862), 80
homestead acts, 80, 206n89
homestead exemptions: constitutional provisions, 39, 104, 109–110, 111, 112, 121–124, *122*, 212n94, 213n101; event history analysis and, 135, 137, 188; in legislation, 69–70, 74, 75; movement for, 36; paternalism and, 124, 213n101
household labor compensation, 61, 162, 174
Housing and Community Development Act (1974), 174
husband-wife relationship. *See* marriage relationship

Idaho reforms, 138
ideal citizen, 5–6, 25–26, 77, 89
Illinois Earnings Act (1869), 63
Illinois reforms, *17*, 63, 123
indebtedness, increase in, 27, 36, 74–75, 109–111, 112
Indiana reforms, 84–85
industrialization, 27, 31, 36, 74, 76, 160
inheritance: antimiscegenation laws and, 83, 107–108; enslaved human property and, 78–79; regional differences, 147; under coverture, 11. *See also* family property protection
interstate reform diffusion, 42–43; vs. coincidence, 133; constitutional provisions and, 89, 109, 116–118, 119–120, 121, 124–128, *127*, 129, 181, 184; decentralized nature of reform and, 4, 43, 145; extent of, 124–128; institutional permeability and, 42; interstate migration and, 43, 117, 121, 146; iterative process and, 44, 170; methodology and, 132, 214n2; participants in, 126, *127*, 128; state court interpretations and, 163. *See also* event history analysis; text analysis
Iowa reforms, 116–117, 145
iterative reform process, 34, 35, 38–41; constitutional provisions and, 4, 38–39, 40, 41; interstate reform diffusion and, 44, 170; methodology and, 43–44; reform legislation and, 38; reform timing and, 147; state court interpretations and, 38, 39–41, 153

joint property rights, 29, 60–61, 86
Jones, Bradford, 185
Jones, James Holland, 113
Jones-Rogers, Stephanie, 78, 146
judicial interpretations. *See* state court interpretations

Kansas reforms, *100*, 126, 144, 147
Kerber, Linda, 11
Kingdon, John, 35, 200n1
Koudijs, Peter, 77

land speculation, 36, 75, 118–119, 158–159
Lebsock, Suzanne, 109, 123

legal identity, 11
legislatures. *See* reform legislation
Lemke, Jayme, 31, 133
liberalism, 6, 76
liberalization, 6–7
Livermore, Mary, 63
Lockwood, Belva, 64
logit models. *See* event history analysis
Louisiana reforms, 14, *95*, 126, 147, 209n19

Maine Earnings Act (1857), 86
Maine reforms, *18*, 86
male beneficiaries, 34; debt relief and, 75–76; homestead exemptions and, 69–70; importance of, 37; industrialization/commercialization and, 6, 27; iterative process and, 153; iterative reform process and, 41; personal motivations of, 1, 3, 75–76; reform limits and, 86; reform pathways and, 35; state court interpretations and, 152; suffrage movement and, 62; women's rights activism and, 28–29. *See also* state power
male political actors. *See* male beneficiaries
marital rape, 12
marriage: civic importance of, 37; frequency of, 2; state power and, 175. *See also* marriage relationship; marriage settlements
marriage relationship: debtor protection and, 118; reform limits and, 6, 86, 162–163; state court interpretations, 162–163; under coverture, 11–12
marriage settlements, 13, 83

married women's property reform: ambivalence about, 36–37; common pathways to, 34–35, 45, 51; decentralized nature of, 4, 43, 144–145; economics research on, 22, 30–32; historical studies of, 21–22, 25–30; impacts of, 31, 58, 144; liminal nature of, 89, 104–105, 128; limits of, 6, 85–86, 162–163, 170; malleability of, 35–36, 58, 200n1; state projects and, 37, 56, 80–82; two-level process of, 33, 169–170. *See also* reform types
Maryland reforms, 39, *103*
Massachusetts reforms, *17*, 144
Matsuda, Mari, 81
Mayes, Edward, 161
McCammon, Holly, 29
McGrane, Reginald Charles, 75
methodology, 43–45, 51, 177–189; case studies, 44–45, *46–48*; interstate reform diffusion and, 132, 214n2; statute dating, 30–31, 177, *178–181*, *182–184*. *See also* event history analysis; text analysis
Michigan reforms, *16*, *103*, *104*, 126
middle class, growth of, 27
Mississippi reforms: Chickasaw tribal law and, 25; codification movement, 66; constitutional provisions, 39, 91–92, 109–112, 114–115, 122, 162, 209n30, 210n34; economic forces and, 75–76, 79; enslaved human property and, 1, 26, 45, 78, 79; homestead exemptions, 75, 109–110, 111, 121; interstate reform diffusion and, 131; migration and, 146; overview, *46*; paternalism and, 84; state court interpretations, 156–163, 217n29; timing of, 45, *49–50*, 145

Missouri reforms, 69
Moncrief, Sandra, 75
Montana reforms, 138
Murrell, Ethel Ernest, 173

National Woman Suffrage Association (NWSA), 61
Native Americans: miscegenation laws and, 83. *See also* settler colonialism
Nebraska reforms, *18*, 139
negative rights, 102, 104, 105
Netterville v. Barber, 161
Nevada reforms: constitutional provisions, *100*, 119–121, 123; homestead exemption, 123; interstate reform diffusion and, 145–146; overview, *48*; timing of, *54–56*
New York reforms: codification movement and, 67, 68–69; constitutional provisions, 116–117; historical studies of, 25; interstate reform diffusion and, 116–117, 144, 145; overview, *47*; paternalism and, 84; state court interpretations, 154–156; timing of, 45, *52–53*
North Carolina reforms, *98*, 126, 128, 209n19
North Dakota reforms, *101*. *See also* Dakota Territory reforms
northern/midwestern states, reforms in: overviews, 45, *47*; timing of, *52–53*, 148. *See also specific states*

Ohio reforms, 45, *47, 52–53*, 144
Oregon reforms, *100*, 121

Panic of 1837, 27, 75
Panic of 1857, 27
partial rights: codification movement and, 66; constitutional provisions and, 114; state court interpretations and, 40, 76, 150, 152, 153, 156
partisan politics, 70–71, *72–73*, 204n50; bipartisan agreement, 71, 74, 107, 114–115, 120–121

Pascoe, Peggy, 83
paternalism: ambivalence about reform and, 36–37; constitutional provisions and, 84–85, 109, 112–114, 115, 118, 120, 121; homestead exemptions and, 124, 213n101; reform legislation and, 28, 83–85; state court interpretations and, 150, 155, 159, 161, 165
Pelan, Sarah, 158
Pelzer v. Campbell, 163–165
percentage female. *See* gender imbalances
policy diffusion, 132. *See also* interstate reform diffusion
political parties. *See* partisan politics
positive rights, 39, 89–90; debtor protection and, 104; iterative reform process and, 4, 38; liminal nature of reform and, 89, 104–105, 128; as social safety net, 102; in southern constitutions, 45, 108, 111–112; state court interpretations and, 162; in statehood constitutions, 116
post-Reconstruction constitutional provisions, 38, 90, *91–93, 94, 96–97*, 209n19; positive rights in, 111–112; racial hierarchies and, 106, 107, 111, 115; state court interpretations and, 167; woman suffrage and, 111, 167
property: Black codes and, 79–80; earnings and, 20, 165–166; positive vs. negative rights and, 105; societal views of, 20, 27–28, 36, 165–166
property registration, 19, 39, 105, 116, 128

protective motivations. *See* debtor protection; family property protection; paternalism

Rabkin, Peggy, 67
racial hierarchies: antimiscegenation laws and, 82–83, 108; Black codes and, 79–80; constitutional provisions and, 88, 89, 105–106, 107, 111, 115, 121, 167; frontier territories/states, 147; homestead acts and, 80, 206n89; reform legislation and, 2, 79–80. *See also* enslaved human property
Radical Republicans, 109, 112, 115, 123
Randolf, B. F., 113
Ranney, Joseph, 63, 83
Ray, Amanda, 204n50
Reconstruction: interracial marriages and, 108; partisan politics and, 204n50. *See also* Reconstruction constitutions
Reconstruction constitutions, 38, 90, *91–92*, *94–98*; homestead exemptions in, 123; interstate reform diffusion and, 124–125; Mississippi case study, 109–111; racial inclusivity in, 106–107; South Carolina case study, 112–114, 115
Reconstruction, end of. *See* post-Reconstruction constitutional provisions
reform legislation, 57–87; antimiscegenation laws and, 82–83; codification movement and, 28, 64–69, *65*; coverture exceptions and, 196n23; debtor-creditor disputes and, 38; economic forces and, 74–76, 79; gender imbalances and, 59, *60*; group mobilization and, 57–58; homestead exemptions and, 69–70, 74, 75; iterative reform process and, 38; partisan politics and, 70–71, *72–73*, 74; paternalism and, 28, 83–85; racial hierarchies and, 2, 79–80; temperance movement and, 63–64; text analysis on, 138–139, 141–144, *141*, *142*, *143*, 184–185
reform timing, 22, 23, 24, 25; case studies and, 45; decentralized nature of reform and, 43, 145; methodology and, 30–31, 177, *178–181*, *182–184*; northern/midwestern states, 52–53, 148; southern states, 49–51, 148; variations in, 147–148; western territories/states, 54–56, 81–82, *82*, 147–148
reform types, 15, *16–18*, 131–132; property registration, 19, 39, 105, 116, 128; wills laws, *18*, 20–21, 25, 45, *143*, *180–181*. *See also* control-and-management provisions; debt-free separate estates exemptions; earnings acts; sole-trader provisions
Republican Party, 70–71
rights guarantees. *See* positive rights
Ritter, Gretchen, 5
Roberts, Evan, 31
Rowland, Dunbar, 66
Runnels, H. G., 146

Salisbury, Laura, 77
Salmon, Marylynn, 11
Schuele, Donna, 68
Scott, William, 165
secession. *See* Civil War
separate estates exemptions. *See* debt-free separate estates exemptions
settler colonialism: economic boom and, 75; frontier settlement projects

and, 5, 26, 37, 81, 106, 147;
homestead acts and, 80; statehood
constitutions and, 106. *See also*
frontier settlement projects
Shannon, William, 117, 146
Shire, Laurel Clark, 106, 147
Siegel, Reva, 28–29
single women, 11
slavery. *See* enslaved human property
sole-trader provisions: constitutional
provisions, 119–120; as coverture
exceptions, 12–13; event history
analysis and, 137; fraud concerns
and, 120; interstate reform diffusion
and, *143*; overview, *18, 20*; reform
timing, 24; state court
interpretations and, 161, 163–164;
statute dating methods, *180*. *See also*
feme-sole provisions
South Carolina reforms: constitutional
provisions, 40, *91*, 108, 112–114, 115;
overview, *46*; state court
interpretations and, 153, 163–167;
timing of, 45, *49–51*
South Dakota reforms, *101*. *See also*
Dakota Territory reforms
Southern Homestead Act (1866), 206n89
southern states: defined, 209n17;
frontier status of, 197nn31,33. *See
also* Reconstruction constitutions;
southern states, reforms in
southern states, reforms in: Black codes
and, 79–80; constitutional
provisions, 39, *91–98*, 106–115,
209nn17,30, 210n34; overviews, 45,
46; paternalism and, 83–84; timing
of, *49–51*, 148. *See also* enslaved
human property; racial hierarchies;
specific states
Spanish civil law, 14, 51, 117

Spencer, Sarah, 157
Stanton, Elizabeth Cady, 63
state court interpretations, 3–4,
149–168, 200n5; court-legislature
relationships and, 150–153, 156;
enslaved human property and, 157,
158; historical studies of, 29;
importance of, 167–168; iterative
reform process and, 38, 39–41, 153;
Mississippi case study, 156–163,
217n29; New York case study,
154–156; partial rights and, 40, 76,
150, 152, 153, 156; partisan
agreement on, 107; South Carolina
case study, 153, 163–167
statehood constitutions: conventions,
88, 90; reform provisions, *99–102*,
115–121
state institutions, 5, 42, 44. *See also*
constitutional conventions; iterative
reform process; reform legislation;
state court interpretations
state legislatures. *See* positive rights;
reform legislation
state paternalism. *See* paternalism
state power, 3, 5, 32, 33, 35, 57, 58, 175.
See also enslaved human property;
frontier settlement projects;
paternalism
suffrage movement: activist focus on,
60–61, 62; impact on economic
reform progress, 29, 60, *61*, 62, 137,
188; post-Reconstruction
constitutional conventions and, 167;
reform goals and, 36. *See also* woman
suffrage; women's rights activism
Sullivan, Kathleen, 196n23
Sunstein, Cass, 105
Supreme Court, 42
Switzer v. Valentine, 155–156

temperance movement, 28, 36, 63–64, 120
Tennyson, Sharon, 30
testamentary power: coverture constraints on, 11–12; wills laws and, *18*, 20–21, *25*, 45, *143*, *180–181*
Texas reforms: constitutional provisions, *96*, *99*, 117, *125*, *126*, 231n101; homestead exemptions and, 69, 231n101; migration and, 146; racial hierarchies in, 147
text analysis: on constitutional provisions, 125, 181, 184; match cutoffs for, 141, 215n17; on reform legislation, 138–139, 141–144, *141*, *142*, *143*, 184–185; reform types and, *140*, 141; software for, 177, 181; state clusters and, 141–144, 185, *186*
Thompson, R. H., 111–112
Thurston, Chloe, 80, 174
Ting, Michael, 133
Toof v. Brewer, 162

universal reform, 63
U.S. Constitution, 102, 105, 153, 155, 216n14
Utah reforms, *101*

VanBurkleo, Sandra F., 13
Viser v. Scruggs, 159
Volden, Craig, 133
voting rights. *See* suffrage movement; woman suffrage

Wallenstein, Peter, 107–108
Warbasse, Elizabeth Bowles, 58, 79
Washington, DC, reforms, 200n8
western territories/states, reforms in: antimiscegenation laws and, 83; gender imbalances, 147; interstate reform diffusion and, 126, 128; overviews, *47–48*; racial hierarchies and, 89; timing of, *54–56*, 81–82, *82*, 147–148; woman suffrage, 81. *See also* frontier settlement projects; frontier territories/states, reforms in; statehood constitutions; *specific states*
West Virginia reforms, *103*, 204n50
white supremacy. *See* racial hierarchies
White v. White, 154–155
Whitworth v. Carter, 158–159
Wicker, Elmus, 74
wills laws, *18*, 20–21, *25*, 45, *143*, *180–181*
Wisconsin reforms, 212n94
woman suffrage: constitutional conventions and, 108, 111, 114, 167; coverture era, 195n12; event history analysis and, 135, 185, 188; frontier settlement projects and, 81; partisan politics and, 71; timing of, *62*, *62*, 81. *See also* suffrage movement
women's rights activism, 57, 58–60; credit discrimination and, 173–174; event history analysis and, 135, 137; paternalism and, 84; post-suffrage reforms and, 172–174; radical demands of, 3, 28–29, 60–61, 86, 152; reform timing and, 45; state court interpretations and, 152; temperance and, 63, 64; universal reform and, 63. *See also* suffrage movement
Wyoming reforms, 81, 147

Yamin, Priscilla, 37

Zackin, Emily, 80, 102, 104, 124

GPSR Authorized Representative: Easy Access System Europe, Mustamäe tee 50, 10621 Tallinn, Estonia, gpsr.requests@easproject.com